American Poetry Now

PITT POETRY SERIES
ED OCHESTER, EDITOR

AMERICAN POETRY NOW

Pitt Poetry Series Anthology

edited by ED OCHESTER

UNIVERSITY OF PITTSBURGH PRESS

Published by the University of Pittsburgh Press, Pittsburgh, Pa., 15260

Copyright © 2007, University of Pittsburgh Press

Manufactured in the United States of America

Printed on acid-free paper

10 9 8 7 6 5 4 3 2 1

Library of Congress Cataloging-in-Publication Data
American poetry now : Pitt poetry series anthology / Ed Ochester, editor.
    p.   cm. — (Pitt poetry series)
  ISBN-13: 978-0-8229-4310-5 (cloth : acid-free paper)
  ISBN-10: 0-8229-4310-7 (cloth : acid-free paper)
  ISBN-13: 978-0-8229-5964-9 (pbk. : acid-free paper)
  ISBN-10: 0-8229-5964-X (pbk. : acid-free paper)
  1. American poetry--20th century. I. Ochester, Ed.
  PS615.A4248 2007
  811'.508—dc22   2006100947

5/07
B&T

Thanks to:

Britt Horner for her patience and knowledge of contemporary poetry;

Betsy and Ned Ochester for innumerable instances of support;

*and to my colleagues at the University of Pittsburgh Press for their
suggestions, enthusiasm, and hard work: Cynthia Miller, Ann Walston,
Lowell Britson, Deborah Meade, Maria Sticco, and David Baumann.*

And, of course, to the poets for their wild imaginings: thanks for being there.

CONTENTS

INTRODUCTION

keep the literary scholars out and
stick to the original writing
—CHARLES SIMIC

This book commemorates the fortieth anniversary of the Pitt Poetry Series and the thirtieth year of my editorship of it. Over the years the series has become "a republic of many voices," which reflects not only many of the forms and styles of American poetry, but the various backgrounds of American poets—in terms of gender, race and ethnicity, class—to a greater degree than any other publisher. It's truly a cross-section of the best of contemporary American poetry.

It was clear to me early in the editing process for this book that if it were going to contain enough poems by each author to make a satisfying introduction to the poet's work we couldn't include selections from every book in print in the series—there are just too many, and I didn't want to produce one of those forbidding anthologies as big and as expensive as a tombstone. I wanted a book easy to browse through and to put in a backpack, a book that would say "there's some pleasure in this" rather than "you have a duty to read it even if it weighs ten pounds, but we are not responsible for eye or back strain or possible hernias." So I made several difficult decisions. I did not include selections from some fine books that for various reasons are difficult to excerpt. I did not include selections from the many fine books we publish as the prizewinners from several competitions: our Starrett first book prize, the Donald Hall Prize of the Association of Writers and Writing Programs, and the Cave Canem Prize—unless the authors had published at least one other book. The series has always supported the publication of first books, is proud of the authors who have come to us through these contests, and will publish many of the winners' subsequent books. We urge you to check out the suggested reading list at the end of this volume, in which prizewinning books are noted.

This is, I hope, an anthology of delight, which will be enjoyed by all readers of poetry, the novice and the veteran alike. I have included here those poems that after long acquaintance interest me and move me. More important than my particular taste, though, is the fact that all of these poems have been tested on other readers and listeners and have met with joy and, in some cases, awe. I've used many of these poems with large success during most of a lifetime of teaching, and I hope that the variety represented here will be particularly useful as a text in poetry reading and writing classes. I hope that it will be a portal for many into a literary genre that Dylan Thomas called the oldest and the greatest of the arts, one that is essential and life-giving. I hope that after using this book readers will not be content with anthologies alone, but will seek out whole books by individual authors. And I hope that readers will also become listeners by attending readings. In most ages of most cultures, poetry was an oral art, not first or merely a book art.

It is true that poetry in the twenty-first century in this country has an audience that is small in relation to the audiences for television or the movies, though it's not as small as many people believe. The audience for poetry has been growing for years, despite the fact that commercial ("trade") publishers are publishing less and less poetry, and the art is represented increasingly by university presses and small independent presses, the garage bands of the publishing industry. While poetry's readership in America is increasing, there are still many people who avoid it. There are many historical and cultural reasons for this. I went to a public high school in the city of New York, and remember that one of our old textbooks—and it was old, kept presumably to be used until it wore out—featured the poetry of Edmund Spenser, the elegant Elizabethan allegorist whose place in the English canon is secure, but who is the worst possible choice for kids who have read next to nothing. In *The Faerie Queene*, Spenser writes about the urgent issues of his day, which are no longer our issues, in a style and diction that are opaque to unsophisticated new readers. What has possessed (and still possesses) some makers of textbooks to do it all backward? Instead of starting with contemporary work and then moving back in time, they emphasize older writers whom students rightly consider dry, and then perhaps offer here and there a few contemporary plums. Yet for many years, I participated in our state's "poets-in-the-schools" program, and found that most students—at all levels of achievement—were interested and often wildly enthusiastic when presented with contemporary poems that spoke to their concerns in their own language.

It's important to emphasize that poetry does not have to be "difficult." This is the hangover from High Modernism. Yes, T. S. Eliot's "Four Quartets" is difficult, and requires and deserves study. Some poetry is difficult because some subjects and some personae are difficult. But most poems from most ages and most cultures have a surface texture, an approachability, that requires no more special reading skills or knowledge than reading a newspaper—and the profit is much greater. The Pitt Poetry Series publishes some poets who are legitimately difficult—Reginald Shepherd and Larry Levis, for example—but poets like Billy Collins, Ted Kooser, and Denise Duhamel exemplify accessibility. As I choose books for the series I try to avoid *manufactured* difficulty. My critical principle in such matters is that poetry should be as difficult as it needs to be, but not more so. It's a kind of Occam's razor for poetry

(Occam's razor is the principle in science that among competing hypotheses that explain sets of facts one should choose the simplest that does the job); of course, one needs to be a fairly experienced reader to judge what is "more difficult than it needs to be," but the principle is important. As one easily approachable (and wonderful) poet, Edward Field, says: "a lot [of poetry] seems irrelevant and boring, of interest only to scholars, and I don't see being a poet [as] a scholarly occupation" (*The Man Who Would Marry Susan Sontag*, 213). My emphasis on "ease of approach" may seem heretical or just plain anti-intellectual to some, but it reflects the nature of the art. Academic critics like difficult poets because their difficulty feeds the critical production essential to promotion. Don't be taken in. Randall Jarrell, one of the two best critics of poetry in the last century (the other was T. S. Eliot), wrote: "The habit of philosophizing in poetry—or of seeming to philosophize, of using a philosophical tone, images, constructions, of having quasi-philosophical daydreams—has been unfortunate. . . . Poetry is a bad medium for philosophy. Everything in the philosophical poem has to satisfy irreconcilable requirements: for instance, the last demand we should make of philosophy (that it be interesting) is the first we make of a poem" (*No Other Book*, 116). With any art, the more you learn about the craft, the greater your appreciation is likely to be, but you don't have to be a specialist to enjoy a good song, or a good movie, or a good poem.

Some readers avoid poetry in general because they want to read only the "great poems." To my mind, that's akin in its intelligence to such thoughts as: "I only eat great meals," "I only play great games of tennis," "I only go to great movies," and "I only have great sex." Translated, such a sentiment usually means: "I was forced to take a course in 'Great Poems of the English Language' once, and I didn't like it much, but in any event I've done it and haven't had to read a poem again in years." A related question is: "where are the great poets of today?" The proper answer is: "we don't know yet." Even Shakespeare was not the acknowledged master of English literature in his lifetime. Walt Whitman was much less famous during his life than Longfellow during his, but time has reversed that judgment. As Eric McHenry writes in *Poets & Writers* magazine (May/June 2003): "Who knows which of today's poets will be, in retrospect, our [Wallace] Stevens? How many Americans knew, in 1930, that Stevens was their Stevens?" Usually, many years pass before reputations are sorted out, and if there's one thing the novice poetry reader can immediately dismiss, it's a claim by a reviewer—or even a learned professor—that a contemporary's work will last forever. One of the pleasures of any art is discovering what matters to *you*. A guidebook may be useful, or a class, or a critical book, but because those things can't tell you what you love or hate or moves you in other ways, ultimately you have to trust yourself to browse among different poets. When you do, you'll discover contemporary poems that will move you and that just possibly may change your life. Poetry is the most personal of the arts.

The word "great" has connotations of "monumental," "philosophical," "serious"—something like Milton's *Paradise Lost*. But as far as I'm concerned one of the "great" poems written in America during the last century is Robert Frost's "The Silken Tent," a sonnet of incomparable grace whose speaker is "merely" complimenting a particular woman. He proves the truth and sincerity of the emotion he's claiming by the exactness and rightness of the extended metaphor. As for "serious"—there's a snobbery that holds that the only serious poems are somber poems. Let me be quite emphatic here: "serious" does not mean "somber," necessarily. Laughter is OK, and sometimes it's the best way to approach a serious subject. Look, for example, at the poems of Daisy Fried or Christopher Bursk. Think of works of poetry—or any art—as being like radioactive isotopes. Like them, all poems have half-lives. Some half-lives are very long, some are very short. But even poems that may not endure for long may be perfect for their moment, and be enjoyable. Only very narrow and Puritanical casts of mind—like Shakespeare's Malvolio—would banish innocent and ephemeral pleasures from their lives *because* they're ephemeral. As Shakespeare asks: do you like cakes and ale or not?

Some people assume that as long as something rhymes, it is poetry, which simply isn't true. Rhyme is just one of many tools that poets may use, but the first English poetry—Anglo-Saxon—didn't rhyme. In the Western tradition, rhyme was used by illiterate medieval monks simply as a mnemonic device to help in memorizing their lessons. As a device in poetry, it has certainly over the centuries been trivialized by bad poets, in large part because English, unlike the Romance languages, is rhyme-poor. The mistaken notion that metrical regularity and heavy end-rhyme is "poetic" has led to an infinite number of bad poems. Shakespeare satirizes the tendency in *A Midsummer Night's Dream;* Bottom mistakes noisiness and heavy end-rhyme for poetry:

> The raging rocks
> And shivering shocks
> Shall break the locks
> Of prison gates,
> And Phibbus' car
> Shall shine from far
> And make and mar
> The foolish Fates.

Not minding the fact that this makes very little sense indeed, Bottom, with great self-satisfaction, observes, "This was lofty." Well, Bottom's notion of what is "lofty" has never died, of course. We find it in innumerable greeting card verses, where the rhyme is everything, and where the aim is to say something very general, sentimental, "pretty"—and meaningless. It's a kind of lying in verse, and is exactly the opposite of what most poets will tell you they're trying to do. On the other hand, some poets, like Ronald Wallace, Paisley Rekdal, and Peter Meinke, have reclaimed—even reinvented—rhyme in ways and with structures that become an integral part of saying something very meaningful.

The option to reinvent the rules is a hallmark of free verse, which has dominated much poetry in English, particularly in America, since the beginning of the twentieth century. No effective poem is "free" in the sense that it's without shape or organization, but the word in this context refers particularly to freedom from metrical restraints, such as iambic pentameter. There's nothing particularly modern about this. In his later plays, such as *King Lear*, Shakespeare was no longer using a regular iambic beat, though he still employed a five-beat line. Later poets, such as William Blake and Heinrich Heine, abandoned conventional metrics well before the twentieth century, as did Walt Whitman's *Leaves of Grass* (1855). The basic unit of the poem became the line, and "the line comes from the breath" (Charles Olson, "Projective Verse"). That is to say, each phrase, bounded by the breath of the writer (just as we all normally take breaths as we speak), determines where the line ends. This facilitates the poet's ability to emphasize important words and images within the text, and also provides the reader of the poem with a means to reproduce the "breath," i.e., the pacing, of the poet. For an example, read these lines from Alicia Ostriker's "The Dogs at Live Oak Beach, Santa Cruz":

> As if there could be a world
> Of absolute innocence
> In which we forget ourselves
>
> The owners throw sticks
> And half-bald tennis balls
> Toward the surf
> And the happy dogs leap after them
> As if catapulted—

Note that the "breath phrase" of each line, with its momentary pause at the end, prevents the reader from reading it straight through, like prose, and that the line breaks may also take the place of conventional marks of punctuation, such as the comma.

Just as many poets have abandoned the use of conventional English metrics, they've sought new ways of organizing poems instead of, or in addition to, using conventional forms such as the sestina or the sonnet (though some contemporary poets, like Peter Meinke, continue to use traditional forms in particularly modern ways—see, for example, "Sonnet on the Death of the Man Who Invented Plastic Roses"). The words "form" and "style" are often used interchangeably. It's more useful, though, to think of form as the deep structure or organizing principle of the poem and style as referring to such surface matters as level of diction, figures of speech, sound effects (alliteration, consonance, etc.) and tone (attitude of the speaker). Poets writing in the early and mid-twentieth century observed that some subjects suggested within themselves the way the poem should be shaped. This idea is usually referred to as "organic form." Denise Levertov wrote "form is never more than a revelation of content. . . . The sounds [of a poem] . . . are a kind of extended onomatopoeia—i.e., they imitate, not the sounds of an experience (which may well be soundless, or to which sounds contribute only incidentally) but the feeling of the experience, its emotional tone, its texture" ("Some Notes on Organic Form," 1965). What she means is reflected in the following lines from Jan Beatty's "Machine Shop of Love." Note how the line breaks and use of slashes determine the pace at which you read the words:

> under the viaduct,
> under the old/railroad bridge of our ancestors/
> immigrant steelworkers/slaves of Carnegie/
> we rocked the back seat of a '69 Chevy/
> you pulled my chuck taylors/your jeans were long gone/
> goodbye to cotton/the rolling stones teeshirt/
> we're spinning in lust and oh
> steamy back windows and nothing
> can stop it/the rolling and tearing/
> machine shop of love, love—

Some contemporary poets are particularly interested in surrealism, that presentation of dream-like states or dream-like fantasies in which the usual principles of cause and effect may be noticeably absent. The impulse toward surrealism may have resulted from the great political, intellectual, and social dislocations that began early in the last century. It may have strengthened with the shocks of later American political life: President Nixon saying "I am not a crook" shortly before it became clear that he was a crook; President Clinton squandering his political authority in a squalid and comic sexual affair with a young intern; President George W. Bush constantly shifting reasons for his preemptive war on Iraq and justifications for torturing captives. Whatever, surrealism is with us, not just in poetry but in other arts as well, as in popular music ever since early Bob Dylan and the Beatles. In the culture at large we've become used to it and, just as in Aesop's fables, that very early nonrealistic writing, the reason for the use of the surreal is often clear in the context of the individual poem. Sometimes, as in Russell Edson's or Dean Young's poetry, the fantastic says more about the "real" than the conventionally realistic can.

Many shorter poems, which is to say most poems, have a two-part structure. The second part, usually brief, alters our perception of the material in the first part. This alteration may occur through a comment of the speaker, an image, a change of tone, or any one of a number of other devices, but the effect is to give a sense of discovery, completeness, or heightened awareness. Here, for example, is Toi Derricotte's "In an Urban School":

> The guard picks dead leaves from plants.
> The sign over the table reads:
> Do not take or *touch* anything on this table!
> In the lunchroom the cook picks up in her dishcloth
> what she refers to as "a little friend,"
> shakes it out,
> and puts the dishcloth back on the drain.
> The teacher says she needs stronger tranquilizers.
> Sweat rises on the bone of her nose,
> on the plates of her skull under unpressed hair.
> "First graders, put your heads down. I'm taking names
> so I can tell your parents
> which children do not obey their teacher."
> Raheim's father was stabbed last week.
> Germaine's mother, a junkie,
> was found dead in an empty lot.

The poem just presents a scene, and yet it improves—extends, intensifies—our understanding of the world and in that way, and perhaps in others, is moving. Note the power of juxtaposition: the first thirteen lines, by themselves, aren't a complete poem; the last three lines, by themselves, aren't a poem at all. But put them together and something electric happens. The two-part, or binary, poem is an ancient construction. The English sonnet is another example: three discrete bundles of information (the three quatrains) with an ending (the final couplet) that "makes sense" of what went before. It's one of many ways that poetry strives to say a lot in a small space in a striking and interesting way. Nor is this a form unique to poetry; most of us have told anecdotes or jokes that depend on a final, brief "punch line."

Efficient use of language is one of the major hallmarks of poetry. For the poet, this means avoiding clumsy or pointless repetition by saying things forcefully and right the first time. It means avoiding abstractions and generalizations in favor of presenting the scene which generated the abstraction. It means that each gesture has its point and no moment of the poem is wasted. For many American poets, such as Charles Olson ("always one perception must must must MOVE, INSTANTER, ON ANOTHER!") and Frank O'Hara in much of his characteristic work, concision means *speed*, telling the poem rapidly, perhaps as a reflection of the hectic pace of American life. That sense of speed, of rush, is evident in Dorothy Barresi's work: "Look, Body says: jumpshot, fadeaway, fakeout, doublepump, / alley-oop—what did you expect, anyway?" O'Hara reinvented for American poetry "the present progressive" (the dramatic monologue), the poem in which the speaker progresses in actual time, from morning to evening for example. Such a stance makes possible a greater sense of immediacy, compared to a static one in which the speaker is delivering a settled, neatly formed view of a scene or event; it allows dramatic representation of the mind of the speaker in action. Condensed speech, however, doesn't necessarily mean brief or telegraphic. Denise Duhamel, for example, has written some wonderfully chatty poems in which the talkative speaker in fact is one of the points of interest as a created character, and in which seemingly random details are juggled very skillfully in the pattern of the whole poem, so that there's no random or functionless language, no mere gab.

Many contemporary poems have a first-person speaker in which the personality or psyche of the speaker is noticeably the subject or part of the subject of the poem. Why "I"? Among many possible reasons, perhaps the most important is that the first-person speaker can present the authority of personal experience without pontificating or claiming to state universal truths; the poem becomes a "test case" of what happens for a particular personality in a particular scene or set of circumstances. Paradoxically, what is most personal, most particular, may lead to the universal; in his essay "Poetry, Personality and Death," Galway Kinnell talks about his wish to go so deeply into the personal in his poems that he discovers he is speaking for everyone. A caution, however: though all writing is autobiographical to some extent (the author has to experience in imagination whatever is written down) that doesn't mean that the "I" of the poem is narrowly autobiographical. William Carlos Williams wrote an amusing poem about what it feels like to be a tree, but he was a medical doctor, not a sugar maple. As Lynn Emanuel puts it in "Homage to Sharon Stone,"

Or you could think of the black car as
Lynn Emanuel, because, really, as an author,
I have always wanted to be a car, even
though most of the time I have to be
the "I," or the woman hanging wash;
I am a woman, one minute, then I am a man,
I am a carnival of Lynn Emanuels:

Critics or ordinary readers often make the mistake of deciding that the poet should have written like somebody else, rather than considering *why* the poet has chosen a particular style or form. That's as wrongheaded as telling Emily Dickinson to write like Walt Whitman. It's as irritating as saying to a happy person, "why do you smile all the time?" or to a quiet person "why are you thinking all the time?" Give the poet a break! Just as one rule of reading in general is "you have to allow the author her subject" another is "you have to allow the poet his style." Figure out *why* he or she is writing that way—what the function of the style is for delivering the content of the poem.

In some circles—and in many anthologies of contemporary poetry—you'll find prejudices against the narrative or story poem and against the comic poem. That's a pity, it seems to me, not only because narrative and comic poems are found at the heart of most poetic traditions, but because narrative and comic poems are very much in evidence these days. The pleasure of listening to a unique character tell his or her story is perhaps the oldest pleasure in literature. And as for the comic poem, I'll let Gabriel Gudding, one of our Starrett Prize winners, comment: "It would be more than nice, for a change, to see anthologies not only recognizing and representing today's great renaissance of comic poetry; it would be an absolute blessing if mainstream American poetry could recognize precisely what is not lofty in us" (*Poetry International* V, 151).

This anthology has many narrative and comic poems. It also represents, I hope, what is "lofty." But any anthology of poetry is an adventure for editor and reader, and no finality is possible. Only a very foolish person would expect that one book could hold a wholly definitive representation of such a vast enterprise as contemporary American poetry. Anyone can argue that a given anthology is unrepresentative, guilty of omitting poet *x*, who, one could claim, is absolutely essential for the understanding of contemporary American poetry. Even critics who in other contexts will argue fiercely that the establishment of a canon—required reading lists!—is impossible or fraudulent, will take this gambit. If one takes it, however, no anthology is possible. If one takes it, one is probably arguing for the centrality of a particular group of poets or school of poetry (read: "poetry gang"), but there is no one center of American poetry now, as New York or Boston or San Francisco used to be, when a handful of white, male, middle- or upper-class, Ivy League–educated poets made up the canon. Not that they were evil. And in the interest of full disclosure I confess that I am white (more or less), male, middle-class, and Ivy League–educated, usually pretty happy with myself and, on some days, delighted. But there's not just one group or one place that matters exclusively anymore. The country is too big for that now. Poetry is too—in the radical sense of the word—popular.

So I'll come back to what I said at the beginning. I've included work here by a large number of poets I've published who've given me and many other people pleasure. They're not the only poets worth reading but they're a pretty good representation and cross-section of what's happening. I hope you enjoy it. Laugh. Cry your eyes out. Be human. Have fun.

—Ed Ochester

American Poetry Now

Maggie Anderson is the author of four books of poems: *Windfall: New and Selected Poems, A Space Filled with Moving, Cold Comfort,* and *Maggie Anderson: Greatest Hits 1984–2004.* She is the editor or coeditor of several books, including *Hill Daughter,* the new and selected poems of Louise McNeill. She has received fellowships from the National Endowment for the Arts, the Ohio Arts Council, and the West Virginia Arts and Humanities Commission. She is the director and a member of the faculty in the Northeast Ohio MFA program at Kent State University, where she also directs the Wick Poetry Center and edits the Wick Poetry Series of the Kent State University Press.

Spitting in the Leaves

In Spanishburg there are boys in tight jeans,
mud on their cowboy boots and they wear huge hats
with feathers, skunk feathers they tell me.
They do not want to be in school, but are.
Some teacher cared enough to hold them. Unlike
their thin disheveled cousins, the boys on Matoaka's
Main Street in October who loll against parking meters
and spit into the leaves. Because of them, someone
will think we need a war, will think the best solution
would be for them to take their hats and feathers,
their good country manners and drag them off somewhere,
to Vietnam, to El Salvador. And they'll go.
They'll go from West Virginia, from hills and back roads
that twist like politics through trees, and they'll fight,
not because they know what for but because what they know
is how to fight. What they know is feathers,
their strong skinny arms, their spitting
in the leaves.

Heart Fire

Three months since your young son shot himself
and, of course, no one knows why. It was October.
Maybe he was following the smell of dying leaves
or the warmth of the fire in the heart, so hard
to locate in a country always readying for war.

One afternoon we sat together on your floor, drinking
tea and listening to Brahms on the radio. He would
have liked this music, you told me. He would have liked
everything I like now and what he wouldn't like I don't
like either. He has made the whole world look like him.

Today, driving into Pittsburgh, I see you are right.
The sky is cold blue like a shirt I once saw him

wear and the bare trees are dark, like his hair.
I see how vulnerable the grasses are, pale and flimsy
by the roadsides, trying to stand straight in the wind.

At Canonsburg, all the pink and green and purple houses
have the same slant of roof toward the hill, like toys
because I'm thinking about children, how sometimes
we want to give them up if they seem odd and distant,
yet even if they die before us, we cannot let them go.

I see your son in landscapes as I drive, in a twist
of light behind a barn before the suburbs start,
or under a suburban street light where a tall boy
with a basketball has limbs like those he had just
outgrown. Because I want to think he's not alone

I invent for him a heart fire even the unenlightened
living are sometimes allowed to see. It burns past
the white fluorescence of the city, past the steel mills
working off and on as they tell us we need, or don't
need, heavy industry for fuel, or war. Your son

keeps me company, driving down the last hill into
Pittsburgh, in the tunnel as I push for good position
in the lanes. He is with me as I spot the shiny cables
of the bridge and gear down, as all the lights beyond
the river come on now, across his safe, perfected face.

Long Story

> To speak in a flat voice
> Is all that I can do.
> —JAMES WRIGHT, "SPEAK"

I need to tell you that I live in a small town
in West Virginia you would not know about.
It is one of the places I think of as home.
When I go for a walk, I take my basset hound
whose sad eyes and ungainliness always draw

a crowd of children. She tolerates anything
that seems to be affection, so she lets the kids
put scarves and ski caps on her head
until she starts to resemble the women who have to dress
from rummage sales in poverty's mismatched polyester.

The dog and I trail the creek bank with the kids,
past clapboard row houses with Christmas seals
pasted to the windows as a decoration.
Inside, television glows around the vinyl chairs
and curled linoleum, and we watch someone old
perambulating to the kitchen on a shiny walker.
Up the hill in town, two stores have been
boarded up beside the youth center and miners
with amputated limbs are loitering outside
the Heart and Hand. They wear Cat diesel caps
and spit into the street. The wind
carries on, whining through the alleys,
rustling down the sidewalks, agitating
leaves, and circling the courthouse steps
past the toothless Field sisters who lean
against the flagpole holding paper bags
of chestnuts they bring to town to sell.

History is one long story of what happened to us,
and its rhythms are local dialect and anecdote.
In West Virginia a good story takes awhile,
and if it has people in it, you have to swear.
that it is true. I tell the kids the one about
my Uncle Craig who saw the mountain move
so quickly and so certainly it made the sun
stand in a different aspect to his little town
until it rearranged itself and settled down again.
This was his favorite story. When he got old,
he mixed it up with baseball games, his shift boss
pushing scabs through a picket line, the Masons
in white aprons at a funeral, but he remembered
everything that ever happened, and he knew how far
he lived from anywhere you would have heard of.

Anything that happens here has a lot of versions,
how to get from here to Logan twenty different ways.
The kids tell me convoluted country stories
full of snuff and bracken, about how long
they sat quiet in the deer blind with their fathers
waiting for the ten-point buck that got away.
They like to talk about the weather,
how the wind we're walking in means rain,
how the flood pushed cattle fifteen miles downriver.

These kids know mines like they know hound dogs
and how the sirens blow when something's wrong.
They know the blast, and the stories, how
the grown-ups drop whatever they are doing
to get out there. Story is shaped
by sound, and it structures what we know.
They told me this, and three of them
swore it was true, so I'll tell you
even though I know you do not know
this place, or how tight and dark the hills
pull in around the river and the railroad.

I'll say it as the children spoke it,
in the flat voice of my people:
down in Boone County, they sealed up
forty miners in a fire. The men who had come
to help tried and tried to get down to them,
but it was a big fire and there was danger,
so they had to turn around
and shovel them back in. All night long
they stood outside with useless picks and axes
in their hands, just staring at the drift mouth.
Here's the thing: what the sound must have been,
all those fire trucks and ambulances, the sirens,
and the women crying and screaming out
the names of their buried ones, who must have
called back up to them from deep inside
the burning mountain, right up to the end.

Black Dog Goes to Art Colony

I like it here. I like it here. They do things in packs.
At night they pile together on the floor.
I lie down on the leather jackets and boots
and the skinny ties I sink my teeth into and shake.
Tonight, as usual, they are listening to someone talk.
I track the smells: linseed oil and mink oil,
bag balm, gasoline and tar, cigarettes.
Tall thin man smell, cologne and sweat.
Great big woman smell, plastic, powder and pastries.
That woman's still talking and now they've got a fire going,
smoke and pine and burning sap, and sulfur.
It's the fire makes them want to drowse and pet a dog.
I move to one side, then the other, to catch the petters
with soft hands, rough hands, shirt cuffs, sweaters.
The guy with the pickup truck takes me with him to the dump;
otherwise I don't have too many duties here.
I've found my place to settle among the brass studs
and the leather, the elbows and knees where
I'm waiting for the shoe to drop, for the talk to stop,
for them to whistle and clap for me,
to call my name, *good dog, good dog.*

Self-Portrait

I was far outside the frame, beyond
the pale, lost in the margins, smudged
like a fingerprint and frankly, nervous
about holding my own. I knew what was coming:
you, toward me, your arms open,
preparing to wrap them around my neck
with the clear determination some people
bring to learning anthropology. I was not
about to be moved, to be swept off my feet
by your exotic bracelets. I'll admit
I sometimes incline toward

the minute particulars of a scene
but never have I been undone by a woman
on account of her accessories. Until now,
when I come into the picture, captivated
by black coral beads, the gold wire of an earring,
the rustle of red scarf against a neckline,
as this pull, this great tug at my heart,
forklifts me into the foreground
at the center of a photograph
of empty beach, empty that is except for
you, and pine and manzanita,
the silver rings and necklaces of white surf.

Dorothy Barresi is the author of three books of poetry, *All of the Above*, *The Post-Rapture Diner*, winner of an American Book Award, and *Rouge Pulp*. Her awards include a fellowship from the National Endowment for the Arts and two Pushcart Prizes. She is professor of English at California State University, Northridge, and lives in Los Angeles with her husband and sons.

The Post-Rapture Diner

A thought you cannot call back,
and empty shoes like
exclamation points
on every road from here to Tucson.

Who will knock their boots against the doorjamb now
and enter shyly?
Who will peel the vegetables?
Pie domes cloud over. Old sugar

makes a kind of weather in there—
webbed, waiting.
Tiers of doughnuts go woozy with collapse.

We deed and we will.
We bow to what providence we understand
and cede the rest: our lies and doubts, our human,
almost necessary
limitations. *Probably I should have,*

we whispered more than once, shaking our heads.
Probably. Now what's left of the past
hangs in a walk-in freezer,
fat-shrouded, bluing,

and all we know of the present
is a spatula in a coffee can
on a cold grill, pointing to heaven.

The Nude Detective, A Complaint

—for God

Your devices are sensitive.

In rain and in snow,
in moonlight that clatters down

its bright plates and crockery
like a voice in the head,

you stay. You lend to our windows
a fishing pole

and a microphone.
But why?

Are you some under-assistant's
last hireling?

Nothing, not even faith or crazy envy explains
how we provoke you to this patience

hour by hour.
And if our daily static can be removed,

our *yeses*
turned to *no* on tape

the way technology puts
plastic hearts in men, or

cheese in jars,
then surely we don't deserve

such a careful listening.
Such bare attention to what we do

only makes us act worse.
A kiss, a gasp—

how long before you drag
your sunburned knuckles in some fleshly

circles on the ground?
How long before you order moo shu pork then drip

plum sauce on the bedsheets?
Mr. Never Kissed and Tell, Mr.

Truly Exposed,
we're speaking out at last.

You wearing just a porkpie hat
like Donatello's *David,*

you with dark circles under wholly
permanent eyes, we wish you'd get a life

and beat it for good this time, you goddamn,
you shivering

angel who loves us more than we love ourselves.

Sock Hop with the New Critics

Crinolines, saddle shoes, blow jobs, Pat Boone.
The bone scripture of words
in a sweating, decorated gymnasium.
Myth builders, punch spikers
dance with themselves
in pairs, "It's a goddamn ghost farm in here,"
Tate churls, missing Pia Verba,
his cupcake who's home,
washing her hair.

The ice sculpture drips.
It's an equal sign on a complicated bed of roses.
Brooks is in drag again, peau de soie, sobbing.
Richards tilts gin
from his wingtip—
"There are seven types of ambiguity, and he's the third,"
nodding at Empson
counting receipts at the door
(the *profanum vulgus* kept out
to keep God in).

For a corsage, a bunch of neuroses.
For music, a polite, black-trained

white hepcat doing doo-wop.
Or is it Roy Cohn in his closet, clearing his throat?
Or young Nixon perspiring, or McNamara? Pol Pot?
One song after another.
"Ask me anything, baby,"
Wimsatt whispers to himself, testing old truth
like pearls against his teeth.
"Anything."
The world understood
is a tiny world.
Someone forgot to invite the girls.

Glass Dress

Lily St. Cyr is dead.
A de-luxe woman,
stripper extraordinaire.
Blonde, like the cortex of a blazing sun
finding the perfect grammar of its form
in sublime asymmetry,
gams and hips and prodigious rolling ass and elegant
poses for the ghost boys newly back from hell
in 1945,
to sit trembling in the old
ghost palaces of burlesque.

Lily St. Cyr is dead.
No tassel-twirling, minimum wage girl.
No discount moon,
no languishing feminine ruses.
She teases the illimitable body,
Marilyn before Marilyn,
Jayne before Jayne.
What she does not do: sing dirty, cootch, or kiss bald heads.
She never takes off
more than she has on.
Lily St. Cyr is dead. Not another bombshell,

but a real atom smasher
dressed up like Salome or the Jungle Maiden
faking love with a parrot,
which gets her arrested at Ciro's,
but who cares?
No one gets hurt here.

Ask the band, those be-bop gods of insect cool, playing
"Say It Isn't So,"
what the difference is
between naked and undressed.
They know with a terrible clarity.

Her generating curves,
her spirals,
her vector rotation of planes and onstage bubble baths
are the swellest immorality for those
wrecked and crippled boys
in the front row.
Lily St. Cyr is dead.
Knock back a whisky. Dim the spot.
Sweep the dressing room free of parrots, sequins, idolaters.
The Gaiety, the Savoy, the Palace,
the Republic are gone,

and in their place,
vast warehouses of exhausted capital
are erected downtown.
Lily St. Cyr is dead.
The high zero,
the unabashed,
the lithe and swift-leaping—"That's it, boys,
you're not getting any more from me."
Miss Liberty with her bare breasts
striking us dumb! Quick,

before the cops come to shut this show down,
watch her hold up a corner of red velvet curtain
to cover her well-turned
female dexterity.

With a wink and a smile, she is
an ecdysiast of the highest order, "ecdysis" meaning "shedding,"
or "nothing." It's true.
In the end, moaning,

we make our sexual pledge of allegiance.
Shed of shame,
we are mad for anything
made of blue lights and such blood.
But the GIs are crying.
They hide their faces, they disturb the air—
what good are their eyes
now that they've seen
what they've seen?
The house lights roar up like rockets for nothing.
Lily St. Cyr is dead.

Body Says

Body says, meet the animal
who made you.

Body says, I'll take mine
with a little tornado sauce, please,
and cunnilingus on the side.

Body says break and shine.

Body says
a diphtherial cough is not a sign of
interstitial lung disease, but

jazz fans, gun owners, and those
who lack confidence in the president
are among the most
sexually active Americans.

Body says
I think I hear cries for help.

Body says
I'm the kind of guy who'd steal your stove
then come back later
for the smoke.

Body says smoke.

Find a vein.

Body says, butter aside, I never
found Marion Brando
all that convincing in *Last Tango,* and further,

Body says pleasure, ruffle, nipple,
cupcake, home,

tendon, canker, tumor, tongue, mouth agape.
Bloody stool. Metastases—oh, Body says, how embarrassing;

it won't happen again.

Look, Body says: jumpshot, fadeaway, fakeout, doublepump,
alley-oop—what did you expect, anyway?
A perfectly *natural* pain?
Kiss me, Body says.

Body says
I'm talking sublingual, baby, the deep deep, the whole
insane molecular level of you in me right now.

Kiss me,
never the same way twice.
Yes, dear God, like that, like that, I love it when you yes—oh,

by the way, darling,
try to forget me.

It's for the best, Body says.
You be Buddy Holly,
I'll be the plane.

Quan Barry teaches at the University of Wisconsin–Madison. She is the author of *Controvertibles* and *Asylum,* which won the Agnes Lynch Starrett Poetry Prize. She has been awarded a National Endowment for the Arts Fellowship as well as a 2003 Pushcart Prize.

the exiled (from "child of the enemy")

> I liked it in South Vietnam.
> —LIEUTENANT WILLIAM CALLEY

Later   when the black
and white photos came in   the rice
sinking in its makeshift grave at the right
of the picture   three children wound
about their mother like meat on a spit   one eye
rolling loose   amazed   in the dead

silence of the frame   the freshly dead
posed hastily   each wound
breaking open like a smile   each eye
cocked as if winking under the black
hood of hair   the stalked rice
a backdrop   nobody wanted to write

the story   after all   no american in his right
mind would rise to this black
mission   109 civilians dead
    gunned down in the eye
of the hunt   it was never about them   the rice
lush in ways their children could never be   wound

so tightly to old wounds
    the chinese   the french   now this blue-eyed
christ seated at the right
of the throne   coming to save them from a black
plague that left so many dead
    rotting in fields like unharvested rice

    this is where it began   in the rice
paddies of vietnam   my mother   her right
hand gripping the earth's black
pillow   the night bleeding like a wound
    the soldier digging into her with the dead
weight of his lust   every star an amazed eye

---

rolling loose in the night   nine months   i
had just one picture taken in saigon   my black
hair sprouting   toes wound
in knots   mouth like a fist   the rice
paper riddled with figures   my right
foot inked   marked like a prayer for the dead

listen   you don't know me   eyes wild as rice
    like wounds scarred black
lieutenant   if revenge is a rite of passage   i need you dead

intermurals

The first time my mother decided to come
somebody lost an eye. Almost, besides,
valedictorian, ivy league-bound, Lone Ardiff had no right
being on the field, the fifteen fibrous seams
basting her eyelid together
a consequence of this. The second time
it was Zoë Burbridge who leaned into it, jumped back
like a dancer with the spirit, her cheekbone split,
fresh as an oyster. After that, my mother stayed home

four long years, not even trekking to the Berkshires, NESN
and the state championship where I made
that incomplete pass out of bounds, hands numb
with December, the ball hard as an explicated rumor, pillaging
free at last. She said she didn't spend the sixties
bra burning so her daughter could master the subtle art
of bloodletting in a kilt. *Suit yourself.* Like marijuana
field hockey led to harsher things—

lacrosse, two semesters of collegiate rugby
where I learned to take it like a man,
dish the dirt, wrap my arms around the enemy's knees
and snap, the contact inflicted with affection. It's only now
I remember the one who didn't get up, the girl
they carried off the field in a fireman's stretcher, leg cocked back

like a carbine. It goes without saying
that I was exultant, frenzied with the power
to cripple. Who wouldn't be?
All those years my mother stayed home
determined like a conscientious objector
to blow this wall tumbling down.

tradition

My mother says   women were made to bleed
   and the whole thing   takes twenty minutes.
She says afterwards   they'll wrap me up like a butterfly
   for forty nights   and I'll drink only camel's milk.
         My mother says   tomorrow
   I'll be a little bride   hands red with henna.
I'll be shining in white   and get to wear as much gold
as I want. She says afterwards   something will get killed
      and the whole clan   will come to eat
         only they won't   sit down
      until I've been washed   in the Nile.
My mother says tomorrow   the blacksmith's wife
   will cut away a part of me   I don't need. She says
      it might hurt   if the blacksmith's wife
uses scissors instead of a knife.   My sister says at her *khefad*
   the blacksmith's wife used glass   and then tied her shut
      with acacia thorns   and horsehair and Mother
   had to remind her to put   a match head in the wound
      so the whole thing   wouldn't heal closed
         and my sister   could still pee.
My aunt says up north   they use something called cautery
   which means they make that place   burn like the sun.
         My mother says I have nothing   to fear
      because women like us   were made to bleed.
      My mother says someday   I'll meet a man
who'll want me smooth and small.   She says we'll marry
      and he'll take a dagger   and slit me open
         like a letter addressed   just to him.

My mother says tomorrow I'll   be a little bride. She says
the whole thing takes   twenty minutes
and after forty days   I'll come out just like her
smooth and small   lips sealed.

crossing the South China Sea as analgesia

One day we will all be like this—the boat's sickening pitch, & the delicateness
needless, consumable.

How everything here naturally passes into night, a room
w/o walls.

Could mindlessness keep us alive? Could bright colors?

Tonight I am thinking of the young woman who dreams of her father
being shot in the head. Imagine needing to believe the one you love
has been destroyed.

Now it is after midnight—the spindrift lunar & diaphanous. Here alone on deck
could I make peace w/it all in thirty seconds—the water's inherent rising, the gasping
for air?

I have never seen such omnipresence, such vast dreamlessness—
but I too am such things.

What does it mean to be eroded? What would be the significance of slipping one leg
over the rail & straddling the indifference?

Yes. Once upon a time we spent three days on a boat out of Kobé, Japan.

All night the waves. All night the somnambulistic urges.

Or how as children we would swim in a hard rain—the lake's surface ragged & torn,
but underneath

the roots of the water lilies like ladders
trailing down into the marvelous.

Emmett Till's Open Casket as *La Pietá*

Today on the radio, news of the great lady's death.

I think of her breaking the coroner's seals, prying her way in
    to him.

How a thousand miles away she heard him crying in the Mississippi night, calling
    her name & when the second black man ever
    stood up in court, he said as much.

This is the litany of injuries: the body waterlogged, monstrous, one eye gouged out,
    hanging halfway down his cheek, the nose broken & mostly missing,
    a hole in the side of his crushed head where the light came through,
    & the marks where they tied the fan w/barbed wire
    to his neck.

Because the child wouldn't beg for his life.

Let them see what I saw.

& we came. For three straight days we came & looked
    at her only son.

They are beating him in the barn.

When Mary holds the dead Christ in her arms
    she has seen everything
    but the Resurrection.

Doug Flutie's 1984 Orange Bowl Hail Mary as Water into Fire

Listen w/o distraction.

Even before its incarnation we were transported, which is to say
    we were there, the Miami night
    larval, charged.

Read this to me when I'm dying, when I'm in the intermediate state—
    my consciousness dissipating through the elements.

Did the child-me know it would be all right, that the next six seconds would represent
　　human existence?

This is the way it always begins: in huddled confusion, then the object
　　churning toward a predetermined end.

There is a plan. There is hope. Then something happens.

Love comes & goes. Anger. Happiness. Decay. A man stands on the other side
　　& holds out his hands.

Something is sailing through the new year.

Teacher, call me by my other name. Tell me to breathe through my eyes, see
　　the path through the luminosity.

We are the ball. We are the arc through the air. We are the no time left on the clock
　　& the disbeliever.

Read this to me when I'm dying, when I'm neither here
　　nor there.

Say, "Grab onto nothing & it will come to you."

Photo by Joyce Connors

Jan Beatty, the author of *Boneshaker* and *Mad River*, is the recipient of the Pablo Neruda Prize for Poetry and two fellowships from the Pennsylvania Council on the Arts. Beatty hosts and produces *Prosody,* a public radio show on NPR affiliate WYEP-FM featuring the work of national writers. She teaches the Madwomen in the Attic Writing Workshop and in the MFA program at Carlow University.

Mad River

Two dollars and sixty-five cents
at the Hot Spot Take-Out Shack
for one chili dog and a coke,
Birmingham, Alabama, 1979.
I kissed a Greyhound bus driver
too many times so I could eat,
I got one chili dog, I wanted two,
thought I'd get two. Lucky I'm not dead.
I asked him about his children, his
fourteen-year-old daughter saved my life,
pulled up his rotten conscience like
regurgitation, black bile memory—I said
How old is your daughter, afraid he'd want
more for his money, and in the slant light
of his dark Chevy he saw a slice
of my young girl face and said,
She's fourteen, I better get you back
to the depot, and the black stench
of his twisted conscience wanted one more
kiss, one more kiss to get me back
to the bus station and my long ride home,
to wanting to spit up the dark beans,
their reddish bodies staining my insides
like a dead baby, like a blood spill,
my heart pumping its mad river with
sixty cents in my pocket and twenty-six
hours till home, I prayed for rain,
I prayed for morning.

Ravenous Blue

—in memory of Scott Prather

We drive up to visit you, talking about school and work,
we don't say you've gone blind, we don't talk about AIDS.
In your mother's living room, you sit on a chair

with blue foam padding, your body too thin to bear
its own weight. I keep looking at the blue,
ravenous blue, remember? We were stoned and running
up and down the aisles of the beauty supply store,
looking for hair color, when I saw RAVENOUS BLUE,
and fell in love with the name.
You tried to talk me out of it, but we dyed
my hair from blond to blue, and shortly after,
young boys in leather started trying to pick me up,
mistaking me for a young thrasher.
The color was so dark, we couldn't cover it,
so we just laughed until it grew out, but
now we're here, just us and this pressing air,
your wide, blind stare, the words we don't say,
and I'm so sorry we are here,
and this is you,
dying.

A Waitress' Instructions on Tipping or Get the Cash Up and Don't Waste My Time

Twenty percent minimum as long as the waitress doesn't inflict bodily harm.
If you're two people at a four top, tip extra.
If you sit a long time, pay rent.
Double tips for special orders.
Always tip extra when using coupons.
Better yet, don't use coupons.
Never leave change instead of bills, no pennies.
Never hide a tip for fun.
Overtip, then tip some more.
Remember, I am somebody's mother or daughter.
No separate piles of change for large parties.
If people in your party don't show up, tip *for* them.
Don't wait around for gratitude.
Take a risk. Don't adjust your tip so your credit card total is even.
Don't ever, ever pull out a tipping guide in public.
If you leave 10% or less, eat at home.

If I call a taxi for you, tip me.
If I hang up your coat for you, tip me.
If I get cigarettes for you, tip me.
Better yet, do it yourself.
Don't fold a bill and hand it to me like you're a big shot.
Don't say, *There's a big tip in it for you if . . .*
Don't say, *I want to make sure you get this,* like a busboy would steal it.
Don't say, *Here, honey, this is for you*—ever.
If you buy a $50 bottle of wine, pull out a ten.
If I serve you one cocktail, don't hand me 35¢.
If you're just having coffee, leave a five.

after sex on a train

canadian rockies fill
my window I am naked
eating blueberry muffins
sipping coke and smelling sperm
lakes and pines no birds fly past
I think of wild blueberries
bleeding juice through pale yellow
the yellow that's almost white
my calves bruised from holding on
rivers moving swollen white
rail ties lie in piles and I
sniff the musk that we all want
telephone poles bending toward
water the white birch the pines

My Father Teaches Me to Dream

You want to know what work is?
I'll tell you what work is.
Work is work.
You get up. You get on the bus.
You don't look from side to side.

You keep your eyes straight ahead.
That way, nobody bothers you—see?
You get off the bus. You work all day.
You get back on the bus at night. Same thing.
You go to sleep. You get up.
You do the same thing again.
Nothing more. Nothing less.
There's no handouts in this life.
All this other stuff you're looking for—
it ain't there.
Work is work.

Going Deep for Jesus

> Run to the street light, make a right at the
> blue car, and go deep.
> —SHARON WATSON

1981, I'm on the back of a cherry
red Kawasaki with my boyfriend Stush,
my biker jacket bought with a tax return
from a year of waiting tables, stuffed
in my pocket the bad check I wrote
to see Stevie Ray play the Decade.
Down Beck's Run we hit Carson, my cheek
resting on Stush's firm shoulder till
the ground rises up with the hulk of J&L
across the river, steel house that burns it all,
an up-against-the-wall-fuck, thick &
ripping, everything is smokestacks
& yellow blaze. We ride the river roads,
looking for deserted two-lanes,
newspapers stuffed under our leather
for warmth. I want to forget my name—
everything but the sharp lean into
the next turn, the cheap slap of the wind.
Stush brags about his water-cooled,
two-stroke engine, but I just want

the contact high of leather, metal,
and the slow burn of a few joints.
Past the bridges & bridges, we ride
away from our fast-food jobs and
run-down apartment, toward the smell
of the Ohio, its perpetual mire, the rotting
docks and lean-tos, *to what we knew.*
I knew the muscles in his back & his
low voice would make me come
back to my self. We stop near the bog
of the river's edge to have hard sex
on the ground, our jeans still on,
trying to shotgun a moment, to split open
our lives in the brilliant light until
we *were* the mills, we *were* the fire.
It was then I decided god and orgasm
were the same thing, that if jesus
had an address, it would be a dark two-lane,
if god were here, she'd shove down
like a two-stroke in a rainstorm,
she'd let it fly.

Zen of Tipping

My friend Lou
used to walk up to strangers
and tip them—no, really—
he'd cruise the South Side,
pick out the businessman on his way
to lunch, the slacker hanging
by the Beehive, the young girl
walking her dog, and he'd go up,
pull out a dollar and say,
Here's a tip for you.
I think you're doing a really
good job today. Then Lou would
walk away as the tippee stood

in mystified silence. Sometimes
he would cut it short with,
Keep up the fine work.
People thought Lou was weird,
but he wasn't. He didn't have much,
worked as a waiter. I don't know
why he did it. But I know it wasn't
about the magnanimous gesture,
an easy way to feel important,
it wasn't interrupting the impenetrable
edge of the individual—you'd
have to ask Lou—maybe it was
about being awake, hand-to-hand
sweetness, a chain of kindnesses,
or fun—the tenderness
we forget in each other.

Machine Shop of Love

I like the way you play your guitar.
That's what I said the first time we met—
there's no explanation for being this corny—
just love or deception.
So,

                    under the viaduct,
        under the old/railroad bridge of our ancestors/
        immigrant steelworkers/slaves of Carnegie/
        we rocked the back seat of a '69 Chevy/
        you pulled my chuck taylors/your jeans were long gone/
        goodbye to cotton/the rolling stones teeshirt/
        we're spinning in lust and oh
        steamy back windows and nothing
        can stop it/the rolling and tearing/
        machine shop of love, love—

its big plans/blue eyes/its you/
looking straight through the body/

in search of the heart/for two
weeks I waited until I proposed/
Let me think, you said/but no—

                              the body,
it has its own light/own scent/
own can't-turn-your-back-on-it-glue/
I'll wait, I said, and did—

                        for the touch
of your hair, the tender of hands/I love
the way you play your guitar/
compression/precision/the rock &
burn of it/the playing the/*yes*, you said—

Photo by Miriam Goodman

Robin Becker's six collections of poems include *Domain of Perfect Affection*, *The Horse Fair*, *All-American Girl*, and *Giacometti's Dog*. In 2001, The Frick Art and Historical Center published *Venetian Blue*, a limited-edition chapbook of her poems about graphic art. Professor of English at The Pennsylvania State University, Becker has received fellowships from the Bunting Institute of Radcliffe College, the Massachusetts Cultural Council, and the National Endowment for the Arts. Becker writes a column on poetry called "Field Notes" for the *Women's Review of Books*, where she serves as contributing and poetry editor.

The New Egypt

I think of my father who believes
a Jew can outwit fate by owning land.
Slave to property now, I mow
and mow, my destiny the new Egypt.
From his father, the tailor, he learned not
to rent but to own; to borrow to buy.
To conform, I disguise myself and drag
the mower into the drive, where I ponder
the silky oil, the plastic casing, the choke.
From my father, I learned the dignity
of exile and the fire of acquisition,
not to live in places lightly, but to plant
the self like an orange tree in the desert
and irrigate, irrigate, irrigate.

Now

Now that I have the whole afternoon to myself
I can forget my twenty-five-year plan of living
on the Paros beach with friends as the school year begins.

Now that the rain has moved inland
I can surrender the old Madison Square Garden
dressage dream of perfect balance on a horse's back.

Now that the forecast says clear weather through Friday
I can give up the dream that my parents live to one-hundred-
and-twenty, still driving and doing their own grocery shopping.

Now that I have three hours to spend before I go
to the dump, and leftovers with which to make a chicken sandwich,
I can forego my dream of breeding standard poodles,

though I like to picture many pens with black puppies sprawling
over my groomed lawn, though a handsome poodle
meets me at the door with a glass of white wine.

Now that my neighbor has finished his mowing
I can hear myself think. About death: how it occupies
every living space I can imagine, though I can't hold the thought—

Now that a breeze permits me to understand this day
will not merge with others into a synopsis of the summer,
now that I've gone this far, now that you've come with me,

I can give up my dream of biking from Boston to San Francisco
in a skintight jersey covered with ads, mid-semester, reciting the names
of North American birds and whistling all the way to the Pacific.

OK, Tucker

You win. My arm got tired of throwing the ball
before you got tired of scrambling up the river-
bank to fetch it. OK, Tucker, you can come, too.
Since you open the door with your clever snout
I'm not about to shove you back in. You win
the beauty contest, the most finicky eater award,
and the like-a-dog-with-a-bone prize; you win
the first-one-in-the-car sweepstakes. Look,
Tucker, we had no choice when we squared off
in your adolescence, we had to get along, it was a live-
and-let-live situation, both of us in love with her.
OK, I bribed you with biscuits and rides;
you conned me with a handshake and a smile.
Remember hide-and-seek in the cornfield,
the jack-in-the pulpit, the lady slipper?
That week at the beach with smelly gulls
wrapped in slime and tangled lines of seaweed?
And a pen of chickens? You had it made, but no!
Old girl, you chased the phantom squirrel
up the slope again and again, returned
slack-jawed, refused to come off the porch,
stood your ground in freezing November rain,

showed your dog's teeth when I showed my human
fear and for good measure ran circles around me—
when I was her woman, but you were her dog.

Adult Child

Now that my parents are old, they love me fiercely,
and I am grateful that the long detente of my childhood
has ended; we stroll through the retirement community.
My father would like to call the woman who left me
and tell her that I will be a wealthy woman someday.
We laugh, knowing she never cared about money
but patiently taught him to use his computer and program
the car phone. In the condo, my mother navigates
a maze of jewelry, tells me the history of watches,
bracelets, rings, pearls. She says I may sell
most of it, she just wants me to know what's what.
I drive her to the bank where we sign a little card
and walk, accompanied, into the vault, gray boxes
stacked like bodies. *Here,* she says, *are the titles and deeds.*

Why We Fear the Amish

Because they are secretly Jewish and eat matzoh on Saturday.
Because they smell us in fellowship with the dead works
of darkness and technology. Because we doubt ourselves.
We find their clothing remorseless; we find their beards unsanitary.
Who among us is not ashamed, speeding, to come upon a poor
horse pulling a cart uphill, everyone dressed the same?
We believe in the state and they believe in the button.

With their fellow Pennsylvanians, the Quakers, they hold noisy pep rallies.
They know the quilting bee, the honey bee and the husking bee
are the only proper activities for women.
Even their horses are thrifty and willing to starve for Christ.
In the Poconos, the men vacation with Hassidim and try on

each other's coats. Back home, no tractors with pneumatic tires.
Pity the child who wants a radio and must settle for a thermos.

When the world shifts to Daylight Savings Time, there's no time
like slow time, to stay out of step. In Standard Time
their horses trot faster than ours, for the Amish
set their clocks ahead. In January, they slaughter the animals.
In March, they go to the sales. In April, they plant potatoes.
In June, they cut alfalfa. In August, they cut alfalfa again.
In October they dig potatoes. In December they butcher and marry.

They modify the milk machine to suit the church, they change
the church to fit the chassis, amending their lives with hooks-and-eyes.
Their dress is a leisurely protest against chairmindedness.
We know their frugality in our corpulence. We know their sacrifice
for the group in our love for the individual. Our gods are
cross-dressers, nerds, beach-bums, and poets. They know it.
By their pure walk and practice do they eye us from their carts.

Spiritual Morning

I am as virtuous as a rabbinical student
after my morning run, God in the body awake, God
of the May apple and wild ginger. Even the little
stiff hands of the whistle pig reach
toward me in death's perfection. Once,
in Katmandu at dawn, I watched a monk in a saffron robe
brush his teeth on the roof of a temple and spit—
and from his mouth flew peach and azure birds
fluttering in the milky sweetness of the air.

       This morning of Pennsylvania
woodchuck and wild geranium, I grasp the
connection among all sentient beings and feel
communion with the wretched of all species and the dead.
The orange swallowtail looping overhead, for example,
is really my old grandmother, back to remind me

to learn Yiddish, the only international language.
I'd like her to sit on my finger
so we could talk face-to-face, but she flies
out of sight, shouting, *Big talker! Don't run on busy streets!*

The Bath

I like to watch
your breasts float like two birds
drifting downstream; you like a book,
a glass of wine on the lip
of the porcelain tub,
your music. It is your way of dissolving
the day, merging the elements of your body
with this body. The room fills with steam
like mist off a river—
as intimate to imagine you
pleasuring yourself: watery fingers, slow
movement into fantasy.
You call me in and take my hand
in your wet hand. I have to shield my eyes
from the great light
coming off your body.
When you ask me to touch you
I kneel by the water like a blind woman
guided into the river by a friend.

The Story I Like to Tell

In a drugstore north of Ft. Lauderdale
you stand in line to buy a roll of film, and I'm suddenly
aware of desire, how it fills the body
at inconvenient moments. We stare innocently at the magazines.
We are hours away from making love, months away from summer
in our real home, up north. But here, eighty degrees
in mid-December, reports of bad weather arrive

like messages from a distant star. You know I want you
and you smile, for the inopportune
appeals to you. Come closer. If we can't make love,
I'll tell you a story.
My bedroom opened onto olive trees and grapevines.
It was too hot for sheets. Mornings, she walked naked
around the mill, we drank strong coffee, I watered red
geraniums in the garden. At the sight of my thighs, she gasped.
While Italian cyclists rimmed our hill town,
I swept her with my tongue for hours.

How does it feel? Tales of old lovers, silk beneath denim,
pain and pleasure cresting like a Mediterranean
wave, like the moon slung in a Tuscan window.
Come closer. I know you
like meetings after separations, ambiguous
relations, someone kissing your ear. Let's go
to the beach now; palm fronds quiver on postcards;
pelicans are flying close to shore.
If we can't make love, I'll distract you
with another story
I like to tell, the one set on a distant coast,
in another Romance language.

Photo by Carlos Betancourt

Richard Blanco was made in Cuba, assembled in Spain, and imported to the United States—meaning his mother, seven months pregnant, and the rest of the family arrived as exiles from Cuba to Madrid, where he was born. Only forty-five days later, the family emigrated once more and eventually settled in Miami where he was raised and educated. He is the author of *City of a Hundred Fires,* winner of the Agnes Lynch Starrett Poetry Prize, and *Directions to The Beach of the Dead,* which received a PEN/American Beyond Margins Award. Blanco has taught at Georgetown, American University, and Connecticut State University. He currently lives in Miami, where he writes and works as a consultant engineer.

América

I.

Although Tía Miriam boasted she discovered
at least half a dozen uses for peanut butter—
topping for guava shells in syrup,
butter substitute for Cuban toast,
hair conditioner and relaxer—
Mamá never knew what to make
of the monthly five-pound jars
handed out by the immigration department
until my friend, Jeff, mentioned jelly.

II.

There was always pork though,
for every birthday and wedding,
whole ones on Christmas and New Year's Eve,
even on Thanksgiving day—pork,
fried, broiled, or crispy skin roasted—
as well as cauldrons of black beans,
fried plantain chips, and *yuca con mojito.*
These items required a special visit
to Antonio's Mercado on the corner of Eighth Street
where men in *guayaberas* stood in senate
blaming Kennedy for everything—*"Ese hijo de puta!"*
the bile of Cuban coffee and cigar residue
filling the creases of their wrinkled lips;
clinging to one another's lies of lost wealth,
ashamed and empty as hollow trees.

III.

By seven I had grown suspicious—we were still here.
Overheard conversations about returning
had grown wistful and less frequent.
I spoke English; my parents didn't.
We didn't live in a two-story house
with a maid or a wood-panel station wagon
nor vacation camping in Colorado.

None of the girls had hair of gold;
none of my brothers or cousins
were named Greg, Peter, or Marcia;
we were not the Brady Bunch.
None of the black and white characters
on Donna Reed or on the Dick Van Dyke Show
were named Guadalupe, Lázaro, or Mercedes.
Patty Duke's family wasn't like us either—
they didn't have pork on Thanksgiving,
they ate turkey with cranberry sauce;
they didn't have *yuca,* they had yams
like the dittos of Pilgrims I colored in class.

IV.

A week before Thanksgiving
I explained to my *abuelita*
about the Indians and the Mayflower,
how Lincoln set the slaves free;
I explained to my parents about
the purple mountain's majesty,
"one if by land, two if by sea,"
the cherry tree, the tea party,
the amber waves of grain,
the "masses yearning to be free,"
liberty and justice for all, until
finally they agreed:
this Thanksgiving we would have turkey,
as well as pork.

V.

Abuelita prepared the poor fowl
as if committing an act of treason,
faking her enthusiasm for my sake.
Mamá set a frozen pumpkin pie in the oven
and prepared candied yams following instructions
I translated from the marshmallow bag.
The table was arrayed with gladiolas,
the plattered turkey loomed at the center

on plastic silver from Woolworth's.
Everyone sat in green velvet chairs
we had upholstered with clear vinyl,
except Tío Carlos and Toti, seated
in the folding chairs from the Salvation Army.
I uttered a bilingual blessing
and the turkey was passed around
like a game of Russian Roulette.
"DRY," Tío Berto complained, and proceeded
to drown the lean slices with pork fat drippings
and cranberry jelly—*"esa mierda roja,"* he called it.
Faces fell when *Mamá* presented her ochre pie—
pumpkin was a home remedy for ulcers, not a dessert.
Tía María made three rounds of Cuban coffee
then *Abuelo* and Pepe cleared the living room furniture,
put on a Celia Cruz LP and the entire family
began to *merengue* over the linoleum of our apartment,
sweating rum and coffee until they remembered—
it was 1970 and 46 degrees—
in *América.*
After repositioning the furniture,
an appropriate darkness filled the room.
Tío Berto was the last to leave.

The Silver Sands

Before the revival of quartz pinks and icy blues
on this neon beach of Art Deco hotels and boutiques,
there were the twilight verandas lined with retirees,
the cataract eyes of Mrs. Stein who would take us
for mezzanine bingo and pancakes at Wolfies;
I remember her beautiful orthopedic wobble.

Before sequined starlets popping out of limousine doors
and booze on the breath of every glitter-paved street,
there were the five-year-old summers of flamingo towels,
transistor radios blaring something in Spanish we ignored,

only curious of driftwood, washed-up starfish and jellyfish,
the beauty of broken conchs and our moated sand castles.

Before the widened sidewalks and pretentious cafés
where I take my cappuccino sprinkled with cinnamon,
our mothers were peacocks in flowered bathing caps
posing for sandy Polaroids like pageant contestants;
there were fifteen-cent Cokes to their ruby lips
and there was nothing their beauty couldn't conquer.

Before the demolition of the Silver Sands Hotel,
our fathers spun dominos under the thatch-palm gazebos,
drank then insulted the scenery: *Nada like our Varadero,*
there the sand was powder; the water truly aquamarine.
I remember the poor magic of those voices—
how beautifully they remembered beauty.

El Cucubano

Lucía enjoyed the mystery, the emerald light
captive in the bright belly of *los cucubanos*
she wore clipped to her home-sewn dress
parading like a peacock at the town socials
around the reservoir and sugar mill clock.
All the señoritas flashed their *cucubanos*—
live pendants adorning breasts and hearts
to compete with the swirl of *guajiro* stars
for the attention of prime young caballeros
in linen *guayaberas* and straw hats;
the clock chiming every hour of courting,
denying every second of lustful thought
in the smolders of raped sugarcane fields.

Lucía knew nothing of the nerve stimulations,
the reactions that produced the bound light
of balanced chemicals in glowing abdomens.
What she knew was how the male *cucubanos*
tracked females by following their flashes;

how to trap them in her mother's glass jars
in the hours of the early evening before
the moon rises strong and snuffs their glow;
how to pinch them so they cling to the dress,
near the heart, calling attention to the breasts,
the green fire silhouetting the spell of nipples.

Lucía never questioned the cool light nor Alberto
when he took her, removed her *cucubano,*
said she wouldn't be needing fireflies anymore
now that she'd belong to him and his promises.
Lucía knows how *el cucubano* swirled away
from Alberto's fingers into infinite green spirals
through palm trees and mountains, how soon after
the harvest Alberto also disappeared.
Lucía stares at stars she swears are green,
traps *cucubanos* between her cupped hands,
jade oozing between the seams of her fingers,
the phenomenon of luminescence in her palms—
light without heat, love without love.

Tía Olivia Serves Wallace Stevens a Cuban Egg

The ration books voided, there was little to eat,
so Tía Olivia ruffled four hens to serve Stevens
a fresh *criollo* egg. The singular image lay limp,
floating in a circle of miniature roses and vines
etched around the edges of the rough dish.
The saffron, inhuman soul staring at Stevens
who asks what yolk is this, so odd a yellow?

Tell me Señora, if you know, he petitions,
what exactly is the color of this temptation:
I can see a sun, but it is not the color of suns
nor of sunflowers, nor the yellows of Van Gogh,
it is neither corn nor school pencil, as it is,
so few things are yellow, this, even more precise.

He shakes some salt, eye to eye hypothesizing:
a carnival of hues under the gossamer membrane,
a liqueur of convoluted colors, quarter-part orange,
imbued shadows, watercolors running a song
down the spine of praying stems, but what, then,
of the color of the stems, what green for the leaves,
what color the flowers; what of order for our eyes
if I can not name this elusive yellow, Señora?

Intolerant, Tía Olivia bursts open Stevens's yolk,
plunging into it with a sharp piece of Cuban toast:
It is yellow, she says, *amarillo y nada más, bien?*
The unleashed pigments begin to fill the plate,
overflow onto the embroidered place mats,
stream down the table and through the living room
setting all the rocking chairs in motion then
over the mill tracks cutting through cane fields,
a viscous mass downing palm trees and shacks.

In its frothy wake whole choirs of church ladies
clutch their rosary beads and sing out in Latin,
exhausted *macheteros* wade in the stream,
holding glinting machetes overhead with one arm;
cafeteras, '57 Chevys, uniforms and empty bottles,
mangy dogs and fattened pigs saved from slaughter,
Soviet jeeps, *Bohemia* magazines, park benches,
all carried in the egg lava carving the molested valley
and emptying into the sea. *Yellow,* Stevens relents,
Yes. But then what the color of the sea, Señora?

Photo by Lucia and Doug Deaville

Christopher Bursk is the author of nine poetry collections, including *The First Inhabitants of Arcadia* and *The Improbable Swervings of Atoms*. He is the recipient of fellowships from the Guggenheim Foundation, the National Endowment for the Arts, and Pew Charitable Trusts. A grandfather of six, he teaches at Bucks County Community College in Bucks County, Pennsylvania.

Dr. Livingstone, I Presume

It may have been 1951 in every home in America
but in ours it was 1865 and my brother and I were going to do
what no human had
yet dared: on the backs of elephants carry Christ
into the jungle and diamonds out.
All we needed were machetes, some quinine, and an excuse
and we'd conquer the Congo.
Who better understood mosquitoes than us?
It didn't daunt my brother
that we'd never bicycled past the town limits.
What was fording a few rapids
compared to battling space aliens for the right
to stake a flag into the red dust of the next-door planet?
This time we'd have gravity
on our side. Nothing's easier
than murdering a whole tribe if you've got guns
that don't have to be reloaded
right away and also a proclamation from the president
and pamphlets from the Aborigines Relief Society
and an open market for all the ivory you can hack
off the corpses of creatures who'd evolved
so children in Schenectady could play a little Brahms
and London barristers might chew meat again,
all because of my brother and me
and a few thousand natives born in the wasteful squalor
of the jungle. How could we not punish the heathens
for dropping things along the trail and dying
at the very moment Western civilization most needed them
to bear the burdens with which they'd been entrusted?
At least we weren't Arabs or Catholics or Huns.
For our gardens we'd not make a border
of the natives' severed heads,
nor cut off their sons' hands. We'd not even whip our slaves
unless we had to. We were Americans.
We wouldn't kill anyone

unless they asked for it,
and it grieved us when they did
again and again.

The Barbarians

> We face a hostile ideology, global in scope, atheistic
> in character, ruthless in purpose, and insidious in
> method.
> —DWIGHT DAVID EISENHOWER,
>   JANUARY 17, 1961

My body was already being invaded by an army
I could no more stop than the Romans could
the Visigoths. Stamp out a few
and more popped up. And Eisenhower was worried
about the Communists? I was at the mercy
of vandals, thousands upon thousands
of pillagers with no history
and, therefore, no scruples, even the most private parts of me
under siege, no matter how vigilant I was
patrolling borders. If I looked away for just a moment
I found myself being plundered
anew, the horde back, preoccupied
with doing what a horde is good at.
Whole tribes set up camp in my armpits,
in my groin, digging in roots so deep
it would have been suicide to try
to eradicate them, my body not mine anymore
to do with as I wished.
I ought to have been a good Roman,
imperturbable in the midst of the squalor,
yet here I was:
picking at, scrubbing, swabbing, swathing, trying to
pluck each rebellious hair. No part of me
off-limits: chest, belly, scrotal sac.
What's wrong with me? What's wrong

with me? Even that stalwart defender
of the faith, my penis, had turned
native, traitor, aboriginal
and mutinous. Would nothing ever be safe
from the barbarians?

One Nation, Indivisible, Under God

On the day that the St. Lawrence Seaway opened
for saltwater ships to sail deep into the heart of America,
I was being launched into water too,
my head stuck in the toilet
thanks to the good offices of the student council
vice president, the class treasurer, and the captain
of the volleyball team, all of whom decided
that if I wasn't a faggot, I ought to be. Last week
it'd been my best friend's turn, but luckily today
they'd been kind enough not to
piss in the toilet beforehand. They were doing me a favor,
one boy told me, as another
laid his hands on my head, the way a pastor might
press down a reluctant parishioner
into the baptismal font again
and again, as if once wasn't enough
to cleanse a soul. Each time my face hit the water
it seemed to mock me. Each time
my head was yanked up,
my mouth tried to swallow
enough air for when I'd be pushed down
again. I was already worrying
about how I'd explain to my dad why I'd come home
reeking of disinfectant. What I remember most
are the arms of the eleventh-grade
treasurer, holding me from behind so tightly
he could have been hugging me,
the minty breath of the volleyball captain
as he pressed my head into the toilet,

the hands of the just-elected vice president
on the back of my neck
as if he were trying to teach me to swim
the only way he knew how.

The World of Business

Marcel Proust on Marketing.
Instructions to the Jesuit Brothers Who Manage Haciendas.
George Washington and Truth in Advertising.
Open to any page of the boxed set and there is my father:
talking to Emperor Hadrian or John Wanamaker,
Alexander Hamilton or Bernal Diaz Del Castillo.

My dad could turn anyone into an entrepreneur.
Hitler, Gandhi. No one was safe from my old man:
Stalin's excerpted speech was retitled "New Methods of Work,
New Methods of Management,"
even George Bernard Shaw ended up a poster boy
for life insurance. Tarquin the Proud, Lorenzo de Medici,

Haile Selassie, Boss Tweed, and Dwight David Eisenhower crowded
into my father's thirty-page index, that great hall
where he'd brought together the world's leaders
so they might agree on certain principles: the healing efficacy
of hard work, the virtues of enlightened
self-interest. It is 1964. My father is at his desk
in his mistress's house, just learning

to drink enough to put everything painful out of his head:
his disappointing son, his crazy wife.
He ends his four-volume labor with what he calls *a challenge*
for the second half of our twentieth century
and for the rest of the years that lie ahead waiting for man
to fill them with his busy dreaming
and his busy doing. By the time of publication

those millions my father envisioned
buying *The World of Business*
would have better things to do; boys sent home
in body bags, the country heavily invested in a war
by men not even mentioned in any of the 1135 pages.
If they'd just read my books, my father liked to say,
as if apologizing to everyone indexed in *The World of Business*.

Buddha, Carnegie, Herodotus, Conrad Hilton,
J. Pierpont Morgan, Michelangelo, the prophet Mohammed
knew the importance of consumer research and good PR.
A failure in marketing strategy, he'd sigh
as he'd sweeten his drink. Yes, most of the world's problems
could be attributed to that: *bad marketing.*
It had much to answer for.

Anthony Butts is the author of *Male Hysteria; Little Low Heaven,* winner of the Poetry Society of America's William Carlos Williams Award; *Evolution;* and *Fifth Season.* He has been a member of the creative writing faculty at Carnegie Mellon University since 2001.

Blue Movie

In the hours before dawn I stand in a black-and-white scene, the almost-blue
blackness of the predawn hours, the white of the snow piling neatly on
the streets: a bus that always takes too long to pull up to the curb outside

of Farmer Jack's grocery store. The cold is my companion, more faithful
than any lover. I am too young for girlfriends, my mother says. Better to
wait until high school or college. The white light pours out of the store.

The white light pours out of the streetlamps. There is a pale patina to
mornings like this as the snow continues to plummet perilously toward
earth. In class, I learned about cold Pluto: a snowy ball of ice in the artist's

rendition, with the sun like any ordinary star glimmering in the middle
of the sky. There were natural arches along the landscape mirroring
the manmade ones here in Detroit, the snowy McDonald's sign down

the street. After the seasick trip from Boblo Island, that's all I wanted:
a Big Mac to make it all right. I wanted something to make me
stop thinking about how I couldn't get Wanda's attention; she didn't

think I needed a girlfriend either. This morning, I listened to Devo
as I dressed—thinking of Jermaine Jackson, the only black performer
to sing with them. Maybe integration is possible, if blacks are

allowed to be nerds as well? The bus ride is uneventful, with the usual
workers at River Rouge Ford getting on—their revoked driving privileges
having forced drunken Detroiters to go without their beloved automobiles

for a year or two. It's all they can do to make life seem more interesting
than it is, fuzzy logic in a blurry Great Lakes state. The day will pass
for them, as evenly as it does for Jacquese Wilson, who I've worked

with every day this week—the straight-A student helping the straight-F
student in the teacher's last-ditch attempt to make this right, the fact
that some students ask too many questions and others not enough.

In Mr. Hall's class, Jacquese pulled down his pants in a show of disrespect
to the teacher. It got him the girls he had been after, later telling me that
he and Ray ate butterscotch off their bellies the night before. *You don't*

get any by keeping your pants on! The smell of the slaughterhouse
fills the morning air as I exit the bus. There are few students walking
to school today, their mothers believing their stories while I march on.

Classes would be cancelled that day, though I didn't want to go home.
I wanted to try one more time to make Jacquese see that science was as
easy as the imagination would allow—as he fantasizes about the next girl.

Eros and Thanatos

I am in the bathroom again with the J. C. Penney catalog. Its lingerie
section is more interesting than Sears's. I don't know why I never get caught.
Maybe I want, in some weird way, to be discovered with my pants thrown
off and the book balancing on the edge of the sink? Maybe sex is as dangerous
as it seems on *Fantasy Island,* people getting just what they want in ways

other than they could have imagined? Or, maybe, the woman I will marry
will someday be like Chris Evert Lloyd—a winner who knows how to
get what she wants? Her tiny white tennis skirt flicks with each shot as she
asserts her will. In the past year, I have asked one hundred and forty-six girls
to be my valentine, but no one has responded. It seems improbable that no one

could love me. Maybe it's not like science, with statistical probabilities?
Maybe nerds don't find love? Gail Keith still hasn't gotten over the fact
that I asked her, that look on her face mirrored in so many others—as if
my love were like lemon sucked down. Maybe my place will always be
with the blind kids, people half-retarded and unaware of what's wrong

with them? Maybe mainstreaming won't work, because the world will
not have me with my folder cover of finely etched names of popular
stars: Cyndi Lauper and Madonna? The firmly inked maze that
surrounds their names is like the maze of my life working abnormally.
Doctor Who is on television. He is my friend, the only one who

seems to believe that the universe is worth saving. Pastor Edison
says that Jesus is coming this year, exactly when he doesn't know, but
we should come to church every day this week and pray that God
does not destroy us. There is red everywhere: the red carpet of the
pulpit; red light coming from the cross carved into the collection box;

red everywhere except in the dresses of the women of the church. Their
clothes have muted colors, in order to not offend the Deity. It's so easy
to offend these days. Last month, he said that boys who masturbate are
going to hell—but I don't believe him. There is something odd about
this church, joining it because I had no choice, because I wanted

to be saved in case I died young. One day, I will find a church of love—
because God must be love if the devil is evil. They both can't be out for
my destruction. What kind of world would that be? In homeroom,
Miss Haynor is getting us ready for the day—half blind herself, with her
make-do hairstyle, telling us how well we will do if we have faith in the system.

Trying to Be Human

The two torches of Demeter, given to the couple for their anniversary, sit on
an outdoor patio in their Grecian resplendence. Inside, artwork hangs on the

walls. Inside, children are living with invisibility. There are finely crafted
bowls of cobalt blue filled with fat noodles. On the tables are chopsticks

with which the children have learned to eat. Other cultures can be fascinating.
His mistresses talk with each other over oysters and ouzo about his facility

with Zen, about acceptance and enlightenment. Another man has come to
the conclusion that he doesn't find his girlfriend to be as attractive as the women

he sees on television, so he stops watching. Their blonde visages are like
a Great Lakes road during whiteout, hazy and ever present, as he searches

in the mirror for his own brunette likeness—a mole he can no longer find,
women in their images contaminating the frame. Another man sits with his

girlfriend on a park bench. She is the greatest fascist he has ever known;
he has no choice but to love her. She is never satisfied with the silences

between them, the sound too contemptuous for words. So she talks, constantly
telling him what to do and how to dress in order to impress her. He wears

suspenders, like her father used to, what real men wear when they want
to seem respectable. The torches shine a dim light as the house sits in darkness,

as the children have gone off to bed. The couple is out getting high in the half-
light of the patio. The couple is starting and putting out fires. Sometimes,

the mistresses join them because life is about finding a way to say "yes"
instead of "no." The fascist is watching her boyfriend performing the sex

acts that she likes. He is happy to be useful. They will sleep with the radio
on, because someone must be talking. They awaken and wonder where

the night went. The ordinary boyfriend wakes up to his ordinary girl after
having a dream where the mole was really eating his cheek, where the dot

was put there by the blonde girls on television. She awakens to kiss
the cheek with the mole, making him feel even less honest or wise.

Forgiveness

The little black boy does not cry, because he can't. He has been beaten
and raped so often that he thinks that he deserves a little rest from time
to time. On the wall is a stolen poster for the movie *Contact*. On the floor
are socks that he is afraid to slip on; even that is too sexual. He wants
to become a beam of light because no one would touch it, as he remembers

what it was like the day before when he sat open-legged in the sun with no
one to bother him. The neighbor girls were watching him with their teenage
grins, their hormones out of control. In their house, the liquor and the pot
come out at every card game, barbecue outing, neighborhood knifing where
the sister thinks one of the brothers wanted something forbidden from her.

Across the street, those neighbors are shooting at squirrels because God
gave them dominion over all the animals. They pretend the squirrels
are men who'd come to steal their twenty-year-old station wagon, rusting
in the backyard. They pretend they are gods of weaponry. God goes
by many names, all of them set against each other in the ultimate search

for *truth*. In the neighborhood church, the Jews and the Catholics are
scapegoats. Jesus will come because they don't understand. A few ministers
sit in the chairs of repentance because they have cheated on their wives again,

because as long as they ask for forgiveness they will be saved from both
parishioners and God—and the children know what children are never

supposed to know, that with God all things are possible. Even the resident
dope dealer comes to church in a gaudy gold cross to match his gold tooth.
Even the prostitute, whose son has been parceled out to the men who wanted
something different, believes that she will ultimately be saved. God never
gets tired of forgiving, beam of light shining on the universe that He is.

The little boy doesn't know what it's like to be human, to have feelings
that someone else didn't tell him he had to have. If he did, would he still
want to become an unfeeling beam of light? Would he want to dominate
the universe with his own belief system? Would he want to wander the streets
when he's older, looking for all the things for which he must later be forgiven?

Heritage

Clouds lie like spilled milk across the fringed blue sky. White moths
make their way along gardenias blooming behind a picket fence.
No, this is not a conspiracy: just the way an easy day should go.

A woman in a canary yellow sundress fades into an inconsequential
complacency as the pages blur, as she stops thinking about what each
word might mean, her skin hinting at being pink in the sunlight waning

near the horizon. Her children might be safe as houses as a black man
walks along the periphery of the park. Her children might be like the
children he wants but cannot have. His marriage would be a compromise,

with children who at their best might not be light enough to pass. He knows
his children would never be safe. Better to adopt white ones.
Across the street, a blonde is straining to be heard as she lip-synchs

the words to her latest video playing on a forty-inch television. She seems
almost life-size, almost as realized as a poem. The black man might want
to climb inside and be someone else, with her, with someone like her

who might provide a better future. But the woman, with her children,
are more than currency, more than the sundress wedding dress any dress blues.
We all know it's true, that the ace of spades is a bad-ass card—that the man

who holds it is a motherfucker. Eastern European and Asian babies
flood the market, while blacks lie in wait—growing old like money
that doesn't spend. As the woman on the bench lapses in and out

of her dream, an elderly woman looks hard at the man, as if to say
"I've got my eye on you, even if she doesn't."
It's good to have friends, good to know people like you.

Photo by John Dougall

Lorna Dee Cervantes is the author of *From the Cables of Genocide: Poems on Love and Hunger* and *Emplumada*, which won an American Book Award. She is also coeditor of *Red Dirt*, a cross-cultural poetry journal, and her work has been included in many anthologies including *Unsettling America: An Anthology of Contemporary Multicultural Poetry, No More Masks! An Anthology of Twentieth-Century Women Poets*, and *After Aztlan: Latino Poets of the Nineties*. She lives in Boulder, Colorado.

Emplumada

When summer ended
the leaves of snapdragons withered
taking their shrill-colored mouths with them.
They were still, so quiet. They were
violet where umber now is. She hated
and she hated to see
them go. Flowers

born when the weather was good—this
she thinks of, watching the branch of peaches
daring their ways above the fence, and further,
two hummingbirds, hovering, stuck to each other,
arcing their bodies in grim determination
to find what is good, what is
given them to find. These are warriors

distancing themselves from history.
They find peace
in the way they contain the wind
and are gone.

Meeting Mescalito at Oak Hill Cemetery

Sixteen years old and crooked
with drug, time warped blissfully
as I sat alone on Oak Hill.

The cemetery stones were neither erect
nor stonelike, but looked soft and harmless;
thousands of them rippling the meadows
like overgrown daisies.

I picked apricots from the trees below
where the great peacocks roosted and nagged

loose the feathers from their tails.
I knelt to a lizard with my hands
on the earth, lifted him and held him
in my palm—Mescalito
was a true god.

Coming home that evening
nothing had changed. I covered Mama on the sofa

with a quilt I sewed myself, locked my bedroom
door against the stepfather, and gathered
the feathers I'd found that morning, each
green eye in a heaven of blue, a fistfull
of understanding;

and late that night I tasted
the last of the sweet fruit, sucked the rich pit
and thought nothing of death.

Beneath the Shadow of the Freeway

1
Across the street—the freeway,
blind worm, wrapping the valley up
from Los Altos to Sal Si Puedes.
I watched it from my porch
unwinding. Every day at dusk
as Grandma watered geraniums
the shadow of the freeway lengthened.

2
We were a woman family:
Grandma, our innocent Queen;
Mama, the Swift Knight, Fearless Warrior.
Mama wanted to be Princess instead.
I know that. Even now she dreams of taffeta
and foot-high tiaras.

Myself: I could never decide.
So I turned to books, those staunch, upright men.
I became Scribe: Translator of Foreign Mail,
interpreting letters from the government, notices
of dissolved marriages and Welfare stipulations.
I paid the bills, did light man-work, fixed faucets,
insured everything
against all leaks.

3

Before rain I notice seagulls.
They walk in flocks,
cautious across lawns: splayed toes,
indecisive beaks. Grandma says
seagulls mean storm.

In California in the summer,
mockingbirds sing all night.
Grandma says they are singing for their nesting wives.
"They don't leave their families
borrachando."

She likes the ways of birds,
respects how they show themselves
for toast and a whistle.

She believes in myths and birds.
She trusts only what she builds
with her own hands.

4

She built her house,
cocky, disheveled carpentry,
after living twenty-five years
with a man who tried to kill her.

Grandma, from the hills of Santa Barbara,
I would open my eyes to see her stir mush

---

in the morning, her hair in loose braids,
tucked close around her head
with a yellow scarf.

Mama said, "It's her own fault,
getting screwed by a man for that long.
Sure as shit wasn't hard."
soft she was soft

5
in the night I would hear it
glass bottles shattering the street
words cracked into shrill screams
inside my throat   a cold fear
as it entered the house in hard
unsteady steps   stopping at my door
my name   bathrobe   slippers
outside a 3 a.m. mist heavy
as a breath full of whiskey
stop it   go home   come inside
mama if he comes here again
I'll call the police

inside
a gray kitten   a touchstone
purring beneath the quilts
grandma stitched
from his suits
the patchwork singing
of mockingbirds

6
"You're too soft … always were.
You'll get nothing but shit.
Baby, don't count on nobody."

—a mother's wisdom.
Soft. I haven't changed,

maybe grown more silent, cynical
on the outside.

"O Mama, with what's inside of me
I could wash that all away. I could."

"But Mama, if you're good to them
they'll be good to you back."

Back. The freeway is across the street.
It's summer now. Every night I sleep with a gentle man
to the hymn of mockingbirds,

and in time, I plant geraniums.
I tie up my hair into loose braids,
and trust only what I have built
with my own hands.

Poem for the Young White Man Who Asked Me How I, an Intelligent, Well-Read Person Could Believe in the War Between Races

In my land there are no distinctions.
The barbed wire politics of oppression
have been torn down long ago. The only reminder
of past battles, lost or won, is a slight
rutting in the fertile fields.

In my land
people write poems about love,
full of nothing but contented childlike syllables.
Everyone reads Russian short stories and weeps.
There are no boundaries.
There is no hunger, no
complicated famine or greed.

I am not a revolutionary.
I don't even like political poems.

Do you think I can believe in a war between races?
I can deny it. I can forget about it
when I'm safe,
living on my own continent of harmony
and home, but I am not
there.

I believe in revolution
because everywhere the crosses are burning,
sharp-shooting goose-steppers round every corner,
there are snipers in the schools . . .
(I know you don't believe this.
You think this is nothing
but faddish exaggeration. But they
are not shooting at you.)

I'm marked by the color of my skin.
The bullets are discrete and designed to kill slowly.
They are aiming at my children.
These are facts.
Let me show you my wounds: my stumbling mind, my
"excuse me" tongue, and this
nagging preoccupation
with the feeling of not being good enough.

These bullets bury deeper than logic.
Racism is not intellectual.
I can not reason these scars away.

Outside my door
there is a real enemy
who hates me.

I am a poet
who yearns to dance on rooftops,
to whisper delicate lines about joy
and the blessings of human understanding.
I try. I go to my land, my tower of words and

bolt the door, but the typewriter doesn't fade out
the sounds of blasting and muffled outrage.
My own days bring me slaps on the face.
Every day I am deluged with reminders
that this is not
my land

and this is my land.

I do not believe in the war between races

but in this country
there is war.

Wanda Coleman's recent books include *Ostinato Vamps*, *Wanda Coleman— Greatest Hits 1966–2003*, and *The Riot Inside Me: More Trials & Tremors*, and her poems have been included in anthologies such as *The Best American Poetry*, *The Norton Anthology of African American Literature*, and *Trouble the Water: 250 Years of African American Poetry*. Coleman has received fellowships from the Guggenheim Foundation, the National Endowment for the Arts, and the California Arts Council. She was awarded the 1999 Lenore Marshall Prize from the Academy of American Poets and was a bronze-medal finalist for the 2001 National Book Awards. Born in the Los Angeles community of Watts and raised in South Central, she resides in Southern California with her husband, Austin Straus, and family.

Lady Sings the Blues 1969

1)

i haven't been conceived yet
haven't been born
yet Lady Holiday is singing my blues
twenty-three years later here i am ears deep
into her song, notes burning in my soul
words decades old still too true, caught up
in the same ol' slavery/love-for-a-black-man slavery
get-up-in-the-morning-face-another-day slavery
cry-lonely-in-the-night slavery
listening while Lady swings my blues

burning out my soul
with old names for new tensions
can't pay the rhetoric tensions
dying in The Dream tensions
too-black-for-some-folk tensions
carry epithets in self-defense tensions

twenty-three years deep
into Lady Day wringing the white out my blue

2)

Lady knew about the jive-assed brothers together
with their "philosophy" the big-mouth the big word
the big-wow talking the cause sweet-tongued, zip-witted
zigzag B-bruthas all play all theater all curtain call & no cast party

Lady knew about the hours between gigs
when hunger is blues. the hours between lovings
when hunger is blues. the hours between laughs
trying to kick the ain't-shit blues,
going home to greet the dust and the echo of a life

i'm on my knees rocking
on the floor on my knees groaning on the floor
into the scratchy hi-fidelity
on my knees as i sing along
twenty-three years forever bluesing out my brown eyes

and i wonder as i romance the night
will i be unlucky and live tomorrow?

3)
autumn—not in New York—but in my heart
evergreens and rose-gold October sunsets

going to my head as the air blows in off the sea
Lady—no waterfronts, but cement & neon

care packages of sausages & chocolate,
love-stained letters to my man in Vietnam

autumn—not a leaf turning—but my hope
spinning fantasies from cobwebs & cracks

Lady—no waterfronts, but cement, neon & padlocks

4)
a turn for the blues, i am the sofa-bound odalisque
fending off the workday with a heavy dose
of moonlight chased by sparkling burgundy brew

essence of daze-eyed and haunted, heartbreak never
felt so luminously rendered—so regrettably wise

Los Angeles Nocturne

Eternity ends where Hollywood begins

to be THERE is to scarf and strangle
on those cool thick lids and hot brown eyes
is to possess the unpossessible/fever and cure
is to ignite those cold stars over Avalon
(like stumblers through long-unpaved hearts
looking for the back entrance to love)
is to set them in a dreamscape of asphalt & desire
a sea of tight ambition & loose thighs

southerly off Graham, streetlamps wave like raffia
when earth quakes. nightprowlers
cruise jungle to jungle, anxious to score the light

no reservations tonight. it's a dress-down affair

stilettos like high-pitched hopes heard
stabbing down sidewalks while
behind slammed doors the Molochs tally
ill-gotten dreams and low-hung coupes take
stops doin' the South Central Roll

the unreachable unbreachable unteachables
hands shoved so deep into pockets
they can feel the next world

    remember the Parisian Room
    remember the California Club
    remember Memory Lane

Normandie zigs where Jefferson zags

(you too can touch it. as much
as you want
you too can taste it. as much
as you want

there is everything to feel. there. throbbings
in your palms like my heart)

Eternity ends where Hollywood begins

Soul Traveler

not dispersing but containing blackness

it was the ending and so reruns began
Amazon style, summer came calling,
fried brains and all. dumbfounded
in Los Angeles where mosquitoes drowse

in noonday heat, bloodlust drained from
tropical eyes, the air thin as a haint's brassiere

luxmobiles took the heights like llamas
where dollars shine from foreheads as smooth
as polished fenders, and from oversized
designer pocketbooks toted under shaved
and flavored underarms, breasts revealed
in bright colors, tank tops and bustiers

negra Afro angel

pat those cheeks in Spanish,
those too round strutters—a lingo dug by all

quietly there's reciprocation in snatches
from whistling lips, sunbeams and posters of James Dean

(shy tourist girl, a face all acne and
inexperience, shares her mother's
private smile. "buy something, some trinket.
support the local economy")

the emissary from G.O.D. calls her over,
places the silver cross at her throat, fixes her
with agate eyes, fingers splayed against
her hips. she follows him to the other side
of the moon, counts the hours under azure,
feigns reachings for her pen

note: plastic trash bags, cheap jewelry, the ebony cat in the cradle

she is made of ocean spray,
condor feathers and memories of sin

Baptism

riptide washes over
and the depths of oceanic rhythms
correct every effing mistake.

they are not in this room. just the sounds
(the boomshockaboom rattling floorboards)
marginalized—from the left and the right

i am visiting this stereophonic past
because i'm not only thirsty in general
but a bloodthirsty blood

and water equals peace of mind
an unhurried soak in the tub
to sooth the savage in the veins
like a glass of liver-corrupter

the light languor of liquor going to his head and mind
the unpainted nudes—four hundred pounds
of raw do-it-to-me/the same way snakes dance
the noisy passion of lovers full hitch
this is the place in the music where
the soloist steps up to the mike
and obsesses over an ear
and the couches and tables catch fire
and there's a burning
in the thickness

Exoteric

what is life's purpose?

      change diapers when necessary

how we think about death

      open the window. it's hot in here

what we cling to in the midst of change

      your cold hand. let me warm it

Photo by Juliet van Otteren

Billy Collins was named U.S. Poet Laureate in June 2001 and reappointed to the post in 2002. His collections of poetry include *The Trouble with Poetry; Nine Horses; Sailing Alone Around the Room: New and Selected Poems; Picnic, Lightning; The Art of Drowning;* and *Questions About Angels.* His work has been featured in the Pushcart Prize anthology and has been chosen several times for the annual *Best American Poetry* series. Collins is the editor of *Poetry 180: A Turning Back to Poetry* and *180 More: Extraordinary Poems for Everyday Life,* and was a guest editor for the 2006 edition of *The Best American Poetry*. He is a Distinguished Professor of English at Lehman College, City University of New York.

I Chop Some Parsley While Listening to
Art Blakey's Version of "Three Blind Mice"

And I start wondering how they came to be blind.
If it was congenital, they could be brothers and sisters,
and I think of the poor mother
brooding over her sightless young triplets.

Or was it a common accident, all three caught
in a searing explosion, a firework perhaps?
If not,
if each came to his or her blindness separately,

how did they ever manage to find one another?
Would it not be difficult for a blind mouse
to locate even one fellow mouse with vision
let alone two other blind ones?

And how, in their tiny darkness,
could they possibly have run after a farmer's wife
or anyone else's wife for that matter?
Not to mention why.

Just so she could cut off their tails
with a carving knife, is the cynic's answer,
but the thought of them without eyes
and now without tails to trail through the moist grass

or slip around the corner of a baseboard
has the cynic who always lounges within me
up off his couch and at the window
trying to hide the rising softness that he feels.

By now I am on to dicing an onion
which might account for the wet stinging
in my own eyes, though Freddie Hubbard's
mournful trumpet on "Blue Moon,"

which happens to be the next cut,
cannot be said to be making matters any better.

Shoveling Snow with Buddha

In the usual iconography of the temple or the local Wok
you would never see him doing such a thing,
tossing the dry snow over the mountain
of his bare, round shoulder,
his hair tied in a knot,
a model of concentration.

Sitting is more his speed, if that is the word
for what he does, or does not do.

Even the season is wrong for him.
In all his manifestations, is it not warm and slightly humid?
Is this not implied by his serene expression,
that smile so wide it wraps itself around the waist of the universe?

But here we are, working our way down the driveway,
one shovelful at a time.
We toss the light powder into the clear air.
We feel the cold mist on our faces.
And with every heave we disappear
and become lost to each other
in these sudden clouds of our own making,
these fountain-bursts of snow.

This is so much better than a sermon in church,
I say out loud, but Buddha keeps on shoveling.
This is the true religion, the religion of snow,
and sunlight and winter geese barking in the sky,
I say, but he is too busy to hear me.

He has thrown himself into shoveling snow
as if it were the purpose of existence,
as if the sign of a perfect life were a clear driveway
you could back the car down easily
and drive off into the vanities of the world
with a broken heater fan and a song on the radio.

All morning long we work side by side,
me with my commentary

and he inside the generous pocket of his silence,
until the hour is nearly noon
and the snow is piled high all around us;
then, I hear him speak.

After this, he asks,
can we go inside and play cards?

Certainly, I reply, and I will heat some milk
and bring cups of hot chocolate to the table
while you shuffle the deck,
and our boots stand dripping by the door.

Aaah, says the Buddha, lifting his eyes
and leaning for a moment on his shovel
before he drives the thin blade again
deep into the glittering white snow.

This Much I Do Remember

It was after dinner.
You were talking to me across the table
about something or other,
a greyhound you had seen that day
or a song you liked,

and I was looking past you
over your bare shoulder
at the three oranges lying
on the kitchen counter
next to the small electric bean grinder,
which was also orange,
and the orange and white cruets for vinegar and oil.

All of which converged
into a random still life,
so fastened together by the hasp of color,
and so fixed behind the animated
foreground of your

talking and smiling,
gesturing and pouring wine,
and the camber of your shoulders

that I could feel it being painted within me,
brushed on the wall of my skull,
while the tone of your voice
lifted and fell in its flight,
and the three oranges
remained fixed on the counter
the way stars are said
to be fixed in the universe.

Then all the moments of the past
began to line up behind that moment
and all the moments to come
assembled in front of it in a long row,
giving me reason to believe
that this was a moment I had rescued
from the millions that rush out of sight
into a darkness behind the eyes.

Even after I have forgotten what year it is,
my middle name,
and the meaning of money,
I will still carry in my pocket
the small coin of that moment,
minted in the kingdom
that we pace through every day.

Japan

Today I pass the time reading
a favorite haiku,
saying the few words over and over.

It feels like eating
the same small, perfect grape
again and again.

I walk through the house reciting it
and leave its letters falling
through the air of every room.

I stand by the big silence of the piano and say it.
I say it in front of a painting of the sea.
I tap out its rhythm on an empty shelf.

I listen to myself saying it,
then I say it without listening,
then I hear it without saying it.

And when the dog looks up at me,
I kneel down on the floor
and whisper it into each of his long white ears.

It's the one about the one-ton
temple bell
with the moth sleeping on its surface,

and every time I say it, I feel the excruciating
pressure of the moth
on the surface of the iron bell.

When I say it at the window,
the bell is the world
and I am the moth resting there.

When I say it into the mirror,
I am the heavy bell
and the moth is life with its papery wings.

And later, when I say it to you in the dark,
you are the bell,
and I am the tongue of the bell, ringing you,

and the moth has flown
from its line
and moves like a hinge in the air above our bed.

Taking Off Emily Dickinson's Clothes

First, her tippet made of tulle,
easily lifted off her shoulders and laid
on the back of a wooden chair.

And her bonnet,
the bow undone with a light forward pull.

Then the long white dress, a more
complicated matter with mother-of-pearl
buttons down the back,
so tiny and numerous that it takes forever
before my hands can part the fabric,
like a swimmer's dividing water,
and slip inside.

You will want to know
that she was standing
by an open window in an upstairs bedroom,
motionless, a little wide-eyed,
looking out at the orchard below,
the white dress puddled at her feet
on the wide-board, hardwood floor.

The complexity of women's undergarments
in nineteenth-century America
is not to be waved off,
and I proceeded like a polar explorer
through clips, clasps, and moorings,
catches, straps, and whalebone stays,
sailing toward the iceberg of her nakedness.

Later, I wrote in a notebook
it was like riding a swan into the night,
but, of course, I cannot tell you everything—
the way she closed her eyes to the orchard,
how her hair tumbled free of its pins,
how there were sudden dashes
whenever we spoke.

What I can tell you is
it was terribly quiet in Amherst
that Sabbath afternoon,
nothing but a carriage passing the house,
a fly buzzing in a windowpane.

So I could plainly hear her inhale
when I undid the very top
hook-and-eye fastener of her corset

and I could hear her sigh when finally it was unloosed,
the way some readers sigh when they realize
that Hope has feathers,
that reason is a plank,
that life is a loaded gun
that looks right at you with a yellow eye.

The Death of the Hat

Once every man wore a hat.

In the ashen newsreels,
the avenues of cities
are broad rivers flowing with hats.

The ballparks swelled
with thousands of strawhats,
brims and bands,
rows of men smoking
and cheering in shirtsleeves.

Hats were the law.
They went without saying.
You noticed a man without a hat in a crowd.

You bought them from Adams or Dobbs
who branded your initials in gold
on the inside band.

Trolleys crisscrossed the city.
Steamships sailed in and out of the harbor.
Men with hats gathered on the docks.

There was a person to block your hat
and a hatcheck girl to mind it
while you had a drink
or ate a steak with peas and a baked potato.
In your office stood a hat rack.

The day war was declared
everyone in the street was wearing a hat.
And they were wearing hats
when a ship loaded with men sank in the icy sea.

My father wore one to work every day
and returned home
carrying the evening paper,
the winter chill radiating from his overcoat.

But today we go bareheaded
into the winter streets,
stand hatless on frozen platforms.

Today the mailboxes on the roadside
and the spruce trees behind the house
wear cold white hats of snow.

Mice scurry from the stone walls at night
in their thin fur hats
to eat the birdseed that has spilled.

And now my father, after a life of work,
wears a hat of earth,
and on top of that,
a lighter one of cloud and sky—a hat of wind.

Mark Cox teaches in the Department of Creative Writing at University of North Carolina–Wilmington and in the Vermont College MFA Program. His honors include a Whiting Writers' Award, a Pushcart Prize, and numerous fellowships. He is the author of three books of poems: *Natural Causes, Thirty-seven Years from the Stone,* and *Smoulder.*

Pail of Eggs

The land is only ground now.
No footpaths, no ruins, not even
a slab where the root cellar stood.
Still, there is the slap of a screen door
when my son exits the car,
the squeal of a well pump
when my youngest wants juice,
and there I am in the sprouting field corn,
back brown as mud, crew cut blond
as the pail of eggs I've never put down.

The adults are still patient,
awaiting breakfast in their graves,
the bacon still diminishing
in the blackened pan.
No one knows where I am.
Half-grown, tousled candle of a boy,
I have walked to where the vulture landed,
to his runway of symmetrical rows
where the fox, lame with poison,
swallowed her last breath.
Face up. Eyes widened and clear.
Wherever I go from here,
I will not go hungry.

Sill

On the kitchen sill,
in the square brick house
my aunt aged and died in,
the flawless hand-blown pear
will neither rot nor last.

My daughter, too young
to ever think of this again,

once took it down
and placed it in a bowl,
with the breakfast oranges.
She'd thought it lonely, I guess,
with just the sunlight against it,
that single breath,
exhaled, perhaps, just after lunch,
smelling of cheese and peach schnapps.

Dust is the pollen of our dying,
even children sense this,
and after she'd wiped it clean
with her flowered dress,
she held it suspended
by its delicate, disproportionate stem
and lowered it into the wooden bowl.

Her great-aunt, though,
had little patience with disorder,
couldn't bear the clean, unblemished outline
where it had originally been,
and that was that.

Moments ago, after assurance that her family
would all recognize each other in heaven,
my daughter asked who would take care of her things.
And when I said her babies could, she cautioned
that babies can't even take care of themselves.

Neither can we, of course, never tall enough
to reach the light switch ourselves,
never able to drink from the wall-mounted fountain of awareness,
we stuff our pockets with beads and bottle-caps,
we organize our knick-knacks as best we can.

My aunt's squat, miniature tract house was razed.
Her windowsill exists only in the heaven of children.
The pear, it could be anywhere,

like the last breath of the old German who made it.
Likewise, her porcelain salters
and the hummingbird hovering
at its glass flower.

Like a Simile

Fell into bed like a tree
slept like boiling water
got up from bed like a camel
and showered like a tin roof.
Went downstairs like a slinky
drove to work like a water skier
entered the trailer like a bad smell
where I changed clothes like a burn victim
drank my coffee like a mosquito
and waited like a bus stop.
A whistle blew.
Then I painted like I was in a knife fight for eight hours
drank like a burning building
drove home like a bank shot
unlocked the door like a jeweler
and entered the house like an argument next door.
The dog smiled like a chain saw.
The wife pretended to be asleep
I pretended to eat.
She lay on the bed like a mattress
I sat at the table like a chair.
Until I inched along the stair rail like a sprinkler
entered like smoke from a fire in the next room
and apologized like a toaster.
The covers did *not* open like I was an envelope
and she was a 24-hour teller
so I undressed like an apprentice matador
discovering bullshit on his shoes.

Style

Today, a coed with a black eye
and bruised cheek stopped me
in the hall to ask, anxiously,
where does one put "Jr."
according to standard manuals
on style?

"In jail?" I said. "No, really," she said,
"This is important."

Natural Causes

Because my son saw the round hay bales—
1200 pounds apiece, shrink-wrapped in white plastic—
lining the fields,
we have had to search all evening
for marshmallows.
Two stores were out. Another
had one stale and shrunken bag.
The fourth had three bags, but no wood for fire,
so we went back to the first.
And I needed newspaper to start the kindling,
which is how I know Earl Softy died Monday,
at home, in his sleep, of natural causes. So rarely
we know how we know what we know.
Don't turn the page. Sit with us awhile,
here by the fire in New Hampshire.
Have a marshmallow.
Because my wife and I love each other
and wanted something of, and more than, ourselves;
because my little son has imagined heaven in the pasture land,
even death tastes sweet.

After Rain

Sometimes, night quieted,
what's real soaks in further;
the mesh screens gemmed by halogen,
my neighbors' doorbell switch
like a moon within reach,
the lilies nodding on their stems
like exhausted horsemen.
Denied the old illusion of ownership,
I have opened somehow,
but for once, nothing is leaving or lessened.

The journey is long.
The journey is not long.
Moths drink their fill at the screens,
the caught rain glistening.
What conscious moment
is not, in essence, worship;
what state more vulnerable
than the attentive mind upturned?

We bear forth our sparks from psychic fire,
each family a series of contained blazes,
each patio torch a signal pyre,
our longing eternal,
and though the skin thins,
our inner lives grow cold,
there is, always, this black frock
nightfall offers—
the comfort, finally,
of tenderness and humility and weakness,
the calm after rain
and before the slate's clearing.

Ashes, Ashes

Snow. A nit's weight
on the hair of our necks,
the blessed host of the past,
right there, just so.

Turn into it, this once.
It's time to become the lake surface,
time to claim your face.

Soon the present
will cool enough to touch,
you can lay you down
in the outline you once were,

smoke still adrift
from the original fire.
Cup the moth's spark
in your hands.
Open your mouth and take
the dissolution
on your tongue.

No one else remembers
all that you remember.
If you don't carry it,
who will?

Photo by Jen Saffron

Jim Daniels's books of poems include *Street,* with the photographs of
Charlee Brodsky; *Show and Tell: New and Selected Poems; Blessing the House; Blue
Jesus; No Pets; M-80; Punching Out;* and *Places/Everyone*. He is also the author
of eight chapbooks of poetry, two books of short stories, two screenplays,
including *Dumpster,* an independent feature film that he also produced,
and the one-act play *Heart of Hearts*. He is the editor or coeditor of four
anthologies of poetry, including *Letters to America: Contemporary American
Poetry on Race* and *American Poetry: The Next Generation*. Daniels has received
fellowships from the National Endowment for the Arts and the Pennsylvania
Council on the Arts, and has been awarded a Pushcart Prize. A native of
Detroit, he is currently a professor of English at Carnegie Mellon University
in Pittsburgh, where he directs the creative writing program

Raw October

We toss eggs
at cars, houses,
Crazy Eddie chases
us down the street
Larry rips
his shirt on a fence
Fred loses a shoe
through the backyards
we outrun
yapping dogs, get away
clean to smoke cigarettes
behind Northeast Trucking.

We pry off hubcaps
fling them toward
the puffy white moon
they clatter and roll
echo up and down
the street.

Why do we do this?
Somebody should catch us
and smack us around a little.
Eventually they do.

Digger Pays Off the Mortgage

You write the final check,
lick the final stamp.
Loretta smiles,
hands on your shoulders.

That's that.
You set the envelope aside
and pull her to your lap.
Kiss her on the cheek.

Think of all the extra money
we'll have each month, she says.
How are we going to spend it?
College for the kids, maybe.
Maybe we can get a place up north?

Give us bigger allowances, your daughter
says from the doorway. *Bigger allowances?*
I was getting ready to cut you off—
time for you to get a job.

No way. She's fifteen. She makes a face,
stomps away. Loretta gets up.
Dishes, she says, pecking you hard
on the forehead.

You watch TV, your usual shows, then the news.
Everyone's in bed. You turn out the lamp
by your chair and look out the front window
at the spot on your lawn
where you planted three trees,
where they all died.

Digger's Territory

Some would say
there's not much to
a life lived on your street.
They might say you're dumb
you watch too much TV
you drink too much
fart and belch and laugh too loud
dress funny, eat too many burgers.

But tonight after work
after you wash your hands
eat a good meal
wrestle with the dog a little

after you grab a beer
and sit with your family
on your porch sharing a laugh
with a couple neighbors
while the sun sets behind
the bowling alley, after a man parks
his car carefully behind
your Impala up on blocks
and walks stiff up your driveway
in his suit and briefcase and perfect hair
and holds out a soft hand,
you all smile at each other
because no matter what he knows
you're going to teach him
a few things.

Still Lives: Sweat

The old woman pleads with her son
to leave a neighbor alone—
a fight over a ten-speed.
She dies from a hole in her gut.

The off-speed ice-cream music
twists itself into the rhythm of a siren.
Words barely dent this ambulance air.
Police stand under a street sign
where nothing points in the right direction.

The son's eyes, his hands twisting in cuffs,
sign the snake that swallows our lives.
The eyes of the police are scooped out
by tiny spoons, the repeated scenes.

The neighbor hugs what lies
between his arms: *I don't got no*
bike. Sweat drips down foreheads,

under arms, nothing like tears.
Kids on bikes ride laughing in circles.

The ambulance takes the mother.
The police take the son.
The neighbor follows the tracks
down his arm: *I don't got no, I can't
get no.* Maybe there's a little more room
on our small porches of summer sweat.
Maybe a little less.

Trouble at the Drive-In

The sky is gray and it will be
raining soon and we're waiting in line
for the drive-in, the one on Eight Mile,
the border between Detroit and Warren and the anger
is stewing just like always, every day
guns pointed at our own dumb heads, every day
somebody else dumb enough to pull the trigger
because we're mad, mad and sick and dumb
and we're gonna get ourselves a little piece of something
even if it means taking it away from someone else
who don't have much, or else we're sick and tired
of everybody taking, so we're gonna
protect ourselves, by god, though god
don't seem to help much here—he's getting ripped
off too—and we all want to have our say
one way or another, so there's a lot of guns
in a lot of hands, yes, I'm thinking all this here
as it starts to pour, fucking rain like crazy,
and I say *fuck* to let you know I mean
business, just like I carry a gun,
so it's fucking raining and if you don't like it
then fucking get lost because I'm still going
to the movies—a Clint triple-header—
Fistful, A Few Dollars More, and *Good/Bad/Ugly,*

and all these good, bad, ugly people are leaning
on their horns and some asshole cuts his car into the line
up front and this big fat guy gets out of his car and runs
up to that car and he's screaming *fuck you* so
he means business, and he's pounding on the windows
yanking on the door, and he's getting soaked, but
he don't give a fuck, he is me and he is you,
and the guy in the car is me and you
and we're all kicking each other's asses
while the bosses are safe and dry
in Grosse Point or West Bloomfield or wherever
the fuck they live, laughing at *The New Yorker* cartoons
and thinking Woody fucking Allen is a genius, let me
tell you, Clint ain't no genius, but I understand
his movies, and I understand what's going on
up ahead, and I'm hearing sirens, and me and you,
we're in this together, buddy, just a couple dummies
like those two up there, and nobody's letting us in
and nobody's getting out, and it's only a matter of time
till somebody pulls a gun.

Blessing the House

I step out of the car and stare
at the flat houses with their bristly bushes
wild and short like my old hair.
I want to cut my hair and spread it over this snowy yard
like my own ashes, I want to curl inside a sidewalk square
my ear to the ground, cupped, listening—what could I bring
back to life? Would I hear the rough chalk scrawl over cement?

This house the priest blessed over thirty years ago
when the lawn was mud and boards. *Bless this house,*
I think, standing in the street. The wind blows cold
but I know this wind, its harsh front.
Don't try to bully me, I say. I am home
and my hands are trembling, I am sighing.

The car door slams. I clap my hands
for the hell of it, a clap on a street corner
echoing a little, among friends.

Once I stood here for hours
trying to hit the streetlight with a snowball,
to leave a white smudge. I have left no smudge,
nothing I could call mine. The grey sky presses
down on these small houses, on my parents' house
and its square slab. They are inside,
maybe changing the channel on the TV, maybe
grabbing a beer and a bowl of chips, maybe
flushing the toilet, maybe scrubbing their faces,
maybe peering out a dark window.

I am waiting to step inside for the hug and the kiss,
I am waiting to push away this grey sadness—cement and sky.
I grab a handful of snow and touch it to my forehead
where it melts down my face. I smudge my chest
with an X of snow, I toss handfuls on the yard,
on the scraped sidewalk—ashes, ashes, glowing
in the streetlight before the melting, the disappearing.
Oh glorious snow, I say, *we have missed each other.*
I listen for a moment. I lift my bags from the trunk.
The porch light glows its yellow basket
of tender light. I stomp my boots, and I go in.

Chard deNiord is the author of *Night Mowing, Sharp Golden Thorn,* and *Asleep in the Fire.* He is an associate professor of English at Providence College and directs the low-residency MFA program in poetry at New England College. He lives in Putney, Vermont.

Raiding the Bees

I went out to gather honey from the hives in the sourwood grove.
Put on my garment of honeybee clothes and packed the smoker full
    of burlap.
I thought of Samson on my way to the grove.
His hive inside the lion carcass.
His curse of hair and holy muscle.
I stared at the river when I arrived to steel my nerves.
Lit the rags until they burned, then closed the chimney.
I smoked the threshold bare with a steady cloud
that rose inside the storied chambers.
Cracked the seal of the super's dome and lifted frames
of honeycomb from out of the box.
How many cells filled to the top and sealed with wax for winter meals?
How many quarts of sourwood nectar distilled to gold?
I made a guess as they buzzed around.
No number sticks in the work of hunger.

To Hear and Hear

The hermit thrush is set for six
to sing his song, as if it were
the end of the world and he was stirred
by dusk to sing the same sweet song
again and again in the understory,
as if to say, it's neither words
nor meaning that matters in the end
but the quality of sound, as if we
were deafened by the sun and needed
his song as a key to unlock our ears,
to hear and hear and understand,
to see and see, knowing that this
one day is the end for now,
which it is, *it is,* he claims, with a song
just loud enough to pierce the woods
until the night descends like a thousand
veils, and then just one.

Frog

My tongue leapt out of my mouth
when I lied to her and hopped away
to the stream below the house.
Mute then, I started to write the truth.
My tongue turned wild in the stream,
for which I was glad and unashamed.
I listen now from my porch to the complex things
it says in the distance about my heart.
How hard it is to tell the truth inside my mouth.
How much it needs to sing in the dark.

Whales

—For Heather McHugh

On a whale watch in Maine I saw
finbacks feeding on mackerel at the mouth
of Passamaquoddy Bay.
I imagined leviathans rising to the surface,
then disappearing beneath the waves
until they rose again for air
in a different hectare, spraying
the sea in geysers from out of the holes
in the backs of their heads, rolling
with the waves like waves themselves.
And then they rose at two o'clock,
three glassy backs the color of night and dorsal fin.
With such small eyes and powerful heads,
like scholars deep in their Atlantic stacks,
they must think without the means, I thought,
of getting down their thoughts,
except on water, written and erased
before the human reader can make it out.
I could feel their hearts as they ascended
and sucked the sky into their lungs
and arced again for another dive.
Did you see? Did you see?

Night Mowing

> Memory is a kind of accomplishment.
> —WILLIAM CARLOS WILLIAMS

I remember the drone of Francis Temple's Farmall
mowing in the dark of a mid-September night,
its deep, desultory blasts were also guttural,
half motor, half cat, as it labored in the meadow
back and forth, felling hay in six-foot rows
with a sickle bar that rattled like a snake.
The memory of that mowing grows in my mind,
which is also a field that's overgrown
with every weed and type of grass, no less real
than the tractor itself mowing in the dark.
I wake with a start to the sound of that engine,
the same old Farmall I heard as a boy,
so that I am forever waking and remembering
at the same time to the accompaniment of a tractor
I cannot see in the meadow, but know is there,
as it is tonight, thirty years later, growing
newer instead of older as it takes me back
in its moving forward down the rows of waist-
high hay that fall like hair against the earth.

Through a Train Window

There she was, my old girlfriend,
outside my window in a late-model
Mustang with her new boyfriend,
keeping right up. No farther away
than twenty yards. I waved at her
with both my hands from the other side
of the darkened glass. She laughed
at something and opened the window.
Suddenly, I remembered the sweep
of her hair across my face, how it
engulfed me in her with its lavender scent
and something else—a consanguinity—

with the force of earth I thought was heaven.
How similarly she had ridden in *my* car—
a vintage Chevy with a broken muffler—
to the way she was riding now,
over there, laughing at everything,
undoing her hair. I regarded
the boyfriend and wished him well
as he gripped the wheel with both
his hands, laughing at nothing, watching
the highway that curved away.

An Incident at the Catholic Worker

Sitting in peace in the dining room
of the country community house one Sunday morning,
reading the paper about the latest truce
in Israel, I heard a disturbance in the living room.
People were scurrying and yelling, "Watch out,
he's got a knife!" and "Put her down!"
Then Kenny, the epileptic from Hudson Valley,
appeared at the door with a little dog in one hand
and a cleaver in the other. He said he was going
to take the dog up the hill and throw her in the well.
He said he was tired of how the people in the "community"
were treating him, and he had to kill the dog
in order to change their attitude. He had
a crazed look in his eye while the dog hung limp,
Mrs. Smith's terrier. I followed him up the hill
while the others prayed below. I said, "Kenny,
what good do you think this will do? They'll only take
you back to the hospital." Then it was there interposed
a fit and he dropped the dog beside the well and fell
to the ground and cut himself with the flailing blade.
I stepped on the hand that held the knife and watched
him twist like a snake with its neck pinned down.
He frothed at the mouth and swallowed his tongue.
I tried to stick my finger in and pull it out
but he clenched his teeth in a human vise.

I thought in retrospect I could have cut a hole
in his throat with the knife but he was writhing
to the end, turning blue. I watched his ghost
shut down his skin, then disappear inside the well.
I held his body as a souvenir of the fallen world
and thought no less of him. The little dog began to bark
from the edge of the woods. "Shut up!" I yelled.
"Shut up!" and almost felt what Kenny felt as he held
the dog above the well and dangled it like the angry god
who'd crossed a wire inside his head. It was his hatred
for the little dog that had set him off, just its yapping
every night in Mrs. Smith's adjacent room. He had been
treated kindly by everyone, according to the wishes
of our saintly mother, Dorothy Day, who had always said,
"Treat every stranger as if he were the Christ."

I See Them Now

the invisible bodies rising
from the ground. How slowly
they lift themselves at first
to their elbows, as if they were
still bodies, then suddenly
to their knees, faster and faster,
until they free themselves
from the earth, higher and higher,
these blessed bodies speeding
like arrows toward a hole
in the sky, which is the sky
now that they are rising,
gaining a new oblivious
knowledge as they rise
of what it means to slip away,
to be forgotten, to say
good-bye without ever saying it,
burning as they rise, hotter
and hotter, on the one drop of fuel
that stayed inside them.

Photo by Ted Rosenberg

Toi Derricotte has published four books of poems, *Tender, Captivity, Natural Birth,* and *The Empress of the Death House,* and a memoir, *The Black Notebooks,* which won numerous awards and was a *New York Times* Notable Book of the Year. Her honors include two fellowships in poetry from the National Endowment for the Arts, two Pushcart Prizes, a Rockefeller Foundation Fellowship, and a Guggenheim Fellowship. She is the cofounder of Cave Canem, the first writing workshop and retreat for African American poets. She is a professor of English at the University of Pittsburgh.

Blackbottom

When relatives came from out of town,
we would drive down to Blackbottom,
drive slowly down the congested main streets—Beubian and
    Hastings—
trapped in the mesh of Saturday night.
Freshly escaped, black middle class,
we snickered, and were proud;
the louder the streets, the prouder.
We laughed at the bright clothes of a prostitute,
a man sitting on a curb with a bottle in his hand.
We smelled barbecue cooking in dented washtubs, and our
    mouths watered.
As much as we wanted it we couldn't take the chance.

Rhythm and blues came from the windows, the throaty voice of
    a woman lost in the bass, in the drums, in the dirty down
    and out, the grind.
"I love to see a funeral, then I know it ain't mine."
We rolled our windows down so that the waves rolled over us
    like blood.
We hoped to pass invisibly, knowing on Monday we would
    return safely to our jobs, the post office and classroom.
We wanted our sufferings to be offered up as tender meat,
and our triumphs to be belted out in raucous song.
We had lost our voice in the suburbs, in Conant Gardens,
    where each brick house delineated a fence of silence;
we had lost the right to sing in the street and damn creation.

We returned to wash our hands of them,
to smell them
whose very existence
tore us down to the human.

Boy at the Paterson Falls

I am thinking of that boy who bragged about the day he threw
    a dog over and watched it struggle to stay upright all the
    way down.
I am thinking of that rotting carcass on the rocks,
and the child with such power he could call to a helpless thing
    as if he were its friend, capture it, and think of the cruelest
    punishment.
It must have answered some need, some silent screaming in a
    closet, a motherless call when night came crashing;
it must have satisfied, for he seemed joyful, proud, as if he had
    once made a great creation out of murder.
That body on the rocks, its sharp angles, slowly took the shape
    of what was underneath, bones pounded, until it lay on the
    bottom like a scraggly rug.
Nothing remains but memory—and the suffering of those who
    would walk into the soft hands of a killer for a crumb of
    bread.

In an Urban School

The guard picks dead leaves from plants.
The sign over the table reads:
Do not take or *touch* anything on this table!
In the lunchroom the cook picks up in her dishcloth
what she refers to as "a little friend,"
shakes it out,
and puts the dishcloth back on the drain.
The teacher says she needs stronger tranquilizers.
Sweat rises on the bone of her nose,
on the plates of her skull under unpressed hair.
"First graders, put your heads down. I'm taking names
so I can tell your parents
which children do not obey their teacher."
Raheim's father was stabbed last week.
Germaine's mother, a junkie,
was found dead in an empty lot.

Allen Ginsberg

Once Allen Ginsberg stopped to pee at a bookstore in New
    Jersey,
but he looked like a bum—
not like the miracle-laden Christ with electric atom juice, not
    like the one whose brain is a river in which was plunked the
    stone of the world (the one bathing fluid to wash away
    25,000 year half-lives), he was dressed as a bum.
He had wobbled on a pee-heavy bladder
in search of a gas station,
a dime store with a quarter booth,
a Chinese restaurant,
when he came to that grocery store of dreams:
Chunks of Baudelaire's skin
glittered in plastic;
his eyes in sets, innocent
as the unhoused eyes of a butchered cow.
In a dark corner, Rimbaud's
genitals hung like jerky,
and the milk of Whitman's breasts
drifted in a carton, dry as talcum.
He wanted to pee and lay his head
on the cool stacks;
but the clerk took one look
and thought of the buttocks of clean businessmen squatting
    during lunch hour,
the thin flanks of pretty girls buying poetry for school.
Behind her, faintly,
the deodorized bathroom.
She was the one at the gate
protecting civilization.
He turned, walked to the gutter,
unzipped his pants, and peed.
Do you know who that was?
A man in the back came forth.
Soon she was known as
the woman in the store on Main

who said no to Allen Ginsberg;
and she is proud—
so proud she told this story
pointing to the spot outside, as if
still flowed that holy stream.

The Struggle

We didn't want to be white—or did we?
What did we want?
In two bedrooms, side by side,
four adults, two children.
My aunt and uncle left before light.
My father went to the factory, then the cleaners.
My mother vacuumed, ironed, cooked,
pasted war coupons. In the afternoon
she typed stencils at the metal kitchen table.
I crawled under pulling on her skirt.
What did we want?
As the furniture became modern, the carpet deep, the white
ballerina on the mantel lifted her aims like some girl near
terror;
the Degas ballerinas folded softly in a group, a gray sensual
beauty.
What did we push ourselves out of ourselves
to do? Our hands
on the doors, cooking utensils, keys; our hands
folding the paper money, tearing the bills.

Grace Paley Reading

Finally, the audience gets
restless, & they send me
to hunt for Grace. I find her
backing out of the bathroom, bending
over, wiping up her footprints

as she goes with a little
sheet of toilet paper, explaining,
"In some places, after the lady mops,
the bosses come to check on her.
I just don't want them to think
she didn't do her job."

When My Father Was Beating Me

I'd hear my mother in the kitchen preparing dinner. I'd hear the spoons
hitting the mixing bowl, the clatter of silver falling into the drawer. I'd hear
the pot lids clink and rattle. The normality of the sound was startling; it
seemed louder than usual, as if she weren't ashamed, as if she were making
a point. Perhaps the house was cut in two by a membrane, and, though
her sounds could come to my ears, my screams and cries and whimpers,
his demands and humiliations, the sounds of his hands hitting my body,
couldn't pierce back the other way. I learned to stretch time and space so I
could think what she was thinking. I learned to hear things far away, to live
in a thought that could expand itself even until now: What Einstein said is
true—everything slows down the farther you get from your mother.

It seemed as if she wanted it, that either I was taking her place, or
maybe she thought I deserved it. Maybe there was an overload of violence in
the universe, a short in a wire that had to spill its electricity, and she was glad,
this time, she hadn't felt it.

Maybe there was some arcane connection between her and my father's
hand, his arm let loose and flying, maybe she was in command, making him
hit, telling her side of the story—that I was evil, that I had to be beaten, not
just for the crime I had committed, but for the crime of who I was: hungry,
trying, in every way, to get through barriers set up for my own good. "You're
tearing me apart, you're driving me crazy," my mother would scream.

Sometimes I saw the world from her perspective: she *was* beautiful
and pitiful and overwhelmed, she was also some blood-sucking witch—not
a whole being—able to stretch and contort herself like a cry, something that
hated and was flexible. She wanted to beat me in the same way my father did,
but she knew she couldn't, because I'd fight back, I'd cry that cry that made
her go crazy. "You can't manipulate your father the way you can manipulate
me." She meant it as a compliment for herself, as if she loved me more.

They wanted a stillness, a lack of person, place, agony swallowed. They wanted me to die, or, not to die, to exist with a terrible pain, but have it sewn up—as if they could reach into my ribs, crack them open, put a handful of suffering in there and stitch it back, as if my body had a pocket, a black pocket they could stick a thought in that they couldn't stand.

I would fold, collapse like a marionette. (I beat my dolls for years, pounded and pounded and nobody seemed to notice.) "Just keep trying," my father'd say just before he'd strike me. And I did. I kept trying to be beaten.

•   •   •

Serving the dinner plates with her face bland, as if it were virtuous not to take sides, serving the beautiful food that she had cooked all day—her great gift—to say, *I've given everything I could, I've got nothing left.* Often when my father would hit me she'd say, as if he and I were man and wife, "I'm not going to come between the two of you. You two have to work this out for yourselves." He'd give me a warning. "Wipe that look off your face or I'll knock it off. Dry up," he'd scream, "and eat."

Photo by Nick Carbó

Denise Duhamel's most recent books are *Two and Two* and *Queen for a Day: Selected and New Poems*. She coedited, with Nick Carbo, *Sweet Jesus: Poems about the Ultimate Icon*, and, with Maureen Seaton and David Trinidad, *Saints of Hysteria: A Half-Century of Collaborative American Poetry*. A recipient of a National Endowment for the Arts Fellowship, she teaches at Florida International University in Miami.

Kinky

They decide to exchange heads.
Barbie squeezes the small opening under her chin
over Ken's bulging neck socket. His wide jawline jostles
atop his girlfriend's body, loosely,
like one of those nodding novelty dogs
destined to gaze from the back windows of cars.
The two dolls chase each other around the orange Country Camper,
unsure what they'll do when they're within touching distance.
Ken wants to feel Barbie's toes between his lips,
take off one of her legs and force his whole arm inside her.
With only the vaguest suggestion of genitals,
all the alluring qualities they possess as fashion dolls,
up until now, have done neither of them much good.
But suddenly Barbie is excited looking at her own body
under the weight of Ken's face. He is part circus freak,
part thwarted hermaphrodite. And she is imagining
she is somebody else—maybe somebody middle class and ordinary,
maybe another teenage model being caught in a scandal.

The night had begun with Barbie getting angry
at finding Ken's blow-up doll, folded and stuffed
under the couch. He was defensive and ashamed, especially about
not having the breath to inflate her. But after a round
of pretend-tears, Barbie and Ken vowed to try
to make their relationship work. With their good memories
as sustaining as good food, they listened to late-night radio
talk shows, one featuring Doctor Ruth. *When all else fails,*
just hold each other, the small sex therapist crooned.
Barbie and Ken, on cue, groped in the dark,
their interchangeable skin glowing, the color of Band-Aids.
Then, they let themselves go—Soon Barbie was begging Ken
to try on her spandex miniskirt. She showed him how
to pivot as though he were on a runway. Ken begged
to tie Barbie onto his yellow surfboard and spin her
on the kitchen table until she grew dizzy. *Anything,*
anything, they both said to the other's requests,
their mirrored desires bubbling from the most unlikely places.

Sex with a Famous Poet

I had sex with a famous poet last night
and when I rolled over and found myself beside him I shuddered
because I was married to someone else,
because I wasn't supposed to have been drinking,
because I was in a fancy hotel room
I didn't recognize. I would have told you
right off this was a dream, but recently
a friend told me, *write about a dream,*
lose a reader and I didn't want to lose you
right away. I wanted you to hear
that I didn't even like the poet in the dream, that he has
four kids, the youngest one my age, and I find him
rather unattractive, that I only met him once,
that is, in real life, and that was in a large group
in which I barely spoke up. He disgusted me
with his disparaging remarks about women.
He even used the word "Jap,"
which I took as a direct insult to my husband, who's Asian.
When we were first dating, I told him,
"You were talking in your sleep last night
and I listened, just to make sure you didn't
call out anyone else's name." My future husband said
that he couldn't be held responsible for his subconscious,
which worried me, which made me think his dreams
were full of blonde vixens in rabbit-fur bikinis,
but he said no, he dreamt mostly about boulders
and the ocean and volcanoes, dangerous weather
he witnessed but could do nothing to stop.
And I said, "I dream only of you,"
which was romantic and silly and untrue.
But I never thought I'd dream of another man—
my husband and I hadn't even had a fight,
my head tucked sweetly in his armpit, my arm
around his belly, which lifted up and down
all night, gently like water in a lake.
If I passed that famous poet on the street,
he would walk by, famous in his sunglasses

and blazer with the suede patches at the elbows,
without so much as a glance in my direction.
I know you're probably curious about who the poet is,
so I should tell you the clues I've left aren't
accurate, that I've disguised his identity,
that you shouldn't guess *I bet it's him* ...
because you'll never guess correctly
and even if you do, I won't tell you that you have.
I wouldn't want to embarrass a stranger
who is, after all, probably a nice person,
who was probably just having a bad day when I met him,
who is probably growing a little tired of his fame—
which my husband and I perceive as enormous,
but how much fame can an American poet
really have, let's say, compared to a rock star
or film director of equal talent? Not that much,
and the famous poet knows it, knows that he's not
truly given his due. Knows that many
of these young poets tugging on his sleeve
are only pretending to have read all his books.
But he smiles anyway, tries to be helpful.
I mean, this poet has to have some redeeming qualities, right?
For instance, he writes a mean iambic.
Otherwise, what was I doing in his arms?

The Difference between Pepsi and Pope

I have this blind spot, a dark line, thin as a hair, that obliterates
a stroke of scenery on the right side of my field of vision
so that often I get whole words at the end of sentences wrong
like when I first saw the title of David Lehman's poem
"The Difference Between Pepsi and Coke" and I misread
"Coke" for "Pope." This blind spot makes me a terrible driver,
a bad judge of distances, a ping-pong player that inspires giggles
from the opposite team.
                        I knew a poet who dressed up as a cookie
and passed out a new brand in a crowded supermarket.

The next day he gave the Pepsi Challenge to passersby
in a mall.
                    I felt old-fashioned admitting to this poet that I prefer Coke,
that wavy hyphen that separates its full name Coca ~ Cola.
Like the bar let down in the limbo dance, the Spanish tilde comes down until
not even a lowercase letter can squeeze under it.
I searched for that character recently, writing to David Lehman,
telling him about an electronic magazine, the address of which
had this ~ in it. I couldn't find it, although I stared
at my computer keyboard for more than a few minutes.
I only noticed it today in the upper left hand corner, above the tab,
the alternate of ` , if you hit the shift key. I wonder if I also have a blind spot
in my left eye. I wonder if the poet who dressed as a cookie
is happy in his new marriage. I wonder if you can still get a bottle of Tab
anywhere, that awful soda my forever-dieting aunt used to drink,
with its pink logo, its "a" all swirls, looking like @.
                                        Yesterday,
when my husband was waiting at an intersection, he said, *Is anyone coming?* I looked from
the passenger seat and said confidently, *We can make it*.
Then we were almost run off the road. I said
I'm sorry I'm sorry through the exchange of honks and fists
and couldn't believe when my husband forgave me so quickly.

                                        Not only that,
but I'm a bad proofreader, I thought to myself as I made a mental list
of ways that I felt inadequate. One friend also recently noted that maybe I
talk too much about myself, so I told her the Bette Midler joke,
Enough about me, what do you think of me? which doesn't *really*
bring me back to David Lehman and his poem, but does make me realize
how far away I strayed from my original point,
which was that I thought his poem would be funny because of the title,
not the real title, but my mistaken one. I started to guess his poem
in my head: Pepsi is bubbly and brown while the Pope
is flat and white. Pepsi doesn't have a big white hat. The Pope
can't get rid of fender rust. Pepsi is all for premarital sex.
The Pope won't stain your teeth.
                                But "The Difference
Between Pepsi and Coke" is a tender poem about a father
whom the speaker reveres and I wonder if David Lehman's own father

is alive or dead, which is something I often do—wonder
how much is true—when I read a poem by someone I like,
which I know is not the right way to read a poem even though
Molly Peacock said at her reading that she is the "I"
in all of hers and doesn't use the word "speaker" anymore.

Still,

I feel like a Peeping Tom, although this is really about what I can't see,
my blind spots, and how easy it is for me to doubt my decisions,
how I relate to the father in Lehman's poem who "won't admit his dread
of boredom" and panics and forgives. How easy it is to live for stretches at a time
in that skinny dark line, how easy it is to get so many things all wrong.

Nick at Nite

When growing up, Nick never saw *The Brady Bunch*.
He watched *Eat Bulaga* with Tito, Vic, and Joey,
which he likens to a Filipino version of *The Three Stooges*.
He ate Sky Flakes crackers instead of Ritz
and drank Royal True Orange with pulp bits instead of Sunkist.
He remembers the bells signaling the after-dinner arrival
of Magnolia ice cream–vendors pushing silver coolers,
not driving trucks. I tell him about Apple Jacks,
the cereal that turned a kid's milk pink
and the phenomenon of Banana Quik.
I try to explain Madge, the brassy beautician who dipped
her clients' hands in Palmolive Dishwashing Liquid
between manicures. My husband endures
the moving scrapbook of my childhood
as we watch another round of Nick at Nite.
I teach him all the words to the *Patty Duke Show* theme song
during a break from their sponsors Head & Shoulders.
In the Philippines, dandruff was also an embarrassment.
Nick tells me of a shampoo commercial in English and Tagalog:
A girl loses interest in her dancing partner
when she notices the white patches on his collar
and huffs away as only the truly insulted can.
The famous slogan: "Charlie Balakubak, excuse me!"

My husband and I laugh. We are "East Meets West"
like LaChoy, makers of "Oriental recipes to serve at home."
I sing him "*Ay yay ay yay . . .* I am the Frito Bandito."
Nick, who only started speaking English at six,
translates the original Spanish lyrics. The song, he says,
is really about singing without tears, not the virtues of corn chips.

The Problem with Woody Allen

(even before Soon Yi)
is that he breaks up with people
like Mariel Hemingway (in *Manhattan*)
and Diane Keaton (in *Annie Hall*)
without so much as a joke about his scrawny body,
those parody glasses, his sallow skin.
My friend Rhonda said (about *Deconstructing Harry*),
"Elisabeth Shue should get an Oscar
for making out with Woody Allen
and not throwing up!" At least
Elisabeth gets to dump him, but still—
why does Woody Allen's character cheat
on Judy Davis? I see what he was trying to do
in *Celebrity,* projecting his male fantasies
through Kenneth Branagh, who's a little easier
to look at. But would Melanie Griffith really give
Kenneth Branagh/Woody Allen a blow job?
I understand if she wants to get a part in the movie
Celebrity, but she's already in it, playing a famous actress,
and Kenneth Branagh is supposed to be
a lowly journalist, so, frankly, it doesn't make sense.
Even Winona Ryder, playing a struggling actress,
falling for Branagh is a stretch.
Wasn't she just going out with Matt Damon
in real life?
        So when I stumble upon
Allen's latest film treatment—he's starring in his films again,
he just can't help it—I feel compelled to write to him

about my concerns:

　　　　Dear Mr. Allen, I'm afraid
this time you're really going to embarrass yourself.
A nursing home patient (you) getting sexual gratification
from a student nurse (Gwyneth Paltrow)? I admit
the premise sounds fun, even madcap—Gwyneth
loves you so much that when you beg her
she sneaks you out of Palm Springs's Golden Gables
and takes you cross-country, popping open your cans
of Ensure and playing her "young people" music
while you kvetch and cover your ears.
The fish-out-of-water element is intriguing—
you hyperventilating as Gwyneth forces you to peer
over the Grand Canyon. You reading the ingredients
of Gwyneth's Pepsi One can with a magnifying glass.
But would you really leave Gwyneth
when you meet up with neurotic Drew Barrymore,
a displaced New Yorker teaching philosophy
in North Dakota? Would Drew really be visiting
the Lawrence Welk Museum when you walk in
(because Gwyneth drops you off there
so she can go mall shopping in peace)?
Would Drew really let you move in
immediately, after that first kiss
behind Welk's favorite accordion? Would you really
leave your oxygen tank behind in Gwyneth's trunk?
Would Gwyneth in a rage really flush all your prescriptions?
Would Drew risk everything for you, even her tenure?
Would you (as a runaway nursing home patient) really
be able to balance on the back of Drew's Harley
all the way from Grand Forks to the Upper East Side?

Noah and Joan

It's not that I'm proud of the fact
that 20 percent of Americans believe
that Noah (of Noah's Ark) was married

to Joan of Arc. It's true. I'll admit it—
Americans are pretty dumb and forgetful
when it comes to history. And they're notorious
for interpreting the Bible to suit themselves.
You don't have to tell me we can't spell anymore—
Ark or Arc, it's all the same to us.

But think about it, just a second, timeline aside,
it's not such an awful mistake. The real Noah's missus
was never even given a name. She was sort of milquetoasty,
a shadowy figure lugging sacks of oats up a plank.
I mean, Joan could have helped Noah *build* that ark
in her sensible slacks and hiking boots. She was good with swords
and, presumably, power tools. I think Noah and Joan
might have been a good match, visionaries
once mistaken for flood-obsessed and heretic.

Never mind France wasn't France yet—
all the continents probably blended together,
one big mush. Those Bible days would have been
good for Joan, those early times when premonitions
were common, when animals popped up
out of nowhere, when people were getting cured
left and right. Instead of battles and prisons
and iron cages, Joan could have cruised
the Mediterranean, wherever the floodwaters took that ark.

And Noah would have felt more like Dr. Doolittle,
a supportive Joan saying, "Let's not waste any time!
Hand over those boat blueprints, honey!"
All that sawing and hammering would have helped
calm her nightmares of mean kings and crowns,
a nasty futuristic place called England.
She'd convince Noah to become vegetarian.
She'd live to be much older than nineteen, those parakeets
and antelope leaping about her like children.

Russell Edson lives in Connecticut with his wife, Frances. His books include, among others, *Appearances; A Stone Is Nobody's; The Very Thing That Happens; The Brain Kitchen; What a Man Can See; The Childhood of an Equestrian; The Clam Theater; Ridderen af Gyngehesten; The Falling Sickness* (four plays); *The Intuitive Journey & Other Works; The Reason Why the Closet-Man Is Never Sad; With Sincerest Regrets; Gulping's Recital* (a novel); *The Wounded Breakfast; Tick Tock; The Song of Percival Peacock* (a novel); *The Tunnel: Selected Poems; The Tormented Mirror; The House of Sara Loo; O Túnel;* and *The Rooster's Wife.*

The Secret Graveyard

Elephants like burlap underwear. It wears better than silk and has more style.

They're shy about this appetite. Underwear embarrasses them.

When the desire overtakes them they head for the secret graveyard of elephants. No one knows where that is. They feel safe there.

Surrounded by the bleached bones of their ancestors they shyly submit themselves to the delicious feel of burlap. They feel more naked wearing it. They don't know why, and so they giggle.

Of course they cannot reenter the forest wearing underwear. A hyena might laugh. Tarzan is another thought . . .

Sadly they must leave their underwear in the bones of their ancestors. They remember to murmur brief prayers as they leave . . .

The Key

An old woman was working her husband's beard into her shawl with her crocheting hook.

What's happening? said the sleepy old man blinking awake, his beard tangled in the old woman's shawl.

I think I've found the key to the universe, said the old woman showing the old man her crocheting hook. Look how it unlocks your beard and my shawl and relocks them as one. Why, you hardly tell where the one ends and the other begins.

But why is my secondary sexual characteristic becoming part secondary sexual characteristic and part shawl, even as a shawl becomes part shawl and part secondary sexual characteristic?

Because, while the key opens something, it must necessarily close something else . . .

Baby Pianos

A piano had made a huge manure. Its handler hoped the lady of the house wouldn't notice.

But the lady of the house said, what is that huge darkness?

The piano just had a baby, said the handler.

But I don't see any keys, said the lady of the house.

They come later, like baby teeth, said the handler.

Meanwhile the piano had dropped another huge manure.

What's that, cried the lady of the house, surely not another baby?

Twins, said the handler.

They look more like cannon balls than baby pianos, said the lady of the house.

The piano dropped another huge manure.

Triplets, smiled the handler . . .

The Alfresco Moment

A butler asks, will Madam be having her morning coffee alfresco?

If you would be so kind as to lift me out of my bed to the veranda I would be more than willing to imbibe coffee alfresco.

Shall I ask the Master to join the Madam for coffee alfresco?

But my nightgown's so sheer he might see my pubic delta alfresco. And being a woman of wealth I have the loins of a goddess. While you, being but a lowly servant, have the loins of a child's teddy bear. Yes, have the Master join the alfresco moment. He might just as well be informed of my pubic delta, it's not a state secret. Besides, he carries an organ worthy of a bull. While you, being but a lowly servant, have the loins of a caterpillar.

Very good, Madam . . .

The Message

The Captain becomes moody at sea. He's afraid of water; such bully amounts that prove the seas . . .

A glass of water is one thing. A man easily downs it, capturing its menace in his bladder and pissing it away.

A few drops of rain do little harm, save to remind how grief looks upon the cheek.

One day the water is willing to bear you and your ship upon its back like a liquid elephant. The next day the elephant has no more willingness to have you on its back.

At sea this is a sad message.

The Captain sits in his cabin wearing a parachute, listening to what the sea might say . . .

The Square Wheel

A mad scientist has cloned himself. It was an accident. He had been trying to invent a square wheel, when all of a sudden there was another mad scientist trying to invent a square wheel.

Theory: If the circle can be squared, why not the wheel?

Meanwhile, the first mad scientist is beginning to feel redundant. He may have to share his wife. Or even a Nobel Prize. Or, come to think of it, his toothbrush!

But, as it is always getting to be too late, the clone trying to invent a square wheel has already cloned another mad scientist trying to invent a square wheel, who has accidentally cloned another mad scientist madly seeking the square wheel . . .

Angels

They have little use. They are best as objects of torment.
No government cares what you do with them.

Like birds, and yet so human . . .
They mate by briefly looking at the other.
Their eggs are like white jellybeans.

Sometimes they have been said to inspire a man to do more with his life than he might have.

But what is there for a man to do with his life?

... They burn beautifully with a blue flame.

When they cry out it is like the screech of a tiny hinge; the cry of a bat.
No one hears it ...

The Bath

A man was taking a bath in a tub of turkey gravy; floating a rubber duck
to while away eternity. Eating mashed potatoes, dipping forkfuls in his
bath ...
It was gorgeous, the whole thing, he thought, me in soak with a duck,
having mashed potatoes and gravy, while out there a whole crazy world ...

Thus Spake Polly

A man had a parrot named Polly who was always saying, Polly wants a
cracker.
The man asked her why she was always referring to herself in the third
person.
Polly said, we are not amused.
And now why the royal *we*?
Because you had a common ancestor with modern apes. So break out the
crackers with your opposable thumbs. And don't forget the Brie cheese, we
are still not amused ...

Wings

In the wing of some old house, mounted under glass, a collection of
wings ...
The wing of a butterfly decorated with a false eye that occasionally
blinks.
A thimble acting the urn that holds the ashes of a moth's.
One of scrotum and finger bones that had grasped the night like a
terrible hand, dark as the night it grasped.

The wing of a white crow.

A mosquito's veined with human blood.

A winglet still unegged, featherless, mounted on a shard of shell.

The invisible one like something in a pawnshop waiting to be redeemed by an angel.

The wing of some famous nose mounted on a toothpick like an hors d'oeuvre, still flared with its last contemptuous breath . . .

Wings that had managed the air in such a way as to be free of the earth, gliding, fluttering. Sometimes soaring so high that the earth seemed hardly there at all . . .

Photo by Mark Lustgarten

Lynn Emanuel is the author of *Hotel Fiesta, The Dig,* and *Then, Suddenly—*, which won the Eric Matthieu King Award from the Academy of American Poets. She has taught at the Bread Loaf Writers' Conference, the Bennington Writers' Conference, The Warren Wilson Program in Creative Writing, and the Vermont College Creative Writing Program. Currently, she is a professor of English at the University of Pittsburgh.

inside gertrude stein

Right now as I am talking to you and as you are being talked to, without letup, it is becoming clear that gertrude stein has hijacked me and that this feeling that you are having now as you read this, that this is what it feels like to be inside gertrude stein. This is what it feels like to be a huge typewriter in a dress. Yes, I feel we have gotten inside gertrude stein, and of course it is dark inside the enormous gertrude, it is like being locked up in a refrigerator lit only by a smiling rind of cheese. Being inside gertrude is like being inside a monument made of a cloud which is always moving across the sky which is also always moving. Gertrude is a huge galleon of cloud anchored to the ground by one small tether, yes, I see it down there, do you see that tiny snail glued to the tackboard of the landscape? That is alice. So, I am inside gertrude; we belong to each other, she and I, and it is so wonderful because I have always been a thin woman inside of whom a big woman is screaming to get out, and she's out now and if a river could type this is how it would sound, pure and complicated and enormous. Now we are lilting across the countryside, and we are talking, and if the wind could type it would sound like this, ongoing and repetitious, abstracting and stylizing everything, like our famous haircut painted by Picasso. Because when you are inside our haircut you understand that all the flotsam and jetsam of hairdo have been cleared away (like the forests from the New World) so that the skull can show through grinning and feasting on the alarm it has created. I am now, alarmingly, inside gertrude's head and I am thinking that I may only be a thought she has had when she imagined that she and alice were dead and gone and someone had to carry on the work of being gertrude stein, and so I am receiving, from beyond the grave, radioactive isotopes of her genius saying, take up my work, become gertrude stein.

Because someone must be gertrude stein, someone must save us from the literalists and realists, and narratives of the beginning and end, someone must be a river that can type. And why not I? Gertrude is insisting on the fact that while I am a subgenius, weighing one hundred five pounds, and living in a small town with an enormous furry male husband who is always in his Cadillac Eldorado driving off to sell something to people who do not deserve the bad luck of this merchandise in their lives—that these facts would not be a problem for gertrude stein. Gertrude and I feel that, for instance, in *Patriarchal Poetry* when (like an avalanche that can type) she is burying the patriarchy, still there persists a sense of condescending affection. So, while I'm a thin, heterosexual sub-genius, nevertheless gertrude has chosen me as her tool, just as she chose the patriarchy as a tool for ending the patriarchy. And because I have become her tool, now, in a sense, gertrude is inside me. It's tough. Having gertrude inside me is like having swallowed an ocean liner that can type, and, while I feel like a very small coat closet with a bear in it, gertrude and I feel that I must tell you that gertrude does not care. She is using me to get her message across, to say, I am lost, I am beset by literalists and narratives of the beginning and middle and end, help me. And so, yes, I say, yes, I am here, gertrude, because we feel, gertrude and I, that there is real urgency in our voice (like a sob that can type) and that things are very bad for her because she is lost, beset by the literalists and realists, her own enormousness crushing her, and we must find her and take her into ourselves, even though I am the least likely of saviors and have been chosen perhaps as a last resort, yes, definitely, gertrude is saying to me, you are the least likely of saviors, you are my last choice and my last resort.

Halfway Through the Book I'm Writing

> This is the wonderful thing about art,
> it can bring back the dead...

My father dies and is buried in his Brooks Brothers suit.
But I can't seem to keep him underground.
Suddenly, I turn around and there he is just
as I'm getting a handle on the train-pulls-

into-the-station poem. "What gives?"
I ask him. "I'm alone and dead," he says,
and I say, "Father, there's nothing I can do about
all that. Get your mind off it. Help me with the poem

about the train." "I hate the poem about the train,"
he says. But since he's dead and I'm a patient woman
I turn back to the poem in which the crowds have gone home
and the janitor pushes the big mustache of his broom across the floor,
and I ask, "Dad, is that you in there?"

"No, it's not."

A black cloud in the shape of Magritte's bowler,
plump and sleek and stark, hanging over the train station, says,
"I want to go to a museum; put one in the poem beside the station."

where it's morning and the ticket window is selling
tickets to a man in a hat and an enormous
trench coat, wrinkled and jowly, a woman
in white looks as cool as a martini in a chrome
shaker, a woman in red seethes in a doorway,
eager to become one of Those Beginning the Journey
and from the horizon's molten light the trains crawl out.

"And when I get to the museum I want to see
Soutine, Miró, Picasso, or Dali, I want eyes in my armpits
and my fingers, eyes in the air, the trees, the dirt."

"Father," I say, "you already are an eye-in-the-dirt."

It's early morning. In the pine tree I hear the phoebe's stressed
squeak, *fee-bee, fee-bay,* like the creak of the old guard at the museum
snoozing in his rocker before Soutine's still life of the butchered cows.

"Father," I say, "do you see them?"
And the phoebe says, Yes-squeak-
yes-squeak-yes-squeak-yes-squeak.

Homage to Sharon Stone

It's early morning. This is the "before,"
the world hanging around in its wrapper,
blowzy, frumpy, doing nothing: my
neighbors, hitching themselves to the roles
of the unhappily married, trundle their three
mastiffs down the street. I am writing this
book of poems. My name is Lynn Emanuel.
I am wearing a bathrobe and curlers; from
my lips, a Marlboro drips ash on the text.
It is the third of September nineteen**.
And as I am writing this in my trifocals

and slippers, across the street, Sharon Stone,
her head swollen with curlers, her mouth
red and narrow as a dancing slipper,
is rushed into a black limo. And because
these limos snake up and down my street,
this book will be full of sleek cars nosing
through the shadowy ocean of these words.
Every morning, Sharon Stone, her head
in a helmet of hairdo, wearing a visor
of sunglasses, is engulfed by a limo
the size of a Pullman, and whole fleets
of these wind their way up and down
the street, day after day, giving to the street
(Liberty Avenue in Pittsburgh, PA)
and the book I am writing, an aspect
that is both glamorous and funereal.
My name is Lynn Emanuel, and in this
book I play the part of someone writing
a book, and I take the role seriously,
just as Sharon Stone takes seriously
the role of the diva. I watch the dark
cars disappear her and in my poem
another Pontiac erupts like a big animal
at the cool trough of a shady curb. So,
when you see this black car, do not think
it is a Symbol For Something. It is just
Sharon Stone driving past the house
of Lynn Emanuel who is, at the time,
trying to write a book of poems.

Or you could think of the black car as
Lynn Emanuel, because, really, as an author,
I have always wanted to be a car, even
though most of the time I have to be
the "I," or the woman hanging wash;
I am a woman, one minute, then I am a man,
I am a carnival of Lynn Emanuels:
Lynn in the red dress; Lynn sulking
behind the big nose of my erection;

then I am the train pulling into the station
when what I would really love to be is
Gertrude Stein spying on Sharon Stone
at six in the morning. But enough about
that, back to the interior decorating:
On the page, the town looks bald
and dim so I turn up the amps on
the radioactive glances of bad boys.
In a kitchen, I stack pans sleek with
grease, and on a counter there is a roast
beef red as a face in a tantrum. Amid all
this bland strangeness is Sharon Stone,
who, like an engraved invitation, is asking
me, *Won't you, too, play a role?* I do not
choose the black limo rolling down the street
with the golden stare of my limo headlights
bringing with me the sun, the moon, and
Sharon Stone. It is nearly dawn; the sun
is a fox chewing her foot from the trap;
every bite is a wound and every wound
is a red window, a red door, a red road.
My name is Lynn Emanuel. I am the writer
trying to unwrite the world that is all around her.

Portrait of the Author

Today I write about the house
of the body and about myself,

its shadowy proprietor,
coming and going.

Above the street, beside a fan
and a half-inch of bourbon

floating in a tumbler, someone's
white face pokes a hole

in a dark window. It's me,
in the body of a man named Raoul.

The rain stings the window
and the nothing beyond.

The rain throbs steadily
as the heart's dull return and lob.

Bending over the woman on the bed,
Raoul says, *Take off your dress.*

I'll take my dress off, the woman says.
And then the sibilant whisper

of a black silk frock.
(*A what?*)

Frock. On the floor.
Also hosiery. Also black.

Suddenly naked or wearing
only flawless technique

and the dark eyes of staring
breasts, the story ends

either (A)

Bending over her
beautiful and tragic face

against the pillows, Raoul says,
Oh Lynn, Lynn, you bring me to my knees.

or (B)

Gazing up into my own
beautiful and tragic face, I say,

Oh, Raoul, you bring me to my knees.

Photo by Micha Langer

Peter Everwine is the author of seven collections of poetry, including *Collecting the Animals*, which won the Lamont Poetry Prize (now the James Laughlin Award). He retired from California State University, Fresno, in 1992.

Drinking Cold Water

Almost twenty years
since you put on your one good dress
and lay down in the shale hills of Pennsylvania.
What you expected from life was nothing much,
and it came
and so it was.
In California I mourned and then forgot,
though sometimes, in a mirror,
I saw someone walk from the weeds,
stepping from a shine of water,
and it was you, shining.

Tonight I brought my bundle of years
to an empty house.
When I opened it, a boy walked out—
drinking cold water, watching the
moon rise slim and shining over your house.
Whatever it was I wanted
must have come and gone.

Twenty years, grandmother.
Here I stand
in the poverty of my feet,
and I know what you'd do:
you'd enter your black shawl,
step back into the shadows of your hair.
And that's no help tonight.
All I can think of is your house—
the pump at the sink
spilling a trough of clear
cold water from the well—
and you, old love,
sleeping in your dark dress
like a hard, white root.

Perhaps It's as You Say

Perhaps it's as you say
That nothing stays lost forever

How many times have I said No No
There is a darkness in the cell

And opened my hands to cup emptiness
Tasting its bitten face

I do not know if our loves survive us
Waiting through the long night for our step

Or if they will know us then
Entering our flesh with the old sigh

I do not know
But I think of fields that stretch away flat

Beneath the stars their dry grasses
Gathering a light of honey

The few houses wink and go out
Across the fields an asphalt road darkens

And disappears among the cottonwoods by the dry creek
It is so quiet so quiet

Meet me there

Sorting the Tools

—Fire I leave to my children

This is the hammer
and the nails.
I enter my brother's house
for the last time.

This is the miner's lamp,
the bit and the sack of dust.
This is the bread
that stinks of carbide.

These are the numbers
of the sleepless, rising
in the power
of their true names:

In the name of crowbar
which is 1.
In the name of broken back
which is 2.

This is the penis
that lugs and sweats like a horse.
These are hands
in their crust of dead lights.

Let the sun and moon go,
the black roof,
the seams of the earth
gathering water.

This is the animal
that grew tired and slept.
These are words
left out in the rain.

In the Last Days

In the last days of my father's illness
he lived on, separate from us, in a tiny room
with a window in it, where we could look in and watch
him laboring at his heavy sleep.

And only once did he startle up
from the pillow, wide eyed, and slapped one palm
across the other—*Phsst!* he said, and smiled, and shook his head
as if in disbelief down into sleep again.

I don't know what my father saw then, wandering
in some mazy episode of time.
That was forty years ago. Forty years, like yesterday.
Almost his own age now, I can see

his face before me: his wry smile of wonder,
as if something had leapt up underfoot
in the dark and sped away
as he watched.

Poem Beginning with a Line from Leonardo Sinisgalli

—for C. H.

Perhaps this memory, too, is useless:
A midsummer morning. You stand at my open door,
a boy in worn jeans shifting from foot to foot
and stuttering, as always, your words
long since gone into wind and silence.
You hold out your new mail-order guitar
as an offering, and the early light, falling
through the maples, flares
against its polished wood and metal …
the image suspended in this quiet room
where I write. Charlie, I don't know why
you come to mind. We were never boyhood friends;
our lives were separate. With your thin face
and troubled tongue, you were not
among the favored. I don't know why
you chose my door or why, years later,
you flung yourself from the bridge
into water so sulfurous and foul nothing

would live in it, not even you.
Music did not save you, Charlie.
Words will not save me—
useless, perhaps, yet here you are, unbidden,
standing before me in the mystery
of an otherwise forgotten morning
as if you were not simply a memory
but memory itself, trembling
and inarticulate, your face
shining with joy as you reach out to touch
a single string, its sound
already silence.

From the Meadow

It isn't that you were ignorant:
star thistle, bloodroot, cruciform …
beautiful words, then as now,
unlike pain with its wooden alphabet,
its many illustrations, which are redundant.

You had imagined vistas, an open meadow:
on the far side, water trembles its lights;
cattle come down to their shadow lives
beneath the trees;
the language of childhood is invented anew.

But now you know, right, what lies ahead
is nothing to the view behind?
How breathtaking these nostalgias rising
like hazy constellations overhead!—

little to go by, surely,
though from the meadow where you stand looking
over your shoulder, that tiny figure you see
seems to be calling someone,
you perhaps.

The Heart

We draw it so it looks
like a deer's footprint, smoothing
its redness into a shape we can fill
with sweetness or a track we can follow
through the wilderness of our lives
into a clearing we call love
or sometimes, mercy—Have a heart, we say—
as if one didn't need the other,
as if the heart didn't break.

In a small white room
I saw my heart, after it broke.
It swam up from the dark,
a blind, albino shape, thick
and writhing, twisting and sinking back
in shadows as if it shunned the light
it could only feel, not see.
And it made a sound, not like a slack drum,
but like the whip-poor-will
I listened to as a boy, singing on spring evenings
at the edge of the woods—
whip-poor-will, whip-poor-will—
but sibilant now and urgent,
as if a little hoarse from all the years
of calling out its name to the unanswering dark.
I close my eyes and I can see it,
and sometimes, in quiet moments before sleep,
I imagine I hear it singing still,
so that the woods return, and the boy,
and the spring evenings—
O love, O mercy,
O passing years!

Edward Field's books of poetry include *Magic Words: Poems; Counting Myself Lucky: Selected Poems 1963–1992; New and Selected Poems from the Book of My Life; A Full Heart*, nominated for the Lenore Marshall Prize; and *Stand Up, Friend, with Me*, which was the 1962 Lamont Poetry Selection of The Academy of American Poets. Field has edited anthologies of poetry, translated Eskimo songs and stories, and written the narration for the documentary film *To Be Alive*, which won an Academy Award for best documentary short subject in 1965. Field has also collaborated on several popular novels with Neil Derrick, under the joint pseudonym of Bruce Elliot. He has taught workshops at the Poetry Center of the YMHA, Sarah Lawrence, and other colleges. Although Field makes regular trips to Europe, his permanent residence is in New York City.

Frankenstein

The monster has escaped from the dungeon
where he was kept by the Baron,
who made him with knobs sticking out from each side of his neck
where the head was attached to the body
and stitching all over
where parts of cadavers were sewn together.

He is pursued by the ignorant villagers,
who think he is evil and dangerous because he is ugly
and makes ugly noises.
They wave firebrands at him and cudgels and rakes,
but he escapes and comes to the thatched cottage
of an old blind man playing on the violin Mendelssohn's "Spring Song."

Hearing him approach, the blind man welcomes him:
"Come in, my friend," and takes him by the arm.
"You must be weary," and sits him down inside the house.
For the blind man has long dreamed of having a friend
to share his lonely life.

The monster has never known kindness—the Baron was cruel—
but somehow he is able to accept it now,
and he really has no instincts to harm the old man,
for in spite of his awful looks he has a tender heart:
Who knows what cadaver that part of him came from?

The old man seats him at table, offers him bread,
and says, "Eat, my friend." The monster
rears back roaring in terror.
"No, my friend, it is good. Eat-gooood"
and the old man shows him how to eat,
and reassured, the monster eats
and says, "Eat-gooood,"
trying out the words and finding them good too.

The old man offers him a glass of wine,
"Drink, my friend. Drink-gooood."
The monster drinks, slurping horribly, and says,

"Drink-gooood," in his deep nutty voice
and smiles maybe for the first time in his life.

Then the blind man puts a cigar in the monster's mouth
and lights a large wooden match that flares up in his face.
The monster, remembering the torches of the villagers,
recoils, grunting in terror.
"No, my friend, smoke-gooood,"
and the old man demonstrates with his own cigar.
The monster takes a tentative puff
and smiles hugely, saying, "Smoke-gooood,"
and sits back like a banker, grunting and puffing.

Now the old man plays Mendelssohn's "Spring Song" on the violin
while tears come into our dear monster's eyes
as he thinks of the stones of the mob, the pleasures of meal time,
the magic new words he has learned
and above all of the friend he has found.

It is just as well that he is unaware
being simple enough to believe only in the present
that the mob will find him and pursue him
for the rest of his short unnatural life,
until trapped at the whirlpool's edge
he plunges to his death.

Nancy

When scolded by Aunt Fritzy Ritz
Nancy seems to lose her wits.
Nancy is very often cross
but Fritzy's the undisputed boss.
She sits in the house reading the papers
supervising Nancy's capers.

Aunt Fritzy's a peculiar sort:
She has no visible means of support.
She never seems to earn a bean
and there's no "uncle" on the scene.

The questions seem to rise a lot:
Is Fritzy Nancy's aunt, or not?
If Fritzy is related to
that awful Mrs. Meany who
Annie Roonie had to flee,
then who can Nancy really be?

Rumors are flying thick and fast;
stories from mouth to ear are passed:
"Who is Fritzy Ritz indeed
but someone overcome by greed.
Welfare pays a monthly sum
to keep that orphan in her home.
Although she looks like Etta Kett
She's older, more depraved, in debt."

One scandalous version I have heard
(of which I don't believe a word)
says Nancy's father, coming back
a little early from the track,
found his wife and Fritzy in
a most revolting act of sin.
With a knife he tried to nip

this lesbian relationship:
Saw red, and stabbed; the blow went wild
and made an orphan of his child.
His wife was dead, he got the chair,
the court named Fritzy Ritz as heir.
The child, the house, the bank account,
were left to Fritzy Ritz, the "aunt."

No one will make Aunt Fritzy crawl
now that she's in charge of all:
the house, the grounds, the little brat.
She'll teach her to remember that!

Poor Nancy's nature has been bent
by this negative environment.
She never will grow up at all
but stay forever three feet tall.

Unwanted

The poster with my picture on it
Is hanging on the bulletin board in the post office.

I stand by it hoping to be recognized
Posing first full face and then in profile

But everybody passes by and I have to admit
The photograph was taken some years ago.

I was unwanted then and I'm unwanted now
Ah guess ah'll go up echo mountain and crah.

I wish someone would find my fingerprints somewhere
Maybe on a corpse and say, You're it.

Description: Male, or reasonably so
White, but not lily-white and politically a pinko

Thirty-fivish, and looks it lately
Five-feet-nine and one-hundred-thirty pounds: no physique

Black hair going gray, hairline receding fast
What used to be curly, now fuzzy

Brown eyes starey under beetling brow
Mole on chin, probably will become a wen

It is perfectly obvious that he was not popular at school
No good at baseball, and wet his bed

His aliases tell his history: Dumbbell, Good-for-nothing,
Jewboy, Fieldinsky, Skinny, Fierce Face, Greaseball, Sissy.

Warning: This man is not dangerous, answers to any name
Responds to love, don't call him or he will come.

The Tailspin

Going into a tailspin
in those days meant curtains.
No matter how hard you pulled back on the stick
the nose of the plane wouldn't come up.

Spinning round, headed for a target of earth,
the whine of death in the wing struts,
instinct made you try to pull out of it that way, by force,
and for years aviators spiraled down and crashed.

Who could have dreamed that the solution
to this dreaded aeronautical problem
was so simple?
Every student flier learns this nowadays:
You move the joystick in the direction of the spin
and like a miracle the plane stops turning
and you are in control again
to pull the nose up out of the dive.

In panic we want to push the stick away from the spin,
wrestle the plane out of it,
but the trick is, as in everything,
to go with the turn willingly,
rather than fight, give in, go with it,
and that way come out of your tailspin whole.

In Praise of My Prostate

While most men I know are having theirs irradiated,
scooped out, or surgically removed,
we're enjoying a blissful Indian summer.

The more horror stories I hear
the more I'm determined to hold on to you—
you're my own and I want you just the way you are.

Yes, I pee all night like any guy my age,
and if I'm rarely rock hard anymore,
I'm not complaining—

rock hard's often numb as a stone,
whereas you're a living bulb,
if bulbously encrusted by our long voyage,

and you still expand, your amazing flowers
bursting forth throughout my body,
pistils and stamens dancing.

The Lost, Dancing

When the drums come to your door
do not try to shut them out,
do not turn away and resist them,
for they have come to tell you what you need to hear,
they are your fate.
When Antony heard them
he knew then that he had lost Egypt forever.
He did not shriek or tear his clothes
for he always knew they would come someday.
What the drums speak to you
is so inevitable you have to agree with them
nothing else could be right.
So when the drummers and dancers come to your door
your life changes,
and with no bitterness
but with a sad smile
—after all what you had you had,
you loved the way few men love—
and as someone who was worthy of such a kingdom,
join the army of the lost, dancing,
follow the drums
and turn and wave goodbye
to the Alexandria you are losing.
                                    —after Cavafy
                                    Carnival, Rio de Janeiro, 1974

Garbo

Her eyes never blink—
higher beings do not blink,

nor people in remote lands
who stare at you from the fields—
but that's innocence, like animals.

If blinking is a kind of flinching,
she never flinches.
She doesn't adopt any facial expression—
it's her feelings she shows
or none at all. Nor does she put on
mannerisms like we do, meaning
we're desperate for attention.
If she says she wants to be alone
she's the only one we believe it of.

It's no devices then that make her beautiful
but the lack of them. Still, the awkwardness
of her grace shows that being graceful
is not an easy victory—
there's that permanent mournfulness in the mouth
and the testimony of those eyes—
no blinking back,
it's all there.

Can't we make the same commitment,
risk shedding evasions, devices, defenses
—in short, our faces—
and look unblinking at each other, vulnerable
to what in our hearts we long for,
whatever the cost, wherever it leads?

Or does she affirm that for mere mortals
the price is too great,
though for herself
she could not, would not, choose another fate?

Photo by Pierce Backes

Daisy Fried is the author of *My Brother Is Getting Arrested Again*, a finalist for the James Laughlin Prize, and *She Didn't Mean to Do It*, which won the Agnes Lynch Starrett Poetry Prize. Her other awards include a Guggenheim Fellowship, a Pushcart Prize, and a Pew Fellowship. She is currently the Grace Hazard Conkling Writer-in-Residence at Smith College and lives in Northampton, Massachusetts, and Philadelphia.

She Didn't Mean to Do It

Oh, she was sad, oh, she was sad.
She didn't mean to do it.

Certain thrills stay tucked in your limbs,
go no further than your fingers, move your legs through their paces,
but no more. Certain thrills knock you flat
on your sheets on your bed in your room and you fade
and they fade. You falter and they're gone, gone, gone.
Certain thrills puff off you like smoke rings,
some like bell rings growing out, out, turning
brass, steel, gold, till the whole world's filled
with the gonging of your thrills.

But oh, she was sad, she was just sad, sad,
and she didn't mean to do it.

A Story Having to Do with Walt Whitman

A friend of mine used to be, and still is, but only
legally, married to a dancer. The girl, this dancer,
his wife, had a teacher, one of those beautiful menschy
dancer men, who was dying of AIDS. He, the teacher,
as I imagine it, though it's not always true for dancers
in his company, had done nothing in his life but dance.
Well, that's perfectly enough. But the girl, this dancer, this
wife, who read as well as danced, thought she would bring him
Leaves of Grass, with the not inconsiderable presumption
that it would comfort him to the great end. (Presumptions need
not be false. It would have.) But this girl, the dancer, the wife,
once she realized that she had presumed, ascribing to her
gift and thus to herself a certain importance, worried
about it so much that she put off bringing it to him.

He lay at home and sometimes in the hospital, with
many friends in bright-colored clothes around him (they all used
to wear black and white, but thinking of death, they put on

rainbows). The girl, the wife, the dancer, worried and worried
about walking into the room of many colors. It
was not her wardrobe, she was not worried about that, though
she wore mostly grays, maroons, browns. She worried about
stepping forward in that crowd, having them look at her,
who did not even know if the dying man cared about her.
She worried she would be seen for what she was, not a friend,
but a pupil, and adorer. So he died and she
never brought the book. When she realized her foolishness,
as she always did, immediately after the moment
when it was too late, she just went down to the East River

and sat on a pier and looked at Manhattan and felt shame.
The book, a pretty hardback, in her lap. She sat and read
it, the whole thing. She thought several things as she read. One,
how can you die, not having read everything. Another,
how all actions should be as if for others, even if
none truly are. Three, how awful to die in the summer.
Four. She missed her husband, my friend. Five. She must work harder
at dancing. Six, what did it really matter if he
never read *Leaves of Grass.* Did it matter to the soul?
Seven, oh for goodness sake, what soul? The next day, she
agreed at his funeral to help clean out his
apartment. On his coffee table there was a Monet
with bad reproductions, Richardson's *Life of Picasso,*
Vol. 2 (the cubist years), autobiographies of

choreographers, and a battered paperback: *Leaves of
Grass,* what do you think? She opened it and found it all marked
up inside, with comments and all. Comments about how one could
make a dance with all this in mind. And she all of a
sudden remembered seeing the title "Afraid of the
Merge" on his list of choreography credits. Inside
the front cover it said "To my darling, from Gary." Instead
of this making this girl, the dancer, the wife laugh, or see the
humor in the whole thing, or at least see that she had read
him right, and picked the right gift, she just felt miserable.
This is why my friend and she had trouble getting along, for

he is not so complex and constipated as this girl, this
dancer, his wife. What happened? Oh, I expect she'll get over
it. Oh, one more thing. I am the girl, this dancer, this wife.

Whatever Works

"I never was much good at blow jobs," she says, driving.
"Couldn't get the right amount of pressure. Or maybe
it was him. He just didn't like them. He said so:
'maybe it's me,' he said. After awhile I just
stopped worrying about it, and here we are." I'm
sitting in the back to keep an eye on her baby.
I nod, thinking what I know, what I don't know. Old
music. Turn off that old radio music. The
baby's crying. More night inside the car than out.
The baby's crying despite she pulled over at
the rest stop to feed it just ten, twenty miles back. I keep on
pushing its rubber nipple at its mouth; it takes
it a moment then goes on crying. Finally,
entering the bridge, she reaches her arm back over the seat,
finds the baby's mouth with her finger. It
knows her skin by taste. Mouths that finger, sucks it,
chews it, falls asleep. "Whatever works," she says,
and keeps on driving fast and crooked around that way.

Aunt Leah, Aunt Sophie and the Negro Painter

Under the lemon, the goblet, the plate of grapes, painterly,
late cubist, by a WPA artist—"the Negro"—
her sister knew in Chicago, my Aunt Leah sits:

"Your father giving his atheist mother
a religious funeral with that schmuck rabbi—why?"
She taps her cigarette, neat fingernail, puts it down,
points the back of her head at the painting.

"Your Aunt Sophie wanted you to have it."
Her cigarette smokes up a thin blue-gray plume.

Sophie was a Socialist. "Communist," Aunt Leah says,
tilting her recliner. "I was the Socialist. Sophie went
to the Peekskill Robeson concert with the Negro painter."
She blows smoke-ribbons up past her eye. "They got
beat up, mobs, cops, nightsticks. I gave them tea—
they came over after. The painter's head was sticky
with blood." Leah exhales nostril-smoke at her chest.
"I laughed at them. 'What did you expect?' I said."

Last time I saw Sophie she was in bed
at the constant care center, cursing
at OJ, fiddling with the edge
of her bedspread. The room stank
of medicine. The painting hung
gray-blue over the TV.

I hoist up from my chair in Leah's home,
look where the palette knife or artist finger
touched wet canvas. I cock my head
side to side; window sun reflects off
the frame-glass, blots out the fruitbowl.
Leah says,

"It's student work, 1938. Sophie told him
'go out to the street, paint *your* people.'
So he did. And never got famous.
Communists were wrong about
art and everything else. That's how Stalin
became a monster and messed everything up—"

To stop another lecture on the purges
I tell Leah how my sister promised
to take my cat while I was on honeymoon;
then, day of my wedding, wouldn't. "I don't
remember why. She screamed. I screamed.

I made my parents do it. My mother's allergic,
so what, it's their fault, they raised us."

I'm six. 1974. Somebody's New York apartment,
white rug, many people. They say "schmatte." They say
"schmooze," they say "schwarze." They wear
bead necklaces, interesting belts, plastic white
sunglasses propped on their heads. Nixon's
resigning on black-and-white TV. He says
nobody gave him anything except a dog.
I climb on Sophie's lap. She smells like olives.
She's drinking a martini. "And," I say to Leah,
2004, "I said something. What did I say?"

"You said 'poor Nixon,'" Leah says. "'Nobody
gave him anything but a little puppy dog—
didn't he have a mommy and poppy?' Nixon's dog speech
was before you were born. You're remembering
a rerun. You were on my lap, not Sophie's. Sophie
was flirting with Arthur."

1980, Leah and Sophie voted for Reagan.
My father wouldn't speak to them for six months.
Now he tells me the good side
of Ariel Sharon. I don't speak to him much.
Leah says: "Arthur was her first Republican.
After Sophie married him, she was happy
for awhile." Leah lights a cigarette off her
burnt-down cigarette—curlicues
of smoke. She says: "I just can't understand how
your father became a Conservative Jew."

I say "I haven't spoken to my sister
for four years. I am unreasonable—
sometimes. I have a hot temper—
sometimes. But I am not envious, I am not
entirely uncharitable,
at all times I try to behave as if I realize

the world does not revolve around
my feelings. Above all, I am
not deranged, I do not take out
my problems on other people's *cats*."

Leah says, "Sophie thought you were like her.
Do you think you're like her?" She puts
her cigarette in the ashtray, I pick it up,
take my first drag in ten years. It burns. Aches.
Sour, it stings. "People still buy his
paintings," Leah says. "For historical
value, I guess. I don't know what he was to her."

Leah twists her head. "Just take it now," she says.
I take down the painting. Leah wipes her eyes.
"I don't know why I'm crying.
If she came in this room now I'd leave.
If she opened her mouth, I'd slap it."

Barbara Hamby is the author of *Babel,* winner of the Donald Hall Prize in Poetry, *Delirium,* which won the Vassar Miller Prize, the Poetry Society of America's Norma Farber First Book Award, and the Kate Tufts Award; and *The Alphabet of Desire,* which won the New York University Poetry Prize and was chosen as one of the twenty-five best books of 1999 by the New York City Public Library. She teaches creative writing at Florida State University.

Ode to American English

I was missing English one day, American, really,
    with its pill-popping Hungarian goulash of everything
from Anglo-Saxon to Zulu, because British English
    is not the same, if the paperback dictionary
I bought at Brentano's on the Avenue de l'Opéra
    is any indication, too cultured by half. Oh, the English
know their dahlias, but what about doowop, donuts,
    Dick Tracy, Tricky Dick? With their elegant Oxfordian
accents, how could they understand my yearning for the hotrod,
    hotdog, hot flash vocabulary of the U. S. of A.,
the fragmented fandango of Dagwood's everyday flattening
    of Mr. Beasley on the sidewalk, fetuses floating
on billboards, drive-by monster hip-hop stereos shaking
    the windows of my dining room like a 7.5 earthquake,
Ebonics, Spanglish, "you know" used as comma and period,
    the inability of 90% of the population to get the past perfect:
I have went, I have saw, I have tooken Jesus into my heart,
    the battle cry of the Bible Belt, but no one uses
the King James anymore, only plain-speak versions,
    in which Jesus, raising Lazarus from the dead, says,
"Dude, wake up," and the L-man bolts up like a B-movie
    mummy. "Whoa, I was toasted." Yes, ma'am,
I miss the mongrel plenitude of American English, its fall-guy,
    rat-terrier, dog-pound neologisms, the bomb of it all,
the rushing River Jordan backwoods mutability of it, the low-rider,
    boom-box cruise of it, from New Joisey to Ha-wah-ya
with its sly dog, malasada-scarfing beach blanket lingo
    to the ubiquitous Valley Girl's *like-like* stuttering,
shopaholic rant. I miss its quotidian beauty, its querulous
    back-biting righteous indignation, its preening rotgut
flag-waving cowardice. *Suffering Succotash*, sputters
    Sylvester the Cat; *sine die,* say the pork-bellied legislators
of the swamps and plains. I miss all those guys, their Tweety-bird
    resilience, their Doris Day optimism, the candid unguent
of utter unhappiness on every channel, the midnight televangelist
    euphoric stew, the junk mail, voice mail vernacular.

On every *boulevard* and *rue* I miss the Tarzan cry of Johnny
        Weismueller, Johnny Cash, Johnny B. Goode,
and all the smart-talking, gum-snapping hard-girl dialogue,
        finger-popping x-rated street talk, sports babble,
Cheetoes, Cheerios, chili dog diatribes. Yeah, I miss them all,
        sitting here on my sidewalk throne sipping champagne
verses lined up like hearses, metaphors juking, nouns zipping
        in my head like Corvettes on Dexedrine, French verbs
slitting my throat, yearning for James Dean to jump my curb.

The Mockingbird on the Buddha

The mockingbird on the Buddha says, Where's my seed,
        you Jezebel, where's the sunshine in my blue sky,
where's the Hittite princess, Pharaoh's temple, where's the rain
        for the misery I love so much? The mockingbird
on the Buddha scolds the tree for trying to stay straight
        in the hurricane of words blowing out of the cold north,
wind like screams, night like brandy on the dark cut of my heart.
        The mockingbird on the Buddha, music is his life,
he hears the tunes of the universe, cacophony of calypso,
        hacking cough in the black lung of desire; he's ruddy
with lust, that sweet stepping puffed-up old grey bird o' mine.
        The mockingbird on the Buddha says, Eat up
while the night is young. Have some peach cobbler, girl,
        have some fried oysters, have some Pouligny
Montrachet, *ma chère*, for the night is coming, and you need meat
        on your bones to ride that wild horse. The mockingbird
on the Buddha says, It's time for a change, little missy. You've
        been in charge too long. It's time for the bird
to take over, because he stays up late, knows what night can be,
        past 12, past two, when trouble's dark and beautiful.
You never knew what hit you, and that's the best feeling
        in the whole wide world. The mockingbird
on the Buddha makes his nest inside my brain: he looks good
        in grey, gets fat on thought, he's my enemy,

my Einstein, my ever-loving monkey boy, every monkey thought
    I blame on him, every night so sweet my body breaks
apart like a Spanish galleon raining gold on the ocean floor.

Ode to the Potato

"They eat a lot of French fries here," my mother
    announces after a week in Paris, and she's right,
not only about *les pommes frites* but the celestial tuber
    in all its forms: rotie, purée, not to mention
au gratin or boiled and oiled in *la salade niçoise*.
    Batata edulis discovered by gold-mad conquistadors
in the West Indies, and only a 100 years later
    in *The Merry Wives of Windsor* Falstaff cries,
"Let the skie raine Potatoes," for what would we be
    without you—lost in a sea of fried turnips,
mashed beets, roasted parsnips? *Mi corazón, mon coeur,*
    my core is not the heart but the stomach, tuber
of the body, its hollow stem the throat and esophagus,
    leafing out to the nose and eyes and mouth. Hail
the conquering spud, all its names marvelous: *Solanum*
    tuberosum, Igname, Caribe, Russian Banana, Yukon Gold.
When you turned black, Ireland mourned. O Mr. Potato Head,
    how many deals can a man make before he stops being
small potatoes? How many men can a woman drop
    like a hot potato? Eat it cooked or raw like an apple
with salt of the earth, apple of the earth, *pomme de terre.*
    Tuber, tuber burning bright in a kingdom without light,
deep within the earth where the Incan potato gods rule,
    forging their golden orbs for the world's ravening gorge.

Fang

I want to be seven feet tall, walk out of the Gabon bush,
    speaking Fang, to gaze into the sky and see
        an overturned bowl of godless blue, a wild storm
    in the heart of the devil, a rocky sea of scudding,

poisoned boats. I want to look into the dark canopy
        of trees and hear the mother of all talking creatures,
fluttering mountains, a green sea swimming with fish that fly.
        I need Fang for revenge—fire smoldering
                in the heart, a quick knife, a sickness
that fells grown men in the midday sun. I want words
        like teeth that could tear the flesh
                from the throat of my worst enemy—her face
        staring at me from every mirror. Every morning
my voice is a bird flying over treetops,
                dropping berries bitter and sweet
                into mouths open and closed. I can hardly bear
the sun on my skin. O Fang, come to me as a suitor
        with two goats and an orchard of pomegranates, woo me
                with your straight back, take me deep
into the night when stars fall like faithless lovers
        on the black trees. I need the mouth of a viper,
                a vampire, a mad dog pulling children
        from their mothers' arms. I want my heart to swell
like a wide brown river carrying trees, huts, limbs
                to the flood-maddened sea. O Fang,
        heart of a snake, body of impenetrable water,
                dark continent of betel nut and monkeypod,
erupt from my tongue, give me a world I cannot give myself.

Ode to Rock 'n' Roll

Tonight the band is so good you have to dance, the lead
        singer's voice like honey at the bottom of a jar,
so deep your hand gets stuck, fingers skimming the last
        bead of sweet, so sticky you remember riding
in a car, an MG or midnight blue Mustang,
        through a fragrant tropical night, 1969 it was,
the radio playing "Ain't Too Proud to Beg,"
        only you were, didn't even know what begging was,
but now you know. Oh, you've done some begging
        in your time, been way down, so low you thought

you'd never get up, because you'd been that bad; you'd lied,
        cheated, stolen, or that's what the falsetto
is singing, swooping down like a crazy mockingbird
        after an alley cat, scratching your skin,
making your tired bones loose in their sockets, and you're
        shaking it, moving your hips like you was some kind
of home girl, jumping up like that skinny cat on a hot
        sidewalk. You're frying eggs, mama, the bald drummer
telling you how to cut that particular rug into a thousand pieces,
        your feet religious, your knees like holy water,
head crazy with hair, the wild Indian your mother
        always said you were, but a Comanche, whose word
for themselves means *the human beings* and that's what you are,
        finally, in this sweltering room in the middle
of December, your arms moving like a semaphore,
        as if you were frantically trying to signal
a distant ship in the doom of the night, an ark filled
        with such fear the Bantu word *mbuki-mvuki,*
to tear off your clothes to dance, is almost lost till it floats
        back on the Mississippi as *boogie-woogie*
in a wild trance of forgetting, and sometimes the spot
        on your sullen heart is the sweetest part,
this collision of Bantu, blues, hillbilly riffs, riding the night
        like a wild stallion filled with a murderous longing.
Oh, let there be fire, a sulfurous kindling of earth and air,
        and in the clear morning may we all be Comanches,
riding the high plains of indifferent grass, fierce with the murmur
        of gods—Leadbelly's growl, Hendrix's response,
Little Richard's screams, heaven sent as our own voices
        were we human enough to heed the call.

Ode to My 1977 Toyota

Engine like a Singer sewing machine, where have you
        not carried me—to dance class, grocery shopping,
into the heart of darkness and back again? O the fruit
        you've transported—cherries, peaches, blueberries,

watermelons, thousands of Fuji apples—books,
         and all my dark thoughts, the giddy ones, too,
like bottles of champagne popped at the wedding of two people
         who will pass each other on the street as strangers
in twenty years. Ronald Reagan was president when I walked
         into Big Chief Motors and saw you glimmering
on the lot like a slice of broiled mahi mahi or sushi
         without its topknot of tuna. Remember the months
I drove you to work singing "Some Enchanted Evening"?
         Those were scary times. All I thought about
was getting on I-10 with you and not stopping. Would you
         have made it to New Orleans? What would our life
have been like there? I'd forgotten about poetry. Thank God,
         I remembered her. She saved us both. We were young
together. Now we're not. College boys stop us at traffic lights
         and tell me how cool you are. Like an ice cube, I say,
though you've never had air conditioning. Who needed it?
         I would have missed so many smells without you—
confederate jasmine, magnolia blossoms, the briny sigh
         of the Gulf of Mexico, rotting 'possums scattered
along 319 between Sopchoppy and Panacea. How many holes
         are there in the ballet shoes in your back seat?
How did that pair of men's white loafers end up in your trunk?
         Why do I have so many questions, and why
are the answers like the animals that dart in front of your headlights
         as we drive home from the coast, the Milky Way
strung across the black velvet bowl of the sky like the tiara
         of some impossibly fat empress who rules the universe
but doesn't know if tomorrow is December or Tuesday or June first.

C. G. Hanzlicek is the author of eight books of poetry, including *Against Dreaming* and *The Cave: Selected and New Poems.* He has translated Native American songs in *A Bird's Companion,* and poems from Czech in *Mirroring: Selected Poems of Vladimir Holan,* which won the Robert Payne Award from the Columbia University Translation Center. In the summer of 2001, he retired from California State University, Fresno, where he taught for thirty-five years and was for most of those years the director of the creative writing program.

Egg

I'm scrambling an egg for my daughter.
"Why are you always whistling?" she asks.
"Because I'm happy."
And it's true,
Though it stuns me to say it aloud;
There was a time when I wouldn't
Have seen it as my future.
It's partly a matter
Of who is there to eat the egg:
The self fallen out of love with itself
Through the tedium of familiarity,
Or this little self,
So curious, so hungry,
Who emerged from the woman I love,
A woman who loves me in a way
I've come to think I deserve,
Now that it arrives from outside me.
Everything changes, we're told,
And now the changes are everywhere:
The house with its morning light
That fills me like a revelation,
The yard with its trees
That cast a bit more shade each summer,
The love of a woman
That both is and isn't confounding,
And the love
Of this clamor of questions at my waist.
Clamor of questions,
You clamor of answers,
Here's your egg.

The Cave

All day long in the forge shop
The drop hammers fell
A full two stories
To mash the red hot metal bars
Into the molds.
We could hear them
In our house a mile away.
There were no ear protectors then,
There was no OSHA;
There was a plant safety man
Who gave it no thought.
Day by day, year by year,
The men went deafer and deafer;
By the time they retired,
Their world must have been as quiet
As the cave we visited
When I was twelve.
No one spoke
As we descended
Into dripping chambers,
Each cooler than the last,
But even in that silence
I could carry a little music with me,
As if my mind was a juke box,
And my memory
A pocket heavy with quarters.
We ended in a wide, round room,
Floodlit from every direction,
Filled with stalactites and stalagmites.
It was like standing inside
A huge marble pipe organ
The moment before hands
Fell to the keys.
"You've never been in darkness
Like this," the guide said,
And then she hit a switch

To suspend us in unimaginable black.
I searched myself in panic
And couldn't find an image anywhere.
"Lord, save my eyes,"
I said to myself as much as to any god
Who might descend so low.
It was just a glimmer then,
But now I know the whole and bitter truth:
Without vision,
I would not, like Milton,
Sit by the fire
In the cavernous dark
And build a book
Of angels.
I would rather leaf through someone's,
Anyone's, photo album—
The trip to the Rockies,
Uncle Ed in his cups
At the family reunion—
Than listen to the teachings of the mystics.
Always it has been for me the seen
High, high above
The unseen world.

Blue Light

In those days I had no one,
And mostly no one to blame for that but myself,
And I took to hanging out
In the town's only piano bar, thinking,
Not altogether wrongly, that the sentimentality
Of those old songs could backfill
The hole I had dug for myself.
The players were booked
Only for a week or two,
And every last one of them

Was on the way down.
They wore their falling years
Like a cheap, wrinkled suit,
And none of them had ever lived
In one place long enough
To smooth out anything in their lives.
The bar horseshoed around the piano,
And my stool was at the tip on the left,
Where I could talk to the player
And catch a little air whenever the door opened.
There were a few booths and tables in the back,
And a single, blue neon tube
Ran all the way around the top of the walls.
The light made the smoke
Look as beautiful and benign
As we thought it was then.
On the night Earl Lincoln showed up to play,
He came in on two canes,
His whole torso twisting left and right
With each step.
When I asked for "But Not For Me,"
He gave me a pleased nod;
He wouldn't have to play "Moon River"
Until the guy with black stitches in his lip
Got drunk enough to ask for it.
After "I Can't Get Started,"
Earl asked, "What's next, Charlie?"
"'Two Septembers,'" I said.
"'Two Septembers?' What the hell is that?
I don't know no 'Two Septembers.'"
"'September Song' and 'September in the Rain.'"
He snapped a laugh and played and sang them both
With a gravelly, slow ease.
And so it went, song after song,
Even through "Moon River."
Whenever the brandy snifter
On the piano had enough tip money,

He'd order a double Early Times.
"Early Times, better times,"
He'd say before the first swallow,
Then, "Not true, but it sounds good."
By last call, his singing
Had turned to slush,
And I knew he wasn't going anywhere
On those hickory canes.
"I'll see you to your room, Earl."
I took one of the canes so he could hold my arm,
And we started off like a busted boat,
But he threw out the anchor after two steps.
"I ain't in the hotel.
Boss thought they wouldn't take kindly
To a black guest, and a drinker at that,
So he put me up in that room over the bar."
He hooked both canes over his right arm,
Hung his left around my neck,
And I hoisted him into my arms,
And up the stairs we went, dangerously,
Stopping three times to rest.
I set him down under an unshaded
Blue bulb in the hallway.
He turned the key slowly,
Like the tumblers were made of stone,
Then lurched into the room
And fell on his back on the bare mattress.
His eyes were closed,
But his voice was clear enough:
"You're a nice boy, Charlie,
But you don't know shit about shit…
You'll never know shit…"

Moment

The moments pass,
Moment by moment,
Like they're on a fast track to somewhere
Worse than Oblivion Depot,
But once in a while,
On a lucky day,
The bullet train stops
And lets you on board.
This day was solid overcast
Except for one thin band
On the eastern horizon,
Where it looked like the gallery
For Chinese landscapes was open for viewing.
The scroll was painted lengthwise,
A long stretch of snowfields
In the high Sierra pure white
In the new sun.
Most days the cloud cover
Will drop back down in minutes,
But we decided to drive east
Until the curtain fell.
One road led into another,
And still the scene held.
Finally we were in foothills
Smeared with mustard flower and fiddleneck,
On a paved road that turned to gravel
At the gate across someone's driveway.
I wonder what it feels like
To come home each evening
To the literal end of the road?
We turned around.
At the crest of the first hill,
A meadowlark perched on a strand of wire
No more than five feet from the car.
He had the yellowest breast
I'd seen on a lark, so I braked

And lowered the window for a clearer look.
He squirted out a quick
White poop as if in greeting,
And then began what may be
The loveliest bird song of all.
Another joined him and then another,
And Dianne rolled down her window,
And I killed the engine,
And suddenly the songs of a whole field
Of larks, fifty of them maybe,
Filled the car.
Fifty meadowlarks singing to each other,
Or maybe singing one to one,
In the early morning,
In the middle of our lives,
In the middle of the San Joaquin Valley.
There were only two houses nearby,
And for a moment I envied
The people who lived there,
In the middle of that sound each morning,
But then I thought maybe it was we
Who should be envied,
For whom the larks sang deeper,
And even, stretching all the way from there
To this very moment,
Sang longer.

Photo by Robert Turney

Bob Hicok, assistant professor of English at Virginia Tech University, is the author of *This Clumsy Living, Insomnia Diary, Animal Soul, Plus Shipping,* and *The Legend of Light.* He is the recipient of the Felix Pollak Prize, a National Endowment for the Arts Fellowship, and two Pushcart Prizes, and a finalist for the National Book Critics Circle Award. His poems have appeared in three volumes of *Best American Poetry.*

Twins

She has a dream and she has the same dream.

She says moon and she says moon and both put their she-phones
to their chests.

She says in my dream I slept between your mattress and box spring
and she nods and she hears her nod.

She says I was in the blue dress before you put it on
and after you put it on, like a soft paper flower she says
and she says yes, like a soft paper flower.

She nestles the phone in her crotch and she nestles the phone
in her crotch and the pubic hairs say it was warm in the dream.

She puts her face against the cool window and they play
where's my face and she guesses against the cool window.

She says I hung up the phone an hour ago and she says
I hung up the phone last year and still we go on talking
she says and she says we go on talking even while I am dead
and even while I am coming back to life.

She is two places at once and she is two places at once
which is four places at once.

She has to go back to sleep now and she has to go back to sleep now.

She says are you asleep now and she says yes and are you asleep now
and she says yes and they go on talking about being asleep now.

She has a dream and she has the same dream and in the dream
she is dreaming what she dreams and she is dreaming what she dreams.

Then it rains.

Team effort

Everyone at the same time if everyone at the same time
looked up from coffee looked up from crotch looked up
if everyone at night at dawn at lunch looked up
at the black at the blue morsel sky at the congress
of clouds of stars looked up from needle from packets
of buzzing from the wedding of dollars if everyone
in Queens in Wembley if everyone in my head if everyone
looked up from electroshock from drift if everyone
threw back the appetite of the eyes threw back the village
of the head the persistence of the skull if everyone thought
I am the vanishing point I am the frontal lobe of wind
if everyone stood and raised their wings and tuned
their orchestra if the census stood the tens of
stood the billions of stood the Earth would move
the circle would move the spinning would move if everyone
at the same time opened their mouth let the wolf
of their uvula go the rivers would stare at us
again would return to our faces the expressions
they carried away to the ocean to bury in the ocean
to save in case we ever came back.

My new neighbor

Looking at a cow one morning last month,
I wondered if the congregation of flies
on the eye of the cow
stared at the eye of the cow
with their compound eyes
and if I had ever seen this many eyes
in this small a space or had a thought
in which the word eye occurred so obsessively.
I wanted to touch the cow
and the cow seemed to ask to be touched,
but when I moved toward the fence,

the cow waddled away and the flies waddled with it.
The cow had a metal tag in its ear,
orange with the black numeral 42.
This will help them make hamburger of the cow,
which is the calling of cows in these parts,
help sellers and buyers and loaders of cows
note the selling and buying and loading of this cow.
I confessed to 42 that I eat cheeseburgers.
I had never addressed my food
before it had reached the plate and technically
not even then. What would I say to chicken teriyaki
by way of lessening the blow or making it feel welcome?
42 has large brown eyes and lives in a field
beside a small Presbyterian church.
I guess this makes 42 a God-fearing cow
and all cows have large brown eyes if 73 and 12
are a fair sampling. They pretty much do
what 42 does seven days a week, which is eat
and which suggests they are atheists after all.
Because of this philosophical bent,
I have taken to asking 42 if agnosticism
is the most reasonable position, my thought being
that the mind cannot dispense with the notion
of a first cause. When 42 blinks at my question,
the flies lift off and come back to what must be
their home planet. It is comforting to talk
to large animals, whether they listen or not.
I said, it is comforting to talk to large animals,
whether they listen or not.

Beasts

Everyone's ordering pan-seared this and foie gras that.
Most of the crowd's down from the symphony, Mahler I think,
four-tops mostly, waiters pushing smiles between tables
and laughter. The Woodward side of the restaurant's

all glass. It's snowing a bit, the flakes too small
for the innocence we ask of the season. Across the street,
the red brick Arts Council building has a steer
or lion in front of it, I can't tell in the dark
which animal is sculpted and out of what, papier-mâché
or stone. Just north of this unknown zoo, Hurley's Wigs
has no door, no windows, is a name in fading paint,
more things have closed than opened in forty years
in Michigan, you could get rich selling plywood, nails,
forgetting. I order a Glenlivet, crab cakes and shrimp,
I'm happy to add Scotland, the ocean to my body.
In an hour, five thousand dollars will be spent
in this restaurant. A woman at my table
leans toward a man in black with silver hair
at the end of the bar, she tells me he's a cellist,
his nose is in a glass of cabernet, I want to ask
if he dreams in music, if he'd die without his hands.
A woman walks by outside. Her coat is made for spring.
She looks in and sees me looking out. These are not eyes
we have but gates. She is old and I think of her
inside one of the Rodins I just visited
at the Detroit Institute of Arts. He was accused
of casting real people inside his sculptures
and I'm certain she was one of them, killed and kept alive
by beauty. I'm always knocking against myself
to get out. More of the day collapses into this moment
of waiting for bread. I'm back to this morning
with Carl on the sidewalk. The sky is gray and pregnant
with snow. He weaves his hands in and out
of each other & his coat pockets. In the three years
I've been away, he's obtained fear, it's below his eyes,
the skin sagging and brown, he has two smokes going,
a man of fire, one on the sidewalk, one burning to knuckles.
We're talking the best ways to kill ourselves.
I suggest chopping parts of my body away and feeding them
to an old-fashioned meat grinder, until I'm just a left hand
turning a handle. I'm not serious but Carl is

because he's about to drive four hundred miles
to work a week at seven dollars an hour packing crates
so he can drive home to that not being enough
and watch men who look like refrigerators wearing heads
haul parts of his life away. Carl's my age, we worked nights
in a foundry, orange flowing steel and orange tipped cigarettes,
whiskey on break under the so many stars, he'd been a fullback
at Stevenson, he could lift everything, I saw him do it,
the world on his back shift after shift, that was his genius,
to ignore gravity. I'm trying once more to explain tenure,
to convince him that the six weeks I have to myself
between semesters isn't a layoff. "I gotta get me some of that,"
he says again, lighting a smoke with a smoke.
I remind him I was once lowered into a sewer
on a rope to unstick a valve. I don't tell him
I traveled to the cave thought to have inspired Dante,
an unremarkable hole suggesting how plain misery can be.
I'm visiting Michigan after three years in western Virginia.
Having worked for twenty years in the automotive industry,
I now teach creative writing. I long ago gave up
trying to explain poetry to people like Carl,
and have recently given up trying to explain people like Carl
to professors. I can't explain to Carl
why I'll go to the museum for the Rodin and Claudel exhibit
when I could be watching football. I can't explain
to most professors why I understand Carl's reservations
when the Colts are on TV and undefeated.
This is just one of the impossibilities of being American.
There's so much black to explain to white to man to woman
to Christian to Jew and so little listening.
There's so much money going places only money knows.
There's so much tearing down to build to tear down to forget
there was anything to remember. I remember a man
lighting himself on fire in Woodhaven Stamping.
I remember the first time I met an art deco building.
I remember working twelve hours a day for a year.
I remember Phil Olson calling Hemut Thoma a rag head.
I remember thinking Nietzsche would have been a horrible

first baseman. I remember the sinews of MLK's dreaming voice.
I remember touching the moon through the Magnavox.
The bread still hasn't come and now I remember Carl
leaning back and putting his hand on WPA
chiseled into the sidewalk. He asks what that means
and I tell him and he says he likes the idea
of building a bridge or anything that lasts. A few hours later,
I'm looking at Rivera murals in the museum and noticing
the red star on the glove of a worker. The murals
were painted in the early thirties, before Americans
completely gave up on Communism. Rivera believed in equality,
equality of man and fucking whoever he wanted.
I believe in Carl five hours away on I-94, screaming along
to "Stairway to Heaven." The only place that Carl exists
with Rivera is in my head. Therefore I am a universe
full of underemployment and frescoes. A universe
featuring the forward pass and anaphora and museums,
which are fortresses of beauty. I wanted Rodin
to tell me something about the disappearance of health insurance.
I wanted Rivera to make people believe in sharing.
The woman has crossed the street and taken her eyes with her.
Not hearing her reminds me of how quiet looking is
in a museum. In each room, maybe ten people stared
at the sculptures, their expressions serious engines. I enjoyed
the studies more than the cast works: a clay face of torment
the size of a thumb, four plaster heads on which Rodin
worked out the sacrificial mouth of Paul Whissant.
My favorite was a plaster mask of Claudel, to which he attached
a left hand that flows out of the back of her skull
and curls around, the ring finger touching her forehead
just barely and wistful. It was worth the backache
of standing for hours on marble to walk away
with the flower of that image, to realize that language
is a torso trying to writhe free of my lips. Finally
the waitress, finally bread, four people chewing, bottomless.

Full flight

I'm in a plane that will not be flown into a building.
It's a SAAB 340, seats 40, has two engines with propellers
is why I think of beanies, those hats that would spin
a young head into the clouds. The plane is red and loud
inside like it must be loud in the heart, red like fire
and fire engines and the woman two seats up and to the right
resembles one of the widows I saw on TV after the Towers
came down. It's her hair that I recognize, the fecundity of it
and the color and its obedience to an ideal, the shape
it was asked several hours ago to hold and has held, a kind
of wave that begins at the forehead and repeats with slight
variations all the way to the tips, as if she were water
and a pebble had been continuously dropped into the mouth
of her existence. We are eighteen thousand feet over America.
People are typing at their laps, blowing across the fog of coffee,
sleeping with their heads on the windows, on the pattern
of green fields and brown fields, streams and gas stations
and swimming pools, blue dots of aquamarine that suggest
we've domesticated the mirage. We had to kill someone,
I believe, when the metal bones burned and the top
fell through the bottom and a cloud made of dust and memos
and skin muscled across Manhattan. I remember feeling
I could finally touch a rifle, that some murders
are an illumination of ethics, that they act as a word,
a motion the brain requires for which there is
no syllable, no breath. The moment the planes had stopped,
when we were afraid of the sky, there was a pause
when we could have been perfectly American,
could have spent infinity dollars and thrown a million
bodies at finding the few, lasering our revenge
into a kind of love, the blood-hunger kept exact
and more convincing for its precision, an expression
of our belief that proximity is never the measure of guilt.
We've lived in the sky again for some years and today
on my lap these pictures from Iraq, naked bodies
stacked into a pyramid of ha-ha and the articles

---

about broomsticks up the ass and the limbs of children
turned into stubble, we are punchdrunk and getting even
with the sand, with the map, with oil, with ourselves
I think listening to the guys behind me. There's a problem
in Alpena with an inventory control system, some switches
are being counted twice, switches for what I don't know—
switches of humor, of faith—but the men are musical
in their jargon, both likely born in New Delhi
and probably Americans now, which is what the flesh
of this country has been, a grafted pulse, an inventory
of the world, and just as the idea of embrace
moves chemically into my blood, and I'm warmed
as if I've just taken a drink, a voice announces
we've begun our descent, and then I sense the falling.

Gray Jacobik is a painter and poet who lives in Deep River, Connecticut. Her collections include *Brave Disguises,* winner of the Associated Writing Programs Poetry Prize; *The Surface of Last Scattering,* winner of the X. J. Kennedy Prize; and *The Double Task,* winner of the Juniper Prize. She is on the faculty of the Stonecoast MFA program.

Pollock's Paintings

This may be music
      moving through the night air
            looking for a Mozart,
or screaming for some as-yet   unrealized
         instrument to be invented.

Jealousy, perhaps, making its way
      toward the hand that will become
    a fist—
        or the drift
    of neurotransmitters
        moving across synapses
in search of
     the right molecules to bind with.

This could be a supernova remnant
      with its gaseous eruptions   spewing forth
particulate matter,
       pocked by antimatter,
    irradiated by gamma rays—

or anything, any force of the natural
      or preternatural world, micro- or macroscopic,
    perhaps wholly
        imagined
        and without analog,
             art creating itself.

Some say Pollock shows us chaos,
    its ubiquity,   its visual flippancies,
the liquid migrations
      of primordial stuff
as it spurts and curls and falls
      through currents
        too minute for us
      to measure—
or the pandemonium of an entropic mind.

Nothing demonic   or divine
          in this, this everywhere
                    and always that spells
          its way through us,   or we through it.

We take his gift of motion, memory, light
          that reaches out
                    through endless
          ropes   and strings   and loops,
probes of paint
          shot forth   or flung
                    in the dance
                              of human energy.

Perhaps this is Dickinson's divine insanity,
          the mental traveler's dream,
                    the journeys of a million lives
inscribed in a lexicon of line,   color,   texture,
          an infinite series of
                    relations graphically
                              displayed.

It is unfathomable, this wordlessness
          finding a technique,
or as Duras says—   *As distant from words*
          as the unknown object
                    of an objectless love—
possibilities visible in the abstract.

The Shabby Truth

The Chowder House on Fisherman's Wharf in Monterey:
across the table, my grown son. I have just told him about
the second time I was raped, at twenty-eight, how it ended
my working in a massage parlor because I couldn't overcome
my fear of men after that. He shows his pain in the scowl
that rips across his face and the downcast look he keeps
a long time. The two of us are stepping across a bridge

toward one another, an abyss under the bridge. He's coming
out of the kind of fog that hugs that peninsula most mornings.
I'm walking outside of pretense as if it's a city I've lived in
all my life and never left before. I needed a lot of cash fast,
I tell him, your father deserted us—you and me and your
sister. The engine had died in my VW bus. I was too
proud to ask for help. Another scowl crosses his face,
then he steadies his gaze, takes me in, leans back in the booth.
I say this because he's just told me how he finds clients
on the Internet, knows their fantasies in detail before he
meets them. He does exactly what they want and they are
the ones in control, he says, these women who send him
a credit card so he can rent a Trans Am at the airport,
reserve a suite, pay the tab at good restaurants. One's
a rock musician who flies in from New York; another's
a plastic surgeon's wife. I am swallowing nausea with
my lemon sole and baked potato, thinking, thinking,
you will not hear me pass judgement on you, I will not
tell you about how love is impossible when money is involved,
how your soul is in peril, as mine was. Souls can be lost forever,
even in the modern world where there is no real devil, it happens.
I will not let fear creep forward, or shame steal this moment.
I was as desperate as you feel, I say, and I believed good could
come of touching people in their deepest most sacred places
even if you don't go there with them. I'm meeting their
natural needs, he says. As in giving a blow job, I don't say,
going down on an iron-bodied businessman who's between
flights at National and catches a cab to the Phase III Health
Club in Alexandria with its black walls and black floors
and ceiling mirrors, with its front room full of sleazily-dressed
women, his mother one. So I know what you must be feeling,
I say, to see these people so starved for touch they fall apart
under your hands. Yes, he says, yes, they do, they fall apart
under your hands, that's right, and then he looks up at me
astonished, wondering, I imagine, is this my mother?
There's no love in their lives, he says, nobody touches them.
It's crazy. Yes I know, I say, and look deep into his green
eyes, my eyes. We sit silent awhile, bewildered in the presence
of our truth, the presence of our lies, the said and the unsaid.

Breasts

I've always enjoyed watching the jouncing breasts
of a woman walking, the easy rise and fall of flesh,
so motherly or erotic, anatomy most personal,
and yet, at times, given so freely to lover or infant,
or palpated by the inquiring hands of the physician,
flattened between the glass and steel of the x-ray,
fatty, duct-rich, nodular, capillarial, the biopsied
or augmented or reshaped, vulnerable to infection,
cyst, tumor; achingly tender at times and too
obvious or not noticeable enough, the coupled
(if she's wearing a bra) or uncoupled (if she's not)
harmonic oscillations, marked by size, firmness,
color of aureole, sign, signal, burden, shame,
always becoming old woman's dugs, striated,
bulbous, drooping downward with age, unlovely,
grotesque, nipples attenuated or inverted,
the body now barren—all this in that graceful
motion, a woman walking past, ageless, primordial,
a Lilith, Miriam, or Ruth, mother, sister, wife,
friend, an ordinary being, her breasts jouncing.

The Lizard Man

A man has tattooed every inch of his body
with half-circular scales colored a vivid green.
Soon, no doubt, copycats—we'll find ourselves
living among creature-people, menageries
of human snails and penguins, butterflies
and great crested auks, each of us branded
decoratively as our high-affinity species.
Rather like a children's picture book where
the animals huddle round second-guessing
one who's run afoul of a farmer's rake,
we'll gossip and speculate about miscreant
breeds. Exclusive tortoise-only country clubs,

gated communities for reptilians or persons
of the bovine persuasion, we'll be species
chauvinists—for, as Heraclitus wrote,
"The ape apes find most beautiful looks
apish to non-apes." I wonder what age
we'll declare to be the age of consent, or will
we call it consecration? *I dedicate myself to the
sloe-eyed anteater… the bloodhound… the ferret…*
Shops, boutiques, industries, devoted to our
favorite living thing, insider gestures, ocelot argot,
off-species jokes. And then there'll be the tragic
crossings when a squirrel decides he's truly a goat,
a cougar a peacock. Tattoo transplant protocols
will be developed, but cross-species dressing,
closeted or flamboyantly exhibited in clubs,
will go unchecked. Big fuss when a gang of scarlet
ibis crash an orgy for orangutans. They'll be purists
predictably crying *cultural abuse!* when a child's raised
in a mixed species home. Yet, like the Lizard Man,
we may enjoy showing off our mottles and feathers,
splotches and stripes, scales and dapplings, and,
with panache, flaunting our etched and tinted skins.

Julia Kasdorf has published two collections of poetry, *Eve's Striptease* and *Sleeping Preacher*, which won the Agnes Lynch Starrett Poetry Prize and the Great Lakes Award for New Writing. She is also the author of a collection of essays, *The Body and the Book: Writing from a Mennonite Life,* and a biography, *Fixing Tradition: Joseph W. Yoder, Amish American*. With Michael Tyrell she has edited the anthology *Broken Land: Poems of Brooklyn*. She teaches creative writing at The Pennsylvania State University, University Park campus, where she is associate professor of English and women's studies.

What I Learned from My Mother

I learned from my mother how to love
the living, to have plenty of vases on hand
in case you have to rush to the hospital
with peonies cut from the lawn, black ants
still stuck to the buds. I learned to save jars
large enough to hold fruit salad for a whole
grieving household, to cube home-canned pears
and peaches, to slice through maroon grape skins
and flick out the sexual seeds with a knife point.
I learned to attend viewings even if I didn't know
the deceased, to press the moist hands
of the living, to look in their eyes and offer
sympathy, as though I understood loss even then.
I learned that whatever we say means nothing,
what anyone will remember is that we came.
I learned to believe I had the power to ease
awful pains materially like an angel.
Like a doctor, I learned to create
from another's suffering my own usefulness, and once
you know how to do this, you can never refuse.
To every house you enter, you must offer
healing: a chocolate cake you baked yourself,
the blessing of your voice, your chaste touch.

Mennonites

We keep our quilts in closets and do not dance.
We hoe thistles along fence rows for fear
we may not be perfect as our Heavenly Father.
We clean up his disasters. No one has to
call; we just show up in the wake of tornadoes
with hammers, after floods with buckets.
Like Jesus, the servant, we wash each other's feet
twice a year and eat the Lord's Supper,
afraid of sins hidden so deep in our organs

they could damn us unawares,
swallowing this bread, his body, this juice.
Growing up, we love the engravings in *Martyrs Mirror:*
men drowned like cats in burlap sacks,
the Catholic inquisitors,
the woman who handed a pear to her son,
her tongue screwed to the roof of her mouth
to keep her from singing hymns while she burned.
We love Catherine the Great and the rich tracts
she gave us in the Ukraine, bright green winter wheat,
the Cossacks who torched it, and Stalin,
who starved our cousins while wheat rotted
in granaries. We must love our enemies.
We must forgive as our sins are forgiven,
our great-uncle tells us, showing the chain
and ball in a cage whittled from one block of wood
while he was in prison for refusing to shoulder
a gun. He shows the clipping from 1916:
Mennonites are German milksops, too yellow to fight.
We love those Nazi soldiers who, like Moses,
led the last cattle cars rocking out of the Ukraine,
crammed with our parents—children then—
learning the names of Kansas, Saskatchewan, Paraguay.
This is why we cannot leave the beliefs
or what else would we be? why we eat
'til we're drunk on shoofly and moon pies and borscht.
We do not drink; we sing. Unaccompanied on Sundays,
those hymns in four parts, our voices lift with such force
that we lift, as chaff lifts toward God.

When Our Women Go Crazy

When our women go crazy, they're scared there won't be
enough meat in the house. They keep asking
but how will we eat? Who will cook? Will there be enough?
Mother to daughter, it's always the same
questions. The sisters and aunts recognize symptoms:

she thinks there's no food, same as Mommy
before they sent her away to that place,
and she thinks if she goes, the men will eat
whatever they find right out of the saucepans.
When our women are sane, they can tomatoes
and simmer big pots of soup for the freezer.
They are satisfied arranging spice tins
on cupboard shelves lined with clean paper.
They save all the leftovers under tight lids
and only throw them away when they're rotten.
Their refrigerators are always immaculate and full,
which is also the case when our women are crazy.

First Gestures

Among the first we learn is good-bye,
your tiny wrist between Dad's forefinger
and thumb forced to wave bye-bye to Mom,
whose hand sails brightly behind a windshield.
Then it's done to make us follow:
in a crowded mall, a woman waves, "Bye,
we're leaving," and her son stands firm
sobbing, until at last he runs after her,
among shoppers drifting like sharks
who must drag their great hulks
underwater, even in sleep, or drown.

Living, we cover vast territories;
imagine your life drawn on a map—
a scribble on the town where you grew up,
each bus trip traced between school
and home, or a clean line across the sea
to a place you flew once. Think of the time
and things we accumulate, all the while growing
more conscious of losing and leaving. Aging,
our bodies collect wrinkles and scars
for each place the world would not give

under our weight. Our thoughts get laced
with strange aches, sweet as the final chord
that hangs in a guitar's blond torso.

Think how a particular ridge of hills
from a summer of your childhood grows
in significance, or one hour of light—
late afternoon, say, when thick sun flings
the shadow of Virginia creeper vines
across the wall of a tiny, white room
where a girl makes love for the first time.
Its leaves tremble like small hands
against the screen while she weeps
in the arms of her bewildered lover.
She's too young to see that as we gather
losses, we may also grow in love;
as in passion, the body shudders
and clutches what it must release.

Eve's Striptease

Lingerie shopping with Mom, I braced myself
for the wedding night advice. Would I seem
curious enough, sufficiently afraid? Yet
when we sat together on their bed, her words
were surprisingly wise:
> Whatever happens, remember this—
> it keeps getting better and better.
She had to be telling the truth. At ten,
I found a jar of Vaseline in her nightstand,
its creamy grease gouged deep, and dusting
their room each week, I marked the decline
of bedside candles. But she didn't say lust
is a bird of prey or tell me the passion
she passed on to me is no protector of borders.
She'd warned me only about the urges men get
and how to save myself from them. Though

she'd flirt with any greenhouse man
for the best cabbage flats, any grease monkey
under the hood, she never kissed anyone but Dad.
How could she guess that with *Jesus Loves Me*
on my tongue, constantly suffering crushes
on uncles, I would come to find that
almost everything gets better and better?
The tiny bird she set loving in me must
keep on, batting the bars of its cage
in a rage only matched by my cravings
for an ample pantry and golden anniversary.
She let me learn for myself all the desires
a body can hold, how they grow stronger
and wilder with age, tugging in every direction
until it feels my sternum might split
like Adam's when Eve stepped out,
sloughing off ribs.

The Sun Lover

The long afternoon after church
a girl lies on the lawn,
glazed thighs slightly parted,
fingers splayed like petals. At sixteen
she is a virgin. While her parents nap
in the quiet house, she knows
the sun is teaching her about love,
how it comes over your body
making every muscle go soft
in its pitiless gaze,

how it penetrates everything,
changing you into something dark
and radiant. She craves it,
knows it is everywhere like God's love,
but difficult to find. She waits,
entirely still, trying to see her eyelids—

not lingering traces, but the lids themselves
luminous and red as the cheeks of the kid
who stuck a flashlight in his mouth at camp.
She squints so the tips of her lashes
flash like iridescent fish scales.

Every hour, she turns over but prefers
to face the sun. All her life
she'll measure loves against this
gentle ravishing. She'll spend afternoons
alone on crowded beaches, and at home
stand naked before mirrors, amazed
by the pale shape of her suit. She'll touch
her cheekbones' tingling pink, and nip
at her lover's shoulder, as if
it were earth she were after.

Sinning

When I was seven, Mom asked if I knew
what rabbits in the hutch were up to.
"Fucking," farm cousins told me long before.
"We call it intercourse," she said
and began the cautionary tales right then—
hurry-up weddings generations back, and look
at the children now: moved away, sloppy,
overweight. Her own name, like the state's,
a reminder forever of a virgin queen,
and her mother's name—Vesta, a pagan
goddess, but her servants were virgins.
At thirteen, I took classes to learn how to ease
my behind into couches without looking down,
to cross legs at the ankles, not knees, and keep hands
cupped on my lap. In *Becoming a Woman*, I read
a fast girl is a blighted rose, no man
wants handled merchandise. I watched sad,
young couples lean together to mumble a confession

before God and a titillated congregation,
earning the kind of church wedding where
everyone turns to check if the bride is showing.
What other sin got such attention? No wonder
I grew weary of bearing that cargo
and finally chose a boy with a saint's name
who would moan from deep in his throat,
"Oh, my God," when I finally broke.

Jesse Lee Kercheval is the author of nine books, including the poetry collections *Dog Angel* and *World as Dictionary;* two story collections, *Alice in Dairyland,* which won the 2006 Prairie Schooner Book Prize, and *The Dogeater,* which won the Associated Writing Programs Award in Short Fiction; the novel *The Museum of Happiness;* and the memoir *Space.* She was the founding director of the University of Wisconsin MFA Program in Creative Writing. Currently, she is the Sally Mead Hands Bascom Professor of English at the University of Wisconsin where she directs the Wisconsin Institute for Creative Writing.

Enter Mecca

Not the center of the Islamic world,
but a sandwich shop across from the red brick towers
of a southern university. I was nineteen,
an English major, and every day we slouched
toward this Bethlehem of lunch counters,
ordered our BLTs or cheeseburgers
from the black short-order cook, paid the black cashier,
both dressed in white like house slaves
and not much better paid, though this was 1979
and civil rights marched here a decade earlier.

In the far booth sat Dr. Rubenstein,
famous for a book declaring God was dead.
Now, he taught courses on the Holocaust.
I looked at him and thought—How can a man
study Auschwitz and Buchenwald and Treblinka
every day with no God to pray to
and still eat tuna on whole wheat for lunch?
I had no answer.

I still don't. Though I have come far enough
from that humid southern believers' air
to doubt God's existence, it's beyond my powers
to imagine the holocaust that killed him.

When I was a minister's wife, briefly and too young
in rural Florida, someone shot a dog
and pushed it through the window
of a neighboring town's church.
There'd been a split in doctrine. Members marched
angrily down the aisle one Sunday and out
into the hot sun and their waiting cars.
The dog crawled the length of the church,
trailing his blood and feces down the aisle
to die alone, underneath the altar.
Who could do that to an animal,

I asked the God I prayed to then,
just to show how much they hated other humans?

Years after watching Dr. Rubenstein
eat his tuna sandwich, a friend called to say
she'd seen my book in the gift shop
at the Holocaust Museum. She heard my silence,
caught herself, *It's not a gift shop, really.*
More a bookstore. But, really, why should I be shocked
to hear the words "gift shop" and "Holocaust"
in the same sentence? In French, language
I was born to, *souvenir* means to remember.
And Dr. Rubenstein, wherever you are now,
I promise that I do.

My daughter, struggling through the dyslexia
of kindergarten, once wrote *doG loves U*
on an Easter card to her grandmother.
Maybe that's what happened.
They shot Him and pushed Him
through the open window of His own church.
God is dead, but he bled and bled
and did not go easily.

The next time, the angry congregants
were less subtle. They set their church
on fire and burned it to the ground.

God, that Dog Angel, looking down.

Not

—*for Wislawa Szymborska*

My sister does not write poems. She uses sign language to teach deaf children
in wheelchairs which color is dangerous red. If something unexpected hap-
pens—say, a child who has a seizure every day, doesn't—she does not rush
from the room to scribble this down. If she has something to say, she calls
me.

In this, she takes after our mother, who likewise did not write poems, not even when she was shot in WWII by a GI sailing home on her hospital ship. He shot the chaplain too—who may or may not have been my mother's lover. The chaplain died. My mother lived to have two daughters and show them the pink scar on her back where the bullet went in, the angry purple welt over her heart where it came spinning out. Not a word on paper about any of this—not about my sister's deaf but swiftly rolling children, or my mother's chaplain who played both pinochle and piano.

In this, they take after my mother's mother—who couldn't read or write and so certainly never wrote a poem—though, once, I am told, she castrated her husband's prize bull with a kitchen knife and calmly promised to do the same to him unless he spent his nights at home. My mother was there. She told me this story. My sister heard it too. But she never imagined it as a poem. But then, looking this over, it probably is not one.

Instead it is like the one family story that does involve the written word: how my mother once flew from Florida to visit me in Wisconsin with a styrofoam cooler of shrimp—marked clearly SHRIMP. On the way home, she wrote NOT in front of SHRIMP and packed her shoes in the cooler. At the airport, the ticket agent, puzzled, asked "What's in the cooler?"

"Not shrimp," my mother said. And let it go at that.

So—think of this as a Not Poem. Think of me as one more Not Poet in a long honorable line of Not Poets.

And let it go at that.

What Max, Age Two, Remembers about Spain

The Cave. Also, Big Churches. But mostly

The Cave.

The boy also named Max, also waiting

to see the cave.

The other Max's father joking (in German) that maybe
there were cave pigs.

There were no pigs. There was a bat.

(In 1905, a farmer looking for guano for fertilizer discovered the cave
and so found something richer than bat dung—tourists)

The old man who owns the cave, who unlocked the iron door, who let
the Maxes in, who lit the lantern so we could see, who locked the door
behind us.

The drawings on the walls—deer, mountains, a (pregnant) horse,
more deer.

Black and red and yellow.

(Also calendars, black hash marks on the wall like those made by prisoners
counting down their days)

In the deepest cave, a big sea fish (though the Mediterranean is fifty
kilometers away across the jagged peaks of the Serrania de Ronda)
and inside the big fish, a small fish, then a smaller fish,

then the smallest fish of all.

That's me, says Max, pointing to the smallest one.

(Max a fish inside his father's arms, inside a cave, inside a mountain
in the south of Spain, on the earth, in our solar system, in a galaxy
some astronomer with a sense of humor or of metaphor named
the Milky Way.

That day in Spain—a hash mark on a dark cave wall, a sooty moment
on the calendar where we stand bathed in lantern light in that infinite
balloon of time we insist on calling now.)

In the cave, Max says, *even day is night.*

The Great Molasses Flood

1919—a four-million-gallon tank burst open
and scalding sugar poured down the street,
smashing houses, twisting El tracks,
carrying people and horses down to the harbor
where dirty water, as well as molasses, filled
their open mouths. One man had his sister, nine,
swept from his arms, was only saved himself
because he wrapped his arms around the Virgin Mary
and refused to let her go.

I read this story in the newspaper
on the 70th Anniversary of the Disaster,
then clipped the article and put it somewhere
I thought I could always find it. Now
I want to know—where, exactly, was the flood?
And where's that clipping?

My daughter, Magdalena, is nine, the age
of the sister lost forever to molasses.
When Magdalena is sad, she cries and says
she misses Daddy Lance, her great-grandfather
who died, age one hundred, when she was only four.
She met him once—a nearly blind old man who shouted,
Girl, come closer. She wouldn't let him near her,
wouldn't let him touch her with his ropey,
shaking hands. So how to explain her grief?
I imagine her taking inventory—mother, father, brother.
Who is missing? *Daddy Lance.* What is missing?
The love only he could give. What is she really missing?
Infanthood with its wet bond of nursing,
the squeeze box of my womb—*God?*

I know this sounds crazy—but sometimes I swear
I can feel God inside me. I just have to think about it,
feel around inside my body as if my soul
were a tongue searching in my mouth,
and there, there—the rough filling in that back molar.

There He is. A foreign presence
grown too familiar to notice every day.

My mother used to say I was slower than molasses
moving uphill in January, so though I know
the molasses pouring from that tank sped
through the town like an express train
bearing down on a drunk—when I imagine it,
the molasses is moving very very slowly.

Still, even after eighty years, the people, the houses
cannot escape their hot, confectionery fate.
Imagine a brown slow wall coming to get you,
to drown you in sweetness.
Imagine one moving slowly toward us all.

When my daughter was little she used to say
we should save the clothes she'd outgrown,
so I could wear them when I was a baby again.
Or she was a baby again. Time flowing
backward, forward, tide pond clock life.
Daddy Lance a baby again, imagine.
The molasses flowing toward us,
then just when the smell is too sweet to bear—
moving backward. Pouring up into the air,
back into the wooden tank that held it,
the boards flying into place, the town below it
golden in a marzipan of calm. Always *both* moments—
the drowning, the not drowning.
Daddy Lance, bald baby, balder old blind man.

Do I believe it? I don't know.
I'm the one whose tongue finds God
inside my dental work, who has a daughter who,
when she learned that everyone who lives must die,
said—*Oh well, I didn't want to be born either
and that turned out okay.*

Imagine the sweet smell of molasses.

Photo by McGuire Studio

Etheridge Knight, widely regarded as one of America's most prominent and liveliest poets, was born in Corinth, Mississippi, in 1931. His books include *The Essential Etheridge Knight; For Black Poets Who Think of Suicide; A Poem for Brother Man; The Idea of Ancestry;* and *Poems from Prison.* Knight received honors from such institutions as the Guggenheim Foundation, the National Endowment for the Arts, and the Poetry Society of America. In 1990 he earned a bachelor's degree in American poetry and criminal justice from Martin Center University in Indianapolis. Etheridge Knight died in 1991.

Hard Rock Returns to Prison from
the Hospital for the Criminal Insane

Hard Rock / was / "known not to take no shit
From nobody," and he had the scars to prove it:
Split purple lips, lumbed ears, welts above
His yellow eyes, and one long scar that cut
Across his temple and plowed through a thick
Canopy of kinky hair.

The WORD / was / that Hard Rock wasn't a mean nigger
Anymore, that the doctors had bored a hole in his head,
Cut out part of his brain, and shot electricity
Through the rest. When they brought Hard Rock back,
Handcuffed and chained, he was turned loose,
Like a freshly gelded stallion, to try his new status.
And we all waited and watched, like a herd of sheep,
To see if the WORD was true.

As we waited we wrapped ourselves in the cloak
Of his exploits: "Man, the last time, it took eight
screws to put him in the Hole." "Yeah, remember when he
Smacked the captain with his dinner tray?" "He set
The record for time in the Hole—67 straight days!"
"Ol Hard Rock! man, that's one crazy nigger."
And then the jewel of a myth that Hard Rock had once bit
A screw on the thumb and poisoned him with syphilitic spit.

The testing came, to see if Hard Rock was really tame.
A hillbilly called him a black son of a bitch
And didn't lose his teeth, a screw who knew Hard Rock
From before shook him down and barked in his face.
And Hard Rock did *nothing.* Just grinned and looked silly,
His eyes empty like knotholes in a fence.

And even after we discovered that it took Hard Rock
Exactly 3 minutes to tell you his first name,
We told ourselves that he had just wised up,
Was being cool; but we could not fool ourselves for long,

And we turned away, our eyes on the ground. Crushed.
He had been our Destroyer, the doer of things

We dreamed of doing but could not bring ourselves to do,
The fears of years, like a biting whip,
Had cut deep bloody grooves
Across our backs.

He Sees Through Stone

He sees through stone
he has the secret eyes
this old black one
who under prison skies
sits pressed by the sun
against the western wall
his pipe between purple gums

the years fall
like overripe plums
bursting red flesh
on the dark earth

his time is not my time
but I have known him
in a time gone

he led me trembling cold
into the dark forest
taught me the secret rites
to make it with a woman
to be true to my brothers
to make my spear drink
the blood of my enemies

now black cats circle him
flash white teeth
snarl at the air

mashing green grass beneath
shining muscles

ears peeling his words
he smiles
he knows
the hunt   the enemy
he has the secret eyes
he sees through stone

The Idea of Ancestry

1

Taped to the wall of my cell are 47 pictures: 47 black
faces: my father, mother, grandmothers (1 dead), grand-
fathers (both dead), brothers, sisters, uncles, aunts,
cousins (1st & 2nd), nieces, and nephews. They stare
across the space at me sprawling on my bunk. I know
their dark eyes, they know mine. I know their style,
they know mine. I am all of them, they are all of me;
they are farmers, I am a thief, I am me, they are thee.

I have at one time or another been in love with my mother,
1 grandmother, 2 sisters, 2 aunts (1 went to the asylum),
and 5 cousins. I am now in love with a 7-yr-old niece
(she sends me letters written in large block print, and
her picture is the only one that smiles at me).

I have the same name as 1 grandfather, 3 cousins, 3 nephews,
and 1 uncle. The uncle disappeared when he was 15, just took
off and caught a freight (they say). He's discussed each year
when the family has a reunion, he causes uneasiness in
the clan, he is an empty space. My father's mother, who is 93
and who keeps the Family Bible with everybody's birth dates
(and death dates) in it, always mentions him. There is no
place in her Bible for "whereabouts unknown."

2

Each fall the graves of my grandfathers call me, the brown
hills and red gullies of mississippi send out their electric
messages, galvanizing my genes. Last yr / like a salmon quitting
the cold ocean-leaping and bucking up his birthstream / I
hitchhiked my way from LA with 16 caps in my pocket and a
monkey on my back. And I almost kicked it with the kinfolks.
I walked barefooted in my grandmother's backyard / I smelled
    the old
land and the woods / I sipped cornwhiskey from fruit jars with
    the men /
I flirted with the women / I had a ball till the caps ran out
and my habit came down. That night I looked at my grandmother
and split / my guts were screaming for junk / but I was almost
contented / I had almost caught up with me.
(The next day in Memphis I cracked a croaker's crib for a fix.)

This yr there is a gray stone wall damming my stream, and when
the falling leaves stir my genes, I pace my cell or flop on my bunk
and stare at 47 black faces across the space. I am all of them,
they are all of me, I am me, they are thee, and I have no children
to float in the space between.

The Warden Said to Me the Other Day

The warden said to me the other day
(innocently, I think), "Say, etheridge,
why come the black boys don't run off
like the white boys do?"
I lowered my jaw and scratched my head
and said (innocently, I think), "Well, suh,
I ain't for sure, but I reckon it's 'cause
we ain't got nowheres to run to."

Feeling Fucked Up

Lord she's gone done left me done packed / up and split
and I with no way to make her
come back and everywhere the world is bare
bright bone white   crystal sand glistens
dope death dead dying and jiving drove
her away made her take her laughter and her smiles
and her softness and her midnight sighs—

Fuck Coltrane and music and clouds drifting in the sky
fuck the sea and trees and the sky and birds
and alligators and all the animals that roam the earth
fuck marx and mao fuck fidel and nkrumah and
democracy and communism fuck smack and pot
and red ripe tomatoes fuck joseph fuck mary fuck
god jesus and all the disciples fuck fanon nixon
and malcolm fuck the revolution fuck freedom fuck
the whole muthafucking thing
all i want now is my woman back
so my soul can sing

Welcome Back, Mr. Knight: Love of My Life

Welcome back, Mr. K: Love of My Life—
How's your drinking problem?—your thinking
Problem? you / are / pickling
Your liver—
Gotta / watch / out for the
"Ol Liver": Love of My Life.
How's your dope
Problem?—your marijuana, methadone, and cocaine
Problem / too?—your lustful problem—
How's your weight problem—your eating problem?
How's your lying and cheating and
Staying out all / night long problem?
Welcome back, Mr. K: Love of My Life

How's your pocket / book problem?—your / being
broke problem? you still owe and borrowing mo'
25 dollar problems from other / po / poets?
Welcome back, Mr. K: Love of My Life.
How's your ex-convict problem?—your John Birch
Problem?—your preacher problem?—your fat
Priests sitting in your / chair, saying
How racist and sexist they / will / forever / be
Problem?—How's your Daniel Moynihan
Problem?—your crime in the streets, runaway
Daddy, Black men with dark shades
And bulging crotches problem?
How's your nixon-agnew—j. edgar hoover
Problem?—you still paranoid? still schizoid?—
Still scared shitless?
How's your bullet-thru-the-brain problem?—or
A needle-in-your-arm problem?
Welcome back, Mr. K:—Love of My Life.
You gotta watch / out for the "Ol Liver."
How's your pussy
Problem?—lady-on-top—
smiling like God, titty-in-your-mouth
Problem? Welcome back, Mr. K:
Love of My Life. How's your peace
Problem?—your no / mo' war
Problem—your heart problem—your belly / problem?—
You gotta watch / out for the "Ol Liver."

Dark Prophecy: I Sing of Shine

And, yeah, brothers
while white / america sings about the unsink-
able molly brown
(who was hustling the titanic
when it went down)
I sing to thee of Shine

the stoker who was hip enough to flee the fucking ship
and let the white folks drown
with screams on their lips
(jumped his black ass into the dark sea, Shine did,
broke free from the straining steel).
Yeah, I sing to thee of Shine
and how the millionaire banker stood on the deck
and pulled from his pockets a million dollar check
saying Shine Shine save poor me
and I'll give you all the money a black boy needs—
how Shine looked at the money and then at the sea
and said jump in mothafucka and swim like me—
And Shine swam on—Shine swam on—
and how the banker's daughter ran naked on the deck
with her pink tits trembling and her pants roun her neck
screaming Shine Shine save poor me
and I'll give you all the pussy a black boy needs—
how Shine said now pussy is good and that's no jive
but you got to swim not fuck to stay alive—
And Shine swam on Shine swam on—

How Shine swam past a preacher afloating on a board
crying save *me* nigger Shine in the name of the Lord—
and how the preacher grabbed Shine's arm and broke his stroke—
how Shine pulled his shank and cut the preacher's throat—
And Shine swam on—Shine swam on—
And when the news hit shore that the titanic had sunk
Shine was up in Harlem damn near drunk

Rehabilitation & Treatment in the Prisons of America

The Convict strolled into the prison administration building to get
assistance and counseling for his personal problems. Inside the main door
were several other doors proclaiming: Doctor, Lawyer, Teacher, Counselor,
Therapist, etc. He chose the proper door, and was confronted with two
more doors: Custody and Treatment. He chose Treatment, went in, and was
confronted with two more doors: First Offender and Previous Offender.

Again he chose the proper door and was confronted with two *more* doors: Adult and Juvenile. He was an adult, so he walked through that door and ran smack into two *more* doors: Democrat and Republican. He was democrat, so he rushed through that door and ran smack into two *more* doors: Black and White. He was Black, so he rushed—*ran*—through that door—and fell nine stories to the street.

Sandra Kohler is the author of *The Ceremonies of Longing*, winner of the Associated Writing Programs Poetry Prize, and *The Country of Women*. She has taught extensively at levels from elementary to university. The recipient of numerous awards, she lives with her husband in Selinsgrove, in central Pennsylvania.

The Game

March enters, tossing and drenching winter's dry sticks.
The news of a marriage, of the war ending, seem stories
made up to go with the weather. Because it is March, because
it is morning, in the thawed mud, in culverts under strata
of oak leaves laid down by autumn storms, something is
stirring: the hot green blades of crocuses. Unexpected emergence,
like the cellar door opening and a man dragging his bike out
into the dim sunlight, the mild air. Every day the possibility
opens of some new loss. The two squirrels chasing each other
up and down the bare oak play their game as if it were life
and death and game at the same time, as it is when I play,
tossing away a prize that means nothing and everything.
Like a child learning to skate, I fall over and over into
the same delusion and as I fall, see, no, not again. Now
is when I want to live forever: this morning, this moment.

The Pond

Why does a man decide to build a pond
on the land of a house he's planning
to sell, a Vermont schoolhouse? Too ashamed
of this decision to tell his wife of forty years,
he calls the contractor, hires him,
commits himself, his shame equaled
by his insistent will: this pond must be.

He should dig the pond himself: fire
the contractor, send away the bulldozer,
the backhoe, begin to spade the thin hard
dirt of Vermont farmland covering the ribs
of stone underneath the way skin covers
an old stringy horse. The pond will come
from the belly of the farm, the loose bowl
of its pelvis. Earth under the hard dry soil
will turn muddy, dense, not friable, still

hostile to the spade, studded with rocks.
It will take days to get down to water.

This man needs to take days. He needs
to sweat in the hot thin October sunlight,
the days that start in cold fog, burning off
slowly, then getting hotter and hotter;
his body, cold in the morning, moving slowly,
by noon hitting a rhythm he puts aside,
sitting down, his back against a tree, to eat
bread, to drink. Then in the short afternoon,
four hot hours, sweating and bending,
his body finding something he thought
it had lost. He must sweat it out
of himself, create the pond, digging it
out of the earth, out of his body.

The End of the Gulf War

The aunts can't believe the war is over. My husband's
aunts, eighty-eight and seventy-seven, each living in her
widowed house within miles of the farm they were born on:
survivors of a harsh childhood among siblings who didn't all
live to adulthood; marriages that spanned a depression, wars;
each the loss, within months, ten years ago, of her husband.
Now the aunts let us take them out to dinner. Aunt Frances
slips into our Honda's backseat like a girl, Aunt Murline needs
help getting her bad leg over what she calls a running board—
like a horse too old to lift its leg to be shoed, she says. We drive
to the cheap restaurant with its more or less honest Dutch food
where they eat a little, always have dessert, talk a little, and steal
the check. Aunt Murline wonders if she'll die waiting for the Moravian
Home to find room for her; she can't bear another summer in
her Main Street house, already sold to the bank next door.
They'll tear it down for a parking lot a month after she's out.
We talk about her plans to "make sale" up at the auction house;
we talk about the war. The aunts can't believe the war is over,

it's always been unreal to them, violating their sense of what
the world is like: we act and act, untouched by consequence,
proud of doing well what we should not do at all.

Tea

The sky steeping, dark brew,
the morning star brilliant and alone.
A sense of disorder. The tea turns
green at the horizon, overhead orange,
mauve. Nights what keeps me awake
is a refusal to give in, allow the day
to end. I dream I'm in New Zealand—
purple skies, thunderous ocean.
Standing on line to see "Waiting for
Godot" I find it's become Japan.
I squat at the front of the tiny theatre
with a man I've met in the queue, tell
him I'm happily married but lonely—
my husband's away for a month.
He thinks I'm neglected and I explain
we each do the things we want not to die
without having done. On stage there is
another sky: turbulent sea of cloud,
seams and layers, troughs. Coffee arrives,
time is short. I can't keep awake. I listen,
I speak; it's only a question of language.
I want to be snow bound and cloud free
at once: wind driven, deep rooted.
On the garage roof there's a patch of
snow like the one white blotch on
a black cow's flank, circle, symbol.
The woods are a dark husband,
the meadow the white ghost of
a bride spectral and waiting.

Write

I can never write on the days I have to walk across
the square to buy cigarettes.
—SOMERSET MAUGHAM

Thank you, Ina, for sending me this fine excuse for

the inexhaustible possibilities of laziness,
the unwillingness of body and spirit to write.
The desire for dense bread, the desire for
sleep, the desire for work to be easy—no, hard,
but clear, glassy, transparent, all-revealing.

The work is a series of counterpanes, blankets
you lift, as if looking for the princess's pea. One
day, it's a pair of shoes I've lost: green suede, but
when I find them, they're gold; transformed like
the orts I make poems: pleasure, life and death.

If the shoe fits, I'll get under the covers and
wait to be transformed, hag into queen. I'm wearing
white taffeta, a dress so ugly I put on a teeshirt
to cover it. I will buy black clothes, I will teach
astronomy, I will stop accounting for myself.

Angering my mother, I make rag dolls out of
the family's secret bones. I am hauling myself from
one floor to another of a huge warehouse full of
shorted-out machinery, in a cage I operate by pulley,
bearing my own weight, the weight of the cage.

It's hard to do it all in one trip. There is only
one trip to do it in. We wear the chains we forge
in life, Miss Beryl reminds us. Encaged, jewels
in a setting. Onyx, amethyst, chalcedony,
Can a jewel make its cage golden?

I am writing for time, clarity, the lucidity of parsed
moments. I am writing to leave a small fossil that
says I lived pressed into the medium that killed me.

Photo by Kathleen Rutledge

Ted Kooser, U.S. Poet Laureate from 2004 to 2006, was born in Ames, Iowa, in 1939. He was educated in the Ames public schools, at Iowa State University, and the University of Nebraska. His collections of poetry include *Flying at Night, Poems 1965–1985; Delights & Shadows; Winter Morning Walks: One Hundred Postcards to Jim Harrison; Weather Central; One World at a Time;* and *Sure Signs.* He is also the author of *Braided Creek: A Conversation in Poetry,* with Jim Harrison, and *Local Wonders: Seasons in the Bohemian Alps.* Kooser's honors include two fellowships from the National Endowment for the Arts, a Pushcart Prize, and the 2005 Pulitzer Prize for Poetry. A visiting professor in the English department of the University of Nebraska–Lincoln, he lives on an acreage near the village of Garland, Nebraska, with his wife Kathleen Rutledge, the editor of the *Lincoln Journal Star.*

Selecting a Reader

First, I would have her be beautiful,
and walking carefully up on my poetry
at the loneliest moment of an afternoon,
her hair still damp at the neck
from washing it. She should be wearing
a raincoat, an old one, dirty
from not having money enough for the cleaners.
She will take out her glasses, and there
in the bookstore, she will thumb
over my poems, then put the book back
up on its shelf. She will say to herself,
"For that kind of money, I can get
my raincoat cleaned." And she will.

A Frozen Stream

This snake has gone on,
all muscle and glitter,
into the woods,
a few leaves clinging,
red, yellow, and brown.
Oh, how he sparkled!
The roots of the old trees
gleamed as he passed.

Now there is nothing
to see; an old skin
caught in the bushes,
bleached and flaking,
a few sharp stones
already poking through.

The Very Old

The very old are forever
hurting themselves,

burning their fingers
on skillets, falling

loosely as trees
and breaking their hips

with muffled explosions of bone.
Down the block

they are wheeled in
out of our sight

for years at a time.
To make conversation,

the neighbors ask
if they are still alive.

Then, early one morning,
through our kitchen windows

we see them again,
first one and then another,

out in their gardens
on crutches and canes,

perennial,
checking their gauges for rain.

How to Make Rhubarb Wine

Go to the patch some afternoon
in early summer, fuzzy with beer
and sunlight, and pick a sack
of rhubarb (red or green will do)
and God knows watch for rattlesnakes
or better, listen; they make a sound
like an old lawnmower rolled downhill.
Wear a hat. A straw hat's best
for the heat but lets the gnats in.
Bunch up the stalks and chop the leaves off
with a buck knife and be careful.
You need ten pounds; a grocery bag
packed full will do it. Then go home
and sit barefooted in the shade
behind the house with a can of beer.
Spread out the rhubarb in the grass
and wash it with cold water
from the garden hose, washing
your feet as well. Then take a nap.
That evening, dice the rhubarb up
and put it in a crock. Then pour
eight quarts of boiling water in,
cover it up with a checkered cloth
to keep the fruit flies out of it,
and let it stand five days or so.
Take time each day to think of it.

Ferment ten days, under the cloth,
sniffing of it from time to time,
then siphon it off, swallowing some,
and bottle it. Sit back and watch
the liquid clear to honey yellow,
bottled and ready for the years,
and smile. You've done it awfully well.

A Widow

She's combed his neckties out of her hair
and torn out the tongues of his shoes.
She's poured his ashes out of their urn
and into his humidor. For the very last time,
she's scrubbed the floor around the toilet.
She hates him even more for dying.

Fort Robinson

When I visited Fort Robinson,
where Dull Knife and his Northern Cheyenne
were held captive that terrible winter,
the grounds crew was killing the magpies.

Two men were going from tree to tree
with sticks and ladders, poking the young birds
down from their nests and beating them to death
as they hopped about in the grass.

Under each tree where the men had worked
were twisted clots of matted feathers,
and above each tree a magpie circled,
crazily calling in all her voices.

We didn't get out of the car.
My little boy hid in the back and cried
as we drove away, into those ragged buttes
the Cheyenne climbed that winter, fleeing.

Shooting a Farmhouse

The first few wounds are nearly invisible;
a truck rumbles past in the dust
and a .22 hole appears in the mailbox

like a fly landing there.
In a month you can see sky
through the tail of the windmill.
The attic windows grow black and uneasy.
When the last hen is found shot in the yard,
the old man and his wife move away.

In November, a Land Rover
flattens the gate like a tank
and pulls up in the yard. Hunters spill out
and throw down their pheasants like hats.
They blow out the rest of the windows,
set beer cans up on the porch rails
and shoot from the hip.
One of them walks up and yells in,
"Is anyone home?" getting a laugh.

By sunset, they've kicked down the door.
In the soft blush of light,
they blast holes in the plaster
and piss on the floors.

When the beer and the shells are all gone,
they drive sadly away,
the blare of their radio fading.
A breeze sighs in the shelterbelt.
Back in the house,
the newspapers left over from packing
the old woman's dishes
begin to blow back and forth through the rooms.

Flying at Night

Above us, stars. Beneath us, constellations.
Five billion miles away, a galaxy dies
like a snowflake falling on water. Below us,
some farmer, feeling the chill of that distant death,
snaps on his yard light, drawing his sheds and barn

back into the little system of his care.
All night, the cities, like shimmering novas,
tug with bright streets at lonely lights like his.

Laundry

A pink house trailer,
scuffed and rusted, sunken
in weeds. On the line,

five pale blue workshirts
up to their elbows
in raspberry canes—

a good, clean crew
of pickers, out early,
sleeves wet with dew,

and near them, a pair
of bright yellow panties
urging them on.

At the Office Early

Rain has beaded the panes
of my office windows,
and in each little lens
the bank at the corner
hangs upside down.
What wonderful music
this rain must have made
in the night, a thousand banks
turned over, the change
crashing out of the drawers
and bouncing upstairs
to the roof, the soft

percussion of ferns
dropping out of their pots,
the ball-point pens
popping out of their sockets
in a fluffy snow
of deposit slips.
Now all day long,
as the sun dries the glass,
I'll hear the soft piano
of banks righting themselves,
the underpaid tellers
counting their nickels and dimes.

Year's End

Now the seasons are closing their files
on each of us, the heavy drawers
full of certificates rolling back
into the tree trunks, a few old papers
flocking away. Someone we loved
has fallen from our thoughts,
making a little, glittering splash
like a bicycle pushed by a breeze.
Otherwise, not much has happened;
we fell in love again, finding
that one red feather on the wind.

Larry Levis was born in Fresno, California, in 1946. His books of poems include *Wrecking Crew,* which won the United States Award from the International Poetry Forum; *The Afterlife,* which won the Lamont Award from the American Academy of Poets; *The Dollmaker's Ghost,* winner of the Open Competition of the National Poetry Series; *Winter Stars;* and *The Widening of the Leaves.* The collection *Elegy* and *The Selected Levis* were published posthumously. Among his awards were three fellowships from the National Endowment for the Arts, a Fulbright Fellowship, and a Guggenheim Fellowship. Levis taught English at the University of Missouri from 1974 to 1980, was an associate professor and directed the creative writing program at the University of Utah from 1980 to 1992, and from 1992 until his death was a professor of English at Virginia Commonwealth University. Larry Levis died in 1996.

Winter Stars

My father once broke a man's hand
Over the exhaust pipe of a John Deere tractor. The man,
Rubén Vásquez, wanted to kill his own father
With a sharpened fruit knife, & he held
The curved tip of it, lightly, between his first
Two fingers, so it could slash
Horizontally, & with surprising grace,
Across a throat. It was like a glinting beak in a hand,
And, for a moment, the light held still
On those vines. When it was over,
My father simply went in & ate lunch, & then, as always,
Lay alone in the dark, listening to music.
He never mentioned it.

I never understood how anyone could risk his life,
Then listen to Vivaldi.

Sometimes, I go out into this yard at night,
And stare through the wet branches of an oak
In winter, & realize I am looking at the stars
Again. A thin haze of them, shining
And persisting.

It used to make me feel lighter, looking up at them.
In California, that light was closer.
In a California no one will ever see again,
My father is beginning to die. Something
Inside him is slowly taking back
Every word it ever gave him.
Now, if we try to talk, I watch my father
Search for a lost syllable as if it might
Solve everything, & though he can't remember, now,
The word for it, he is ashamed....
If you can think of the mind as a place continually
Visited, a whole city placed behind
The eyes, & shining, I can imagine, now, its end—
As when the lights go off, one by one,
In a hotel at night, until at last

All of the travelers will be asleep, or until
Even the thin glow from the lobby is a kind
Of sleep; & while the woman behind the desk
Is applying more lacquer to her nails,
You can almost believe that the elevator,
As it ascends, must open upon starlight.

I stand out on the street, & do not go in.
That was our agreement, at my birth.

And for years I believed
That what went unsaid between us became empty,
And pure, like starlight, & that it persisted.

I got it all wrong.
I wound up believing in words the way a scientist
Believes in carbon, after death.

Tonight, I'm talking to you, father, although
It is quiet here in the Midwest, where a small wind,
The size of a wrist, wakes the cold again—
Which may be all that's left of you & me.

When I left home at seventeen, I left for good.

The pale haze of stars goes on & on,
Like laughter that has found a final, silent shape
On a black sky. It means everything
It cannot say. Look, it's empty out there, & cold.
Cold enough to reconcile
Even a father, even a son.

My Story in a Late Style of Fire

Whenever I listen to Billie Holiday, I am reminded
That I, too, was once banished from New York City.
Not because of drugs or because I was interesting enough
For any wan, overworked patrolman to worry about—
His expression usually a great, gauzy spiderweb of bewilderment

Over his face—I was banished from New York City by a woman.
Sometimes, after we had stopped laughing, I would look
At her & see a cold note of sorrow or puzzlement go
Over her face as if someone else were there, behind it,
Not laughing at all. We were, I think, "in love." No, I'm sure.
If my house burned down tomorrow morning, & if I & my wife
And son stood looking on at the flames, & if, then,
Someone stepped out of the crowd of bystanders
And said to me: "Didn't you once know…?" *No.* But if
One of the flames, rising up in the scherzo of fire, turned
All the windows blank with light, & if that flame could speak,
And if it said to me: "You loved her, didn't you?" I'd answer,
Hands in my pockets, "Yes." And then I'd let fire & misfortune
Overwhelm my life. Sometimes, remembering those days,
I watch a warm, dry wind bothering a whole line of elms
And maples along a street in this neighborhood until
They're all moving at once, until I feel just like them,
Trembling & in unison. None of this matters now,
But I never felt alone all that year, & if I had sorrows,
I also had laughter, the affliction of angels & children.
Which can set a whole house on fire if you'd let it. And even then
You might still laugh to see all of your belongings set you free
In one long choiring of flames that sang only to you—
Either because no one else could hear them, or because
No one else wanted to. And, mostly, because they know.
They know such music cannot last, & that it would
Tear them apart if they listened. In those days,
I was, in fact, already married, just as I am now,
Although to another woman. And that day I could have stayed
In New York. I had friends there. I could have strayed
Up Lexington Avenue, or down to Third, & caught a faint
Glistening of the sea between the buildings. But all I wanted
Was to hold her all morning, until her body was, again,
A bright field, or until we both reached some thicket
As if at the end of a lane, or at the end of all desire,
And where we could, therefore, be alone again, & make
Some dignity out of loneliness. As, mostly, people cannot do.
Billie Holiday, whose life was shorter & more humiliating
Than my own, would have understood all this, if only

Because even in her late addiction & her bloodstream's
Hallelujahs, she, too, sang often of some affair, or someone
Gone, & therefore permanent. And sometimes she sang for
Nothing, even then, & it isn't anyone's business, if she did.
That morning, when *she* asked me to leave, wearing only
The apricot tinted, fraying chemise, I wanted to stay.
But I also wanted to go, to lose her suddenly, almost
For no reason, & certainly without any explanation.
I remember looking down at a pair of singular tracks
Made in a light snow the night before, at how they were
Gradually effacing themselves beneath the tires
Of the morning traffic, & thinking that my only other choice
Was fire, ashes, abandonment, solitude. All of which happened
Anyway, & soon after, & by divorce. I know this isn't much.
But I wanted to explain this life to you, even if
I had to become, over the years, someone else to do it.
You have to think of me what you think of me. I had
To live my life, even its late, florid style. Before
You judge this, think of her. Then think of fire,
Its laughter, the music of splintering beams & glass,
The flames reaching through the second story of a house
Almost as if to—mistakenly—rescue someone who
Left you years ago. It is so American, fire. So like us.
Its desolation. And its eventual, brief triumph.

The Oldest Living Thing in L.A.

At Wilshire & Santa Monica I saw an opossum
Trying to cross the street. It was late, the street
Was brightly lit, the opossum would take
A few steps forward, then back away from the breath
Of moving traffic. People coming out of the bars
Would approach, as if to help it somehow.
It would lift its black lips & show them
The reddened gums, the long rows of incisors,
Teeth that went all the way back beyond
The flames of Troy & Carthage, beyond sheep
Grazing rock-strewn hills, fragments of ruins

In the grass at San Vitale. It would back away
Delicately & smoothly, stepping carefully
As it always had. It could mangle someone's hand
In twenty seconds. Mangle it for good. It could
Sever it completely from the wrist in forty.
There was nothing to be done for it. Someone
Or other probably called the LAPD, who then
Called Animal Control, who woke a driver, who
Then dressed in mailed gloves, the kind of thing
Small knights once wore into battle, who gathered
Together his pole with a noose on the end,
A light steel net to snare it with, someone who hoped
The thing would have vanished by the time he got there.

The Smell of the Sea

Because they could not blind him twice, they drove a pencil
Through the blind king's ear. The pencil could not believe the thing
It had been asked to do, but by then it was already entering the mind,

And there it forgot that it had ever been a pencil.

Darkness reigned in the basement of the record store in Ogden, Utah,
Where all this happened, & there wasn't any king. The other king, the one who
Came in the night, was blind & mad, & owned a record store. And was a Mormon.

So were his ungrateful daughters who would pretend to pry his eyes out
With kitchen spoons, & so, within the kingdom, was everyone except
The Fool who repaired chainsaws & snowmobiles & thought of them as small,

Snarling gods whose faith & hatred of trees was perfect. The man who owned

the record store had once suspected God did not exist & had spent a summer
Lying on the beach at Santa Monica trying hard not to believe in God,
And was unable to. It was 1967. *Wild Thing* was coming from a radio. Her name

Was Dawn. She had dropped a half tab of acid an hour before he picked her up,
And didn't say a word until they were driving back & then she said "Blue lights …
So many blue lights." "Yeah, well, it's the airport. We're driving by the airport now,"

He explained. "Oh," she said. Maybe it was the acid that had made her seem

As distant & withdrawn as the world was, stretched across a quiet evening.
Where was *Wild Thing?* Dawn was hazy, overcast, & about as much
Fun to be with as the third wife at the wedding of a Spanish Fork polygamist.

The woman in her hopeless gingham dress had looked on, smiled at her husband
Then at the teenage bride. "You kin to her?" she had asked him. He had come
With a friend who thought the whole thing would be amusing, he had no idea who

The girl was. "That little slut?" he had wanted to say because he wanted to say
Something shocking. He still wanted to until the woman turned to him & said,
"With so many people showin' up, we're stretching it pretty thin. But we got chili dogs
And ice cream anyway. We splurged." The way someone had carefully trimmed
The yard with its small, parched lawn, & strung balloons on a clothesline, suddenly
Filled him with pity. Faith showed itself in the rib cage. Its bones were visible.
He could see them beneath the too-small bodice of the woman's dress.

Faith resided there, under the shriveled & lost left nipple.

•   •   •

He liked music. He liked hearing it while he worked.

And now he owned the store, although, for an hour or two each night,
He was both blind & mad & believed in kings. And believed he was a king,
And it never once entered his mind that the pencil balanced between

The pulse of his temple & his ear had been invented long after the deaths of kings.
After they had done the scene, he would remember who he was again,
An ordinary man who knew it & would have been insane because of knowing it

If he could not crawl toward Dover on his knees. He couldn't act.

When he dressed in weeds, his Temple garment showed under them.
One day he pretended he was a king who had disguised himself as the owner
Of a record store. The king sold eighteen new Donny & Maries before

He abdicated his vinyl throne & went home. If he fell from a high place it would be
A canyon wall he thought he remembered well enough to climb alone.
The water in the stream beneath him would wrinkle & whiten over the rocks as it

Always had & the trees rushing toward him would show him only that they could not

Help it. He knew who he was. Someone would ask him whether he carried
Brahms' *German Requiem,* or Valery Wellington on an extinct Chicago blues label,
And he had both. Sometimes he was sick of who he was, & the sickness passed.
The two guys who came in that afternoon were AWOL from a nearby army base,
And maybe only intended to rob the place, & had no idea who they were.
There was a young woman who worked afternoons there & her boyfriend had

Stopped by to tease & flirt with her a little. The two men pretended to browse

Through the stacks of record albums for a while, & then made the owner close
The store & marched them down the steps, & made the woman take off her dress,
And made the boyfriend watch as one, & then the other, raped her there.

What happened after that is blind & smells its way to the sea. They forced
The woman & her boyfriend to swallow some Drano from a can, & then flushed
Their mouths with water & made them swallow. But before they found the leftover can

With the snowy crystals in it, or had thought of using it,

One of them must have noticed the owner with the pencil in his ear, then
the short pine two-by-four. "Has the thought ever entered your mind ... ?"
One of them said after they had made the man lie on the floor, made him lie on his side

With his ear exposed, with his ear turned up to them, listening to everything,
Wondering how an ear could feel naked when it never had before. Did the man really
Believe the two of them would let the others live if he would lie as still as possible, as they

Had told him to, & let them do it?

This is usually the moment when the Fool is hanged & the poet disappears because
He doesn't know what happens next & a hunger with a mouth as small as the eye
Of a sewing needle overruns & darkens the flaxen grasses & the willows & the staring
Eyes of ponds, & you know there wasn't any king. There was only a man who owned
A record store & who believed two murderers would be kind, & keep their promises,
And waited for it to happen, lying there on his side, waiting until they were ready to drive

The unbelieving pencil through his ear.

Shara McCallum is the author of two books of poems, *Song of Thieves* and *The Water Between Us*, winner of the Agnes Lynch Starrett Poetry Prize. Originally from Jamaica, McCallum directs the Stadler Center for Poetry and teaches at Bucknell University. She is also on the faculty of the Stonecoast Low Residency MFA program. She lives in Pennsylvania with her family.

Sunset on the Wharf

John crows fill the red sky. Coming in
closer with each swooping pass, they smell

the unsold dead to be discarded. Fishermen,
women with their wares, higglers, pack up

as daylight ends. My father's presence lingers.
With an eight-year-old's eyes, I watch him poised

on one leg frozen in the midst of motion. Right
leg straight, firmly planted in the soil. Left one

bent at the knee, stranded in midair. Walking:
the unfinished step he could not make.

My calling could not retrieve him from that place
he exchanged for me: no *Daddy, Father, Alastair,*

enough to reclaim the eyes averted from my gaze.
What he saw what he went toward, I was left

behind, pulling at his sleeve as people crowded to see
the spectacle: my father: standing grasshopper,

lotus flower against darkening seas, sand turning black,
grains disintegrating under the dying light of the sun.

Jamaica, October 18, 1972

You tell me about the rickety truck:
your ride in back among goats or cows—
some animal I can't name now—

the water coming down your legs,
my father beside you, strumming
a slow melody of darkened skies

and winter trees he only dreamed
on his guitar. The night was cool.
That detail you rely on each time

the story is told: the one story
your memory serves us better
than my own. I doubt even that night

you considered me, as I lay inside you,
preparing to be born. So many nights
after it would be the same.

You do not remember anything,
you say, so clearly as that trip:
animal smells, guitar straining for sound,

the water between us becoming a river.

What my mother taught me:

When God closes a door, there are no windows.
When the Big Bad Wolf knocks, he knows how to get in.
Be afraid of the dark.

Don't scream.
Don't run.
Don't make wishes you can't keep.

If you drag a horse to water enough, she will drink.
If you don't play with fire, it will find you and burn.
Even careful chickens get caught by the hawk.

Calypso

Dese days, I doh even bada combing out mi locks.
Is dread I gone dread now.
Mi nuh stay like dem oda ones, mi luv—
wid mirra an comb,
sunnin demself pon every rock,
lookin man up and down de North Coast.
Tourist season, dem cotch up demself whole time in Negril,
waitin for some fool-fool American,
wid belly white like fish,

fi get lickle rum inna him system an jump in.
An lawd yu should see de grin.
But man can stupid bad, nuh?
I done learn mi lesson long ago
when I was young and craven.
Keep one Greek boy call Odysseus
inna mi cave. Seven years
him croonin in mi ear an him wife nuh see him face.
The two a we was a sight fi envy. I thought
I was goin die in Constant Spring at last
till the day him come to me—
as all men finally do—seyin him tired a play.
Start talkin picknie an home an wife
who can cook an clean. *Hmph.*
Well yu done know how I stay arredi, mi love.
I did pack up him bag and sen him back
to dat oda woman same time.
I hear from Mildred down de way
dat de gal did tek him back, too;
him tell her is farce I did farce him fi stay
an she believe the fool. But lawd,
woman can also bline when she please.
Mi fren, I tell yu
I is too ole for all dis bangarang.
I hear ova Trini way, young man is beatin steel drum,
meking sweet rhyme an callin music by mi name.
Well, dat the only romance I goin give de time a day.
Hmph.

What the Oracle Said

You will leave your home:
nothing will hold you.
You will wear dresses of gold; skins
of silver, copper, and bronze.
The sky above you will shift in meaning
each time you think you understand.
You will spend a lifetime chipping away layers

of flesh. The shadow of your scales
will always remain. You will be marked
by sulphur and salt.
You will bathe endlessly in clear streams and fail
to rid yourself of that scent.
Your feet will never be your own.
Stone will be your path.
Storms will follow in your wake,
destroying all those who take you in.
You will desert your children
kill your lovers and devour their flesh.
You will love no one
but the wind and ache of your bones.
Neither will love you in return.
With age, your hair will grow matted and dull,
your skin will gape and hang in long folds,
your eyes will cease to shine.
But nothing will be enough.
The sea will never take you back.

An Offering

I am the woman at the water's edge,
offering you oranges for the peeling,
knife glistening in the sun.
This is the scent and taste
of my skin: citron and sweet.
Touch me and your life will unfold
before you, easily as this skirt
billows then sinks,
lapping against my legs, my toes
filtering through the river's silt.
Following the current out to sea,
I am the kind of woman
who will come back to haunt
your dreams, move through you
humid nights the way honey
swirls through a cup of hot tea.

Facing It

Always the same questions
of blood and bread breaking,
eaten in communion
with what we know—this chair,
the candle flickering.
With what we don't—the dark
outside the window, night
ashen like the voice of my hands.

If I could again be a child
at my mother's side,
I would believe in the stove,
the lit room; in her skirt
swishing against my face
as I crumpled the hem in my fist,
made my hand a flag to wave
my mother's love into my skin.

*I once was lost
but now am found,* she hummed.
And we were, she and I.
And I believed in the night
more fiercely, believed
in my mother, my hand wrapt
in her skirt, moving back and forth
across my face, her face, the face
of God, the face I loved.

Peter Meinke has published fifteen books of poetry, the most recent being *The Contracted World*. He is also the author of the short story collections *The Piano Tuner* and *Unheard Music*; a book on writing, *The Shape of Poetry*; and two children's books in verse, *The Legend of Larry the Lizard* and *Very Seldom Animals*. His poems have received numerous awards, including two National Endowment for the Arts Fellowships. He taught at Eckerd College for twenty-seven years, and has been writer-in-residence at various colleges and universities. Most recently, he held the Darden Chair in Creative Writing at Old Dominion University in Norfolk, Virginia. Meinke and his wife, the artist Jeanne Clark, have lived in St. Petersburg for over forty years.

Sonnet on the Death of the Man
Who Invented Plastic Roses

The man who invented the plastic rose
is dead. Behold his mark:
his undying flawless blossoms never close
but guard his grave unbending through the dark.
He understood neither beauty nor flowers,
which catch our hearts in nets as soft as sky
and bind us with a thread of fragile hours:
flowers are beautiful because they die.

Beauty without the perishable pulse
is dry and sterile, an abandoned stage
with false forests. But the results
Support this man's invention; he knew his age:
a vision of our tearless time discloses
artificial men sniffing plastic roses.

(Untitled)

this is a poem to our son Peter
whom I have hurt a thousand times
whose large and vulnerable eyes
have glazed in pain at my ragings
thin wrists and fingers hung
boneless in despair, pale freckled back
bent in defeat, pillow soaked
by my failure to understand.
I have scarred through weakness
and impatience your frail confidence forever
because when I needed to strike
you were there to be hurt and because
I thought you knew
you were beautiful and fair
your bright eyes and hair
but now I see that no one knows that

about himself, but must be told
and retold until it takes hold
because I think anything can be killed
after a while, especially beauty
so I write this for life, for love, for
you, my oldest son Peter, age 10,
going on 11.

The Poet, Trying to Surprise God

The poet, trying to surprise his God
composed new forms from secret harmonies,
tore from his fiery vision galaxies
of unrelated shapes, both even & odd.
But God just smiled, and gave his know-all nod
saying, "There's no surprising One who sees
the acorn, root, and branch of centuries;
I swallow all things up, like Aaron's rod.

So hold this thought beneath your poet-bonnet:
no matter how free-seeming flows your sample
God is by definition the Unsurprised."
"Then I'll return," the poet sighed, "to sonnets
of which this is a rather pale example."

"Is that right?" said God. "I hadn't realized…."

Liquid Paper

Smooth as a snail, this little parson
pardons our sins. Touch the brush tip
lightly and—*abracadabra!*—a clean slate.

We know those who blot their brains
by sniffing it, which shows
it erases more than ink
and with imagination anything

can be misapplied … In the army,
our topsergeant drank aftershave, squeezing
my Old Spice to the last slow drop.

It worked like Liquid Paper in his head

until he'd glide across the streets of Heidelberg
hunting for the house in Boise, Idaho,
where he was born. … If I were God
I'd authorize Celestial Liquid Paper
every seven years to whiten our mistakes:
we should be sorry and live with what we've done
but seven years is long enough and all of us

deserve a visit now and then
to the house where we were born
before everything got written so far wrong

Atomic Pantoum

In a chain reaction
the neutrons released
split other nuclei
which release more neutrons

The neutrons released
blow open some others
which release more neutrons
and start this all over

Blow open some others
and choirs will crumble
and start this all over
with eyes burned to ashes

And choirs will crumble
the fish catch on fire
with eyes burned to ashes
in a chain reaction

The fish catch on fire
because the sun's force
in a chain reaction
has blazed in our minds

Because the sun's force
with plutonium trigger
has blazed in our minds
we are dying to use it

With plutonium trigger
curled and tightened
we are dying to use it
torching our enemies

Curled and tightened
blind to the end
torching our enemies
we sing to Jesus

Blind to the end
split up like nuclei
we sing to Jesus
in a chain reaction

Zinc Fingers

Though scientists inform us that criminals
have insufficient zinc I've always believed
it's insufficient gold and silver that gets
them going   The man who slipped his hand into
my front pocket on the jammed Paris *Métro*
wasn't trying to make friends   His overcoat
smelled greasy and it was unpleasant holding
hands above my wallet   pressed in on all sides
like stacked baguettes   There was no way to move or
take a swing Still some action on my part seemed
to be called for: we stood   nose to nose I tried

to look in his eyes but he stared at my chin
shy on our first date   so after a while as
we rattled along toward the Champs-Élysées

I lost concentration and began to think

of our scholarly daughter working at Yale
on a project called Zinc Fingers   scanning a
protein with pseudopods   each with a trace of
zinc   that latch on to our DNA and help
determine what we become   This brought me back
to *mon ami* the pickpocket: I wondered
how he chose his hard line of work and if as
a boy he was good at cards for example
or sewing and for that matter what choice did
I have either so when we reached our stop and
he looked up from my chin at last I smiled at
him and his eyes flashed in fear or surprise and
I called *It's OK* as he scuttled away
Tout va bien!   though I held tight to my wallet

A Meditation on You and Wittgenstein

Wittgenstein never met you face to face
but fancied someone like you when he said
The world is everything that is the case

a maxim hard to fathom   Nevertheless
its rhythms tug like Ariadne's thread:
the world *is* everything that is the case

the world's *everything* that is the case
(you for example sleeping in my bed)
Although Wittgenstein never met you face to face

he guessed logic lies in poetry's embrace
and from the same dark labyrinth has fed
the world being everything that is the case:

---

for love or dreams of love curls at its base
and if you miss it your heart's bled and dead
I wish he could have met you face to face

An ounce of loneliness outweighs a pound of lace:
what strange equations winding through my head!
Poor Wittgenstein never met you face to face
The world is only everything: *that's* the case

Preacher, Said the General

Preacher   said the General
are we not able
to carve a cane or a
stick for the glory of God?
Why art thou wroth?   and why
is thy countenance fallen?

This rifle now, the M-1
I'm offering you   isn't it beautifully balanced
(though obsolete)?   The curve
of burnished stock
fits snugly the shoulder socket
Is it not sweet to hear ka-rack
of the spinning bullet   the downward swerve
of adjusted trajectory
zeroing in to the sheeplike target
SMACK at a mile away?
What do you say: isn't that
satisfactory?

And tell me   isn't
a man-made cloud
a terrific thing?
(harder than fire and
softer than cumulonimbus
warmer than summer
and louder than birth and hot

with the holy desire
of man for dominion
over every thing that moveth
upon the earth)

And is this not
our burnt offering
mounting to God?
Are we not Abel
whose smoke rose
from bubbling flesh
to meat-eating heaven
driving the vegetarian Cain
east of Eden
to the land of Nod?

Photo by Max Brady

Malena Mörling, assistant professor of creative writing at the University of North Carolina, Wilmington, is the author of *Ocean Avenue* and *Astoria*. She has translated works by the Swedish poet Tomas Tranströmer, a selection of which appears in the collection *For the Living and the Dead*.

If There Is Another World

If there is another world,
I think you can take a cab there—
or ride your old bicycle
down Junction Blvd.
past the Paris Suites Hotel
with the Eiffel Tower on the roof
and past the blooming Magnolia and on—
to the corner of 168th Street.
And if you're inclined to,
you can turn left there
and yield to the blind
as the sign urges us—
especially since it is a state law.
Especially since there is a kind of moth
here on the earth
that feeds only on the tears of horses.
Sooner or later we will all cry
from inside our hearts.
Sooner or later even the concrete
will crumble and cry in silence
along with all the lost road signs.
Two days ago 300 televisions
washed up on a beach in Shiomachi, Japan,
after having fallen off a ship in a storm.
They looked like so many
oversized horseshoe crabs
with their screens turned down to the sand.
And if you're inclined to, you can continue
in the weightless seesaw of the light
through a few more intersections
where people inside their cars
pass you by in space
and where you pass by them,
each car another thought—only heavier.

Happiness

How far away is your happiness?
    How many inches?
How many yards?
    How many bus rides to work
and back?
    How many doorways
and stairwells?
    How many hours
awake in the dark
    belly of the night
which contains
    all the world's bedrooms,
all dollhouse-sized?
    How far away is your happiness?
How many words?
    How many thoughts?
How much pavement?
    How much thread
in the enormous sewing machine
    of the present moment?

Gone

    The world
is gone
    like the exact
shape of a cloud
      or the exact shape
of a hand waving
    in the sunlight
from across
    a crowded
train station
    parking lot
to another hand
    that waves back.

Come to think of it,
    everything up to now
is gone.
        And I have also
already left
    even though
I still ride
        the train
through the outskirts
    of the city.

And I still sit
        by the window,
the filthy
    train window
while what is left
        of the demolished
buildings
    goes past
and the empty
        billboards
and the transitory
    architecture.

It's amazing
        we're not
more amazed.
    The world
is here
        but then it's gone
like a wave
    traveling toward
other waves.

        Or like
the delicate white
    spaceships
of the Dogwood
        that float

as if there were
no gravity,
as if there were
no moments
isolated from
any other
moments
anywhere.

Simply Lit

Often toward evening,
after another day, after
another year of days,
in the half dark on the way home
I stop at the food store
and waiting in line I begin
to wonder about people—I wonder
if they also wonder about how
strange it is that we
are here on the earth.
And how in order to live
we all must sleep.
And how we have beds for this
(unless we are without)
and entire rooms where we go
at the end of the day to collapse.
And I think how even the most
lively people are desolate
when they are alone
because they too must sleep
and sooner or later die.
We are always looking to acquire
more food for more great meals.
We have to have great meals.
Isn't it enough to be a person buying
a carton of milk? A simple

package of butter and a loaf
of whole wheat bread?
Isn't it enough to stand here
while the sweet middle-aged cashier
rings up the purchases?
I look outside,
but I can't see much out there
because now it is dark except
for a single vermilion neon sign
floating above the gas station
like a miniature temple simply lit
against the night.

Seemed Pleased

Just after the plane lifted
off the ground with all of its
weight, a small hand, its nails with
partially chipped off red nail

polish, worked itself back
from in between the seats in
front of me and sort of waved.
The next I saw of the person

with the hand was a blue eye
peering back at me and then
the girl stood up on her seat
and smiled. She had brown, just

above the shoulder length hair
and bangs and she wore a blue
and white striped sundress. A
red rose of the same material

as the dress was attached to
the middle of the upper

lining which was also red.
"My mother is dead," she told

me suddenly. "She is already gone—
She is in heaven." The girl seemed
pleased, almost proud at that
moment, to be able to inform

me of this, perhaps as a
handy way of meeting. "This
is my dad," she said, and pointed
to the back of his head of

blond thinning rather unruly
cap of hair. "My dad." She
exclaimed again and again
and hugged his face with all

of her might until she knocked
his glasses off and they ended
up in the aisle. Then she introduced
her brother, engrossed in a book:

"This is Marcus, he is eight.
I am four and a half." And then
she proceeded to demonstrate
the workings of a doodle pad.

On the cover of it was a clown
riding in an airplane waving
his hands in the clouds. And that's
when the trays of food arrived and the girl

whose name I never learned was told
by her father to turn around
and sit down and eat what was
being unwrapped for her on her tray.

In the Yellow Head of a Tulip

In the yellow head of a tulip
in the sound of the wind entangled in the forest
in the haphazard combination of things
for sale on the sidewalk
an iron next to a nail-clipper next to a can of soup
next to a starling's feather
in the silence inside of stone
in tea in music in desire in butter in torture
in space that flings itself out in the universe
in every direction at once without end
despite walls despite grates and ceilings
and bulletproof glass
the sun falls through without refracting
in the wind hanging out its own sheets
on all the empty clotheslines
in the bowels of rats
in their tiny moving architectures
in a world that is always moving
in those who are unable to speak but know how to listen
in your mother who is afraid of her own thoughts
in her fear in her death
in her own derelict loneliness
in the garden late at night
between the alder tree and the ash
she rocks herself to sleep in the hammock
a little drunk and wayward
in everything she is that you are not
in the well of the skull
in the fish that you touch
in the copper water
in its breath of water
in your breath, the single bubble rising
that could be you
that could be me
that could be nothing

A Wake

I called Michael and he told me he just got home from a wake. "Oh, I am sorry," I said. "No, no," he said, "it was the best wake I have ever been to. The funeral home was as warm and as cozy as anyone's living room. We had the greatest time. My friend looked wonderful, much better dead than alive. He wore his red and green Hawaiian shirt. He was the most handsome corpse I'd ever seen. They did such a good job! His daughter was there and a lot of old friends I had not seen in years. You know, he drank himself to death. He'd been on and off the wagon for years, but for some reason this is what he ended up doing." As my friend kept talking, I thought of Lorca and what he wrote about death and Spain: "A dead man in Spain is more alive as a dead man than anyplace else in the world" and "Everywhere else, death is an end. Death comes, and they draw the curtains. Not in Spain. In Spain they open them. Many Spaniards live indoors until the day they die and are taken out into the sunlight."

Photo by David Dwyer

Kathleen Norris is the author of five books of poetry—*Journey, Little Girls in Church, The Middle of the World, Falling Off,* and *The Astronomy of Love*—and three books of nonfiction listed as *New York Times* Notable Books of the Year—*Dakota: A Spiritual Geography, The Cloister Walk,* and *Amazing Grace: A Vocabulary of Faith.* She is also the author of *The Virgin of Bennington,* a memoir of her college days and mentor Betty Kray, and *The Holy Twins,* a children's book done in collaboration with the artist Tomie de Paola.

Perennials

I've betrayed them all:
columbine and daisy,
iris, day-lily,
even the rain barrel
that spoke to me in a dream.

I inherited this garden,
and miss my grandmother
in her big sun hat.
My inexperienced hands
don't know what to hope for.

Still, flowers come: yellow,
pink, and blue. Preoccupied,
I let them go
until weeds produce spikes
and seeds around them.

I never used the rain barrel.
Water froze in the bottom;
too late, I set it on its side.

Now lily-of-the-valley comes
with its shy bloom,
choked by a weed
I don't know the name of. One day,
too late, I'll weed around them,
and pull some lilies by mistake.

Next year we'll all be back,
struggling.

Just look at these flowers
I've done nothing to deserve:
and still, they won't abandon me.

Young Lovers with Pizza

The curve of a smile,
of buttocks,
clothes everywhere,
pizza in a box, laughter
when the telephone intrudes
and you must untangle
legs, breasts, hips
to answer it.
It becomes
a private joke:
the person on the other end
doesn't know a thing.

I envy you,
couples in this town,
in the world:
that first touch, growing,
the dry, breathy heat
and kisses like cool water,
couples lost for a moment
inside each other, inside out.

Don't think of me,
or your duty to God
and telephone. This is silence,
holy and lucky:
a man's hard body,
skin soft to the touch, the giddy
generosity
of a woman's breasts,
as light curves gently
around the spinning earth,
around your smiles and
naked hips, holding
everything you need.

Eve of St. Agnes in the
High School Gym

The saint's been dead too long:
no young girl keeps her vigil. Not one fasts
or prays tonight for a vision
of the man she'll marry.

A band plays—too loudly—
popular tunes a few years out of date.
Young men emerge from a huddle
of teammates, cheerleaders,
fans. They run onto the court,
howling, slapping hands.

Men just a few years older
stand smoking by the door;
their windbreakers advertise a local bar.
Others sit in the stands
holding sleepy children;
the women with them look worried and tired.

Snow falls silently,
snaking through the streets,
while in the gym, done up like spring
in a pale yellow skirt
and lavender sweater,
a pretty girl sleepwalks
on high heels. She carries herself
to a boy on the bench
who doesn't look up; and the old men sigh.

When the game is over
they flee on the storm.
The saint sits in heaven,
and if anyone's praying
on this chilly night,
let it be for love.

How I Came to Drink
My Grandmother's Piano

It has to do with giving,
and with letting go,
with how the earth rotates
on its axis
to make an oblate spheroid.

It has to do
with how it all comes 'round.

There was a piano
in my grandmother's house.
I inherited it,
but never learned to play.
I used it as a bookshelf
and dust collector
and finally gave it to a church up the street.

I was snowed in at a trailer house
in Regent, North Dakota,
when Rita offered me a glass
of dandelion wine.
"That's some glass," I said,
much too fancy for our thrown-together meal
of hamburgers and fried potatoes.
"Yes, isn't it?" she replied,
fingering the cut glass pattern.
"A friend gave it to me.
Someone had given it to her,
but she never used it."

I began to hear that piano
as Rita poured the wine.
The dandelions spun around:
glad to be yellow again,
glad to be free of the dark.

Afterward,

the soldiers argued: did she prove
that God exists?

The corpse of a girl, thirteen at most,
lies bloodied on a hill
named for the cross of Jesus Christ,
nothing left
of her voice crying out,
small as a bird,
singing hymns as they raped her,
one long afternoon, the others
already dead,
twenty-three children bayoneted,
left to burn, the old hacked
and shot, fallen in the dust
of the village square
of El Mozote.

God speaks like fire,
God's words
are a sword. The soldiers
are stunned, too sated with death
to move. When one finally shot her,
she kept on singing,
her voice a bit weaker than before.
Another shot, and still she sang
and the soldiers became afraid.
One unsheathed his machete
and hacked through her neck
until at last, the singing stopped.

Afterward,
they argue: does she prove
that God exists? The soldiers are afraid,
and it burns within:
is it fear,
or singing, that has no end?

Emily in Choir

Emily holds her father's hand,
she dances in place
through the Invitatory
and refuses the book with no pictures.
"This is boring," she whispers,
in the silence between psalms.

Candles lit in honor of the guardian angels
make rivers of air that bend the stone
walls of the abbey church. "Why are the men
wearing costumes?" Emily asks.
"They're the brothers," her father
explains, and Emily says, "Well!
They must have a very strict mother!"

The Grave is strict, says another Emily;
Emily here and now plays with the three
shadows her hands make
on the open page. *While the clergyman
tells Father and Vinnie that "this Corruptible
shall put on Incorruption," it has already done so
and they go defrauded.*

Brimful of knowledge, Emily shakes my arm:
"They're the monks!" she says,
"The men who sing," and she runs
up the aisle, out into the day,

to where the angels are:
*In the name of the Bee—
And of the Butterfly—
And of the Breeze—Amen!*

Sharon Olds's books include *Strike Sparks; Selected Poems 1980–2002; The Unswept Room*, a finalist for the National Book Award and the National Book Critics Circle Award; and *The Dead and the Living*, which was chosen as the Lamont Poetry Selection by the Academy of American Poets and received the National Book Critics Circle Award. Olds teaches in the Graduate Creative Writing Program at New York University, and for eighteen years has helped run a writing workshop at the Sigismund Goldwater Memorial Hospital, a state hospital for the severely physically challenged. From 1998–2000 she was New York State Poet Laureate. She was named the James Merrill Fellow of the Academy of American Poets for 2003, and was inducted into the American Academy of Arts and Science in 2004. She lives in New York City.

Satan Says

I am locked in a little cedar box
with a picture of shepherds pasted onto
the central panel between carvings.
The box stands on curved legs.
It has a gold, heart-shaped lock
and no key. I am trying to write my
way out of the closed box
redolent of cedar. Satan
comes to me in the locked box
and says, *I'll get you out. Say*
My father is a shit. I say
my father is a shit and Satan
laughs and says, *It's opening.*
Say your mother is a pimp.
My mother is a pimp. Something
opens and breaks when I say that.
My spine uncurls in the cedar box
like the pink back of the ballerina pin
with a ruby eye, resting beside me on
satin in the cedar box.
Say shit, say death, say fuck the father,
Satan says, down my ear.
The pain of the locked past buzzes
in the child's box on her bureau, under
the terrible round pond eye
etched around with roses, where
self-loathing gazed at sorrow.
Shit. Death. Fuck the father.
Something opens. Satan says
Don't you feel a lot better?
Light seems to break on the delicate
edelweiss pin, carved in two
colors of wood. I love him too,
you know, I say to Satan dark
in the locked box. I love them but
I'm trying to say what happened to us
in the lost past. *Of course,* he says

and smiles, *of course. Now say: torture.*
I see, through blackness soaked in cedar,
the edge of a large hinge open.
Say: the father's cock, the mother's
cunt, says Satan, *I'll get you out.*
The angle of the hinge widens
until I see the outlines of
the time before I was, when they were
locked in the bed. When I say
the magic words, Cock, Cunt,
Satan softly says, *Come out.*
But the air around the opening
is heavy and thick as hot smoke.
Come in, he says, and I feel his voice
breathing from the opening.
The exit is through Satan's mouth.
Come in my mouth, he says, *you're there*
already, and the huge hinge
begins to close. Oh no, I loved
them, too, I brace
my body tight
in the cedar house.
Satan sucks himself out the keyhole.
I'm left locked in the box, he seals
the heart-shaped lock with the wax of his tongue.
It's your coffin now, Satan says.
I hardly hear;
I am warming my cold
hands at the dancer's
ruby eye—
the fire, the suddenly discovered knowledge of love.

Quake Theory

When two plates of earth scrape along each other
like a mother and daughter
it is called a fault.

There are faults that slip smoothly past each other
an inch a year, with just a faint rasp
like a man running his hand over his chin,
that man between us,

and there are faults that get stuck at a bend for twenty years.
The ridge bulges up like a father's sarcastic forehead
and the whole thing freezes in place, the man between us.

When this happens, there will be heavy damage
to industrial areas and leisure residence
when the deep plates
finally jerk past
the terrible pressure of their contact.

                           The earth cracks
and innocent people slip gently in like swimmers.

Indictment of Senior Officers

In the hallway above the pit of the stairwell
my sister and I would meet at night,
eyes and hair dark, bodies
like twins in the dark. We did not talk of
the two who had brought us there, like generals,
for their own reasons. We sat, buddies
in wartime, her living body the proof of
my living body, our backs to the vast
shell hole of the stairs, down which
we would have to go, knowing nothing
but what we had learned there,

                         so that now
when I think of my sister, the holes of the needles
in her hips and in the creases of her elbows,
and the marks from the latest husband's beatings,
and the scars of the operations, I feel the
rage of a soldier standing over the body of

someone sent to the front lines
without training
or a weapon.

The Sisters of Sexual Treasure

As soon as my sister and I got out of our
mother's house, all we wanted to
do was fuck, obliterate
her tiny sparrow body and narrow
grasshopper legs. The men's bodies
were like our father's body! The massive
hocks, flanks, thighs, elegant
knees, long tapered calves—
we could have him there, the steep forbidden
buttocks, backs of the knees, the cock
in our mouth, ah the cock in our mouth.
            Like explorers who
discover a lost city, we went
nuts with joy, undressed the men
slowly and carefully, as if
uncovering buried artifacts that
proved our theory of the lost culture:
that if Mother said it wasn't there,
it was there.

Station

Coming in off the dock after writing,
I approached the house,
and saw your long grandee face
in the light of a lamp with a parchment shade
the color of flame.

An elegant hand on your beard. Your tapered
eyes found me on the lawn. You looked

as the lord looks down from a narrow window
and you are descended from lords. Calmly, with no
hint of shyness you examined me,
the wife who runs out on the dock to write
as soon as one child is in bed,
leaving the other to you.

                          Your long
mouth, flexible as an archer's bow,
did not curve. We spent a long moment
in the truth of our situation, the poems
heavy as poached game hanging from my hands.

The Language of the Brag

I have wanted excellence in the knife-throw,
I have wanted to use my exceptionally strong and accurate arms
and my straight posture and quick electric muscles
to achieve something at the center of a crowd,
the blade piercing the bark deep,
the haft slowly and heavily vibrating like the cock.

I have wanted some epic use for my excellent body,
some heroism, some American achievement
beyond the ordinary for my extraordinary self,
magnetic and tensile, I have stood by the sandlot
and watched the boys play.

I have wanted courage, I have thought about fire
and the crossing of waterfalls, I have dragged around

my belly big with cowardice and safety,
my stool black with iron pills,
my huge breasts oozing mucus,
my legs swelling, my hands swelling,
my face swelling and darkening, my hair
falling out, my inner sex
Stabbed again and again with terrible pain like a knife.
I have lain down.

I have lain down and sweated and shaken
and passed blood and feces and water and
slowly alone in the center of a circle I have
passed the new person out
and they have lifted the new person free of the act
and wiped the new person free of that
language of blood like praise all over the body.

I have done what you wanted to do, Walt Whitman,
Allen Ginsberg, I have done this thing,
I and the other women this exceptional
act with the exceptional heroic body,
this giving birth, this glistening verb,
and I am putting my proud American boast
right here with the others.

Seventh Birthday of the First Child

The children were around my feet like dogs,
milling, nipping, wetting, slavering,
feed sieving from their chops like plankton.

I slid on their messes, I found their silky bodies
asleep in corners, paws fallen
north, south, east, west,
little sexes gleaming.

Ankle-deep in their smell, their noise,
their crisis, their noses cold and black
or going soft with fever, I waded, I slogged.

crowding around my toes like tits,
they taught me to walk carefully,
to hold still to be sucked.
I worked my feet in them like mud
for the pleasure.

And suddenly there is a head at my breastbone
as if one of the litter had climbed

onto the branch of a dwarf tree
which overnight grew to here
bearing you up, daughter, with your dark
newborn eyes. You sit in the boughs,
blossoms breaking like porcelain cups around you.

The Unjustly Punished Child

The child screams in his room. Rage
heats his head.
He is going through changes like metal under deep
pressure at high temperatures.

When he cools off and comes out of that door
he will not be the same child who ran in
and slammed it. An alloy has been added. Now he will
crack along different lines when tapped.

He is stronger. The long impurification
has begun this morning.

The Mother

In the dreamy silence after bath,
hot in the milk-white towel, my son
announces that I will not love him when I'm dead
because people can't think when they're dead. I can't
think at first—not love him? The air outside the
window is very black, the old locust
beginning to lose its leaves already...
I hold him tight, he is white as a buoy
and my death like dark water is rising
swiftly in the room. I tell him I loved him
before he was born. I do not tell him
I'm damned if I won't love him after I'm
dead, necessity after all being
the mother of invention.

Alicia Suskin Ostriker is a poet and critic whose previous volumes of poetry include *The Imaginary Lover*, which won the William Carlos Williams Award of the Poetry Society of America, and *The Crack in Everything* and *The Little Space, Poems Selected and New 1968–1998*, both National Book Award finalists. Her critical works include *Stealing the Language: The Emergence of Women's Poetry in America, Feminist Revision and the Bible,* and *The Nakedness of Fathers: Biblical Visions and Revisions.* Ostriker teaches in the low residency Poetry MFA Program at New England College.

The Leaf Pile

Now here is a typical children's story
that happens in gorgeous October
when the mothers are coming
in the afternoon, wearing brisk boots
and windy skirts to pick up
the little children from the day care center

Frost in the air
the maples golden and crimson
my son in a leaf pile in the playground dreaming
I am late, the playground is almost
empty, my husband will kill me

I gather my son to go home,
he forgets his sweater in the playground and I send him back
he dawdles, he is playing with leaves
in his mind, it is already a quarter
to six, will you come on I say

and hurry along the corridor, there are yellow and blue rocket
paintings, but I feel bad and ask what did you do today,
do you recognize this story, the way he stands and picks
his nose, move I say, do you want dinner or not
I'm going to make a nice dinner, fried chicken
I wheedle, so could you please walk a little
faster, okay, I walk a little faster and get upstairs
myself, pivot on boot-heel, nobody there,
he is putting something in his mouth, his sable eyelashes
downcast, and I am swooping down the stairwell screaming

damn you
that's filthy
I told you not before dinner

We are climbing the stairs
and I am crying, my son is not crying
I have shaken him, I have pried the sweet from his cheek

I have slapped his cheek like a woman slapping a carpet
with all my strength

> mothers are very strong
> he is too young to do anything about this
> will not remember he remembers it

The mind is a leaf pile where you can bury
anything, pain, the image of a woman
who wears a necklace of skulls, a screaming woman
you dig quickly and deposit the pulpy thing
you drop leaves on it and it stays there, that is the story

that is sticking in my mind as we push
the exit door, and run through the evening wind
to my car where I jerk the gearshift and pick
up a little speed, going along
this neat suburban avenue full of maples
the mark of my hand a blush on my son's cheek.

A Question of Time

I ask a friend. She informs me it is ten years
From when her mother wrote
"I hope at least you are sorry
For causing your father's heart attack,"
To now, when they are speaking
Weekly on the phone
And almost, even, waxing confidential.
I check my watch. Ten years is rather much,
But I am not a Texas fundamentalist,
And you are not a red-headed lesbian,
So it should take us shorter, and I should get
Time off for good behavior
If I behave well, which
I do not plan to do.
No, on the contrary, I plan to play
All my cards wrong,

To pelt you with letters, gifts, advice,
Descriptions of my feelings.
I plan to ask friendly maternal questions.
I plan to beam a steady
Stream of anxiety
Rays which would stun a mule,
Derail a train,
Take out a satellite,
At you in California, where you hack
Coldly away at this iron umbilicus,
Having sensibly put three thousand miles between us.

I remember you told me once, when we were still
In love, the summer before you left
For the hills of San Francisco,
The music of youth,
To stop fearing estrangement:
"Mom, you're not crazy like grandma."
It was the country. We were on the balcony
Overlooking the pond, where your wiry boyfriend
And the rest of the family swam and drank, unconscious.
False but endearing, dear. I *am* my mother.
I am your mother. Are you keeping up
Your drawing, your reading?
Have you written poems?
Are you saving money? Don't
Do acid, it fries the brain,
Don't do cocaine, don't
Get pregnant, or have you already,
Don't slip away from me,
You said you wouldn't,
Remember that. I remember it was hot,
How lightly we were dressed,
And barefoot, at that time,
And how you let me rest
A half a minute in your suntanned arms.

Everywoman Her Own Theology

I am nailing them up to the cathedral door
Like Martin Luther. Actually, no,
I don't want to resemble that *Schmutzkopf*
(See Erik Erikson and N. O. Brown
On the Reformer's anal aberrations,
Not to mention his hatred of Jews and peasants),
So I am thumbtacking these ninety-five
Theses to the bulletin board in my kitchen.

My proposals, or should I say requirements,
Include at least one image of a god,
Virile, beard optional, one of a goddess,
Nubile, breast size approximating mine,
One divine baby, one lion, one lamb,
All nude as figs, all dancing wildly,
All shining. Reproducible
In marble, metal, in fact any material.

Ethically, I am looking for
An absolute endorsement of loving-kindness.
No loopholes except maybe mosquitoes.
Virtue and sin will henceforth be discouraged,
Along with suffering and martyrdom.
There will be no concept of infidels.
Consequently the faithful must entertain
Themselves some other way than killing infidels.

And so forth and so on. I understand
This piece of paper is going to be
Spattered with wine one night at a party
And covered over with newer pieces of paper.
That is how it goes with bulletin boards.
Nevertheless it will be there.
Like an invitation, like a chalk pentangle,
It will emanate certain occult vibrations.

If something sacred wants to swoop from the universe
Through a ceiling, and materialize,

Folding its silver wings,
In a kitchen, and bump its chest against mine,
My paper will tell this being where to find me.

The Dogs at Live Oak Beach, Santa Cruz

As if there could be a world
Of absolute innocence
In which we forget ourselves

The owners throw sticks
And half-bald tennis balls
Toward the surf
And the happy dogs leap after them
As if catapulted—

Black dogs, tan dogs,
Tubes of glorious muscle—

Pursuing pleasure
More than obedience
They race, skid to a halt in the wet sand,
Sometimes they'll plunge straight into
The foaming breakers

Like diving birds, letting the green turbulence
Toss them, until they snap and sink

Teeth into floating wood
Then bound back to their owners
Shining wet, with passionate speed
For nothing,
For absolutely nothing but joy.

What Was Lost

What fed my daughters, my son
Trickles of bliss,

My right guess, my true information,
What my husband sucked on
For decades, so that I thought
Myself safe, I thought love
Protected the breast.
What I admired myself, liking
To leave it naked, what I could
Soap and fondle in its bath, what tasted
The drunken airs of summer like a bear
Pawing a hive, half up a sycamore.
I'd let sun eyeball it, surf and lake water
Reel wildly around it, the perfect fit,
The burst of praise. Lifting my chin
I'd stretch my arms to point it at people,
Show it off when I danced. I believed this pride
Would protect it, it was a kind of joke
Between me and my husband
When he licked off some colostrum
Even a drop or two of bitter milk
He'd say *You're saving for your grandchildren.*

I was doing that, and I was saving
The goodness of it for some crucial need,
The way a woman
Undoes her dress to feed
A stranger, at the end of *The Grapes of Wrath,*
A book my mother read me when I was
Spotty with measles, years before
The breast was born, but I remembered it.
How funny I thought goodness would protect it.
Jug of star fluid, breakable cup—
Someone shoveled your good and bad crumbs
Together into a plastic container
Like wet sand at the beach,
For breast tissue is like silicon.
And I imagined inland orange groves,
Each tree standing afire with solid citrus
Lanterns against the gleaming green,
Ready to be harvested and eaten.

Fix

The puzzled ones, the Americans, go through their lives
Buying what they are told to buy,
Pursuing their love affairs with the automobile,

Baseball and football, romance and beauty,
Enthusiastic as trained seals, going into debt, struggling—
True believers in liberty, and also security,

And of course sex—cheating on each other
For the most part only a little, mostly avoiding violence
Except at a vast blue distance, as between bombsight and earth,

Or on the violent screen, which they adore.
Those who are not Americans think Americans are happy
Because they are so filthy rich, but not so,

They are mostly puzzled and at a loss
As if someone pulled the floor out from under them,
They'd like to believe in God, or something, and they do try.

You can see it in their white faces at the supermarket and the gas station
—Not the immigrant faces, they know what they want,
Not the blacks, whose faces are hurt and proud—

The white faces, lipsticked, shaven, we do try
To keep smiling, for when we're smiling, the whole world
Smiles with us, but we feel we've lost

That loving feeling. Clouds ride by above us,
Rivers flow, toilets work, traffic lights work, barring floods, fires
And earthquakes, houses and streets appear stable,

So what is it, this moon-shaped blankness?
What the hell is it? America is perplexed.
We would fix it if we knew what was broken.

Minnie Bruce Pratt is the author of five books of poetry: *The Sound of One Fork; We Say We Love Each Other; Crime Against Nature; Walking Back Up Depot Street*, chosen as the Lamont Poetry Selection by the Academy of American Poets and a *New York Times* Notable Book of the Year; and *The Dirt She Ate: Selected and New Poems*, winner of the 2003 Lambda Literary Award for Poetry. Pratt has also received a Creative Writing Fellowship in Poetry from the National Endowment for the Arts, and a 2005 Fellowship in Poetry from the New Jersey State Council on the Arts. Pratt is a member of the Graduate Faculty at The Union Institute and University, and lives in New Jersey.

The Blue Cup

Through binoculars the spiral nebula was
a smudged white thumbprint on the night sky.
Stories said it was a mark left by the hand
of Night, that old she, easily weaving
the universe out of milky strings of chaos.

Beatrice found creation more difficult.
Tonight what she had was greasy water
whirling in the bottom of her sink, revolution,
and one clean cup.

               She set the blue cup
down on the table, spooned instant coffee, poured
boiling water, a thread of sweetened milk. Before
she went back to work, she drank the galaxy that spun
small and cautious between her chapped cupped hands.

Learning to Write

I am holding something too big in my hand,
a stick, a fat finger, six fingers instead of five.
My eyes trace, then my fist, the force that moves
down from the white letters on the blackboard,
to march A a B b onto the page in front of me.

How I love that broad untouched expanse, how
it fades into distance when the letters spread their legs
and straddle its surface. Now the letters are mine,
yet they still sit above, staring down, elbows akimbo,
as we copy the morning's lesson: September 12, 1952.

Time divided into days, and my life into years
as I wrote. But what I loved first was the flecked blank
paper, the bound tablet like a book waiting to be
filled, like a basket, a bucket, a grocery bag.

The book of pages waiting to be turned,
an airplane propeller, an album of old photographs,
an empty field, unplowed ground, waiting for my hand.

From "Crime Against Nature"

1

The upraised arm, fist clenched, ready to hit,
fist clenched and cocked, ready to throw a brick,
a rock, a Coke bottle. When you see this on TV,

robbers and cops, or people in some foreign alley,
is the rock in your hand? Do you shift and dodge?
Do you watch the story twitch in five kinds of color

while you eat Doritos, drink beer; the day's paper
sprawled at your feet, supplies bought at the 7-11
where no one bothered you? Or maybe he did. All

depends on what you look like, on if you can smile,
crawl, keep your mouth shut. Outside the store,
I, as usual, could not believe threat meant me, hated

by four men making up the story of their satiated
hot Saturday night and what they said at any woman
to emerge brash as a goddess from behind smoky glass,

how they won, if she would not bend her eyes or laugh,
by one thrusting question, broke her in half,
a bitch in heat, a devil with teeth for a cunt:

What's wrong with you, girl? The grin, gibe, chant.
What's the matter? (Split the concrete under her feet,
send her straight to hell, the prison pit fire,

blast her nasty self.) *You some kind of dyke?*
Sweating, damned if I'd give them the last say,
hissing into the mouth of the nearest face, *Yesss,*

hand jumped to car door, metal slam of escape
as he raised his hand, green bomb of a bottle,
I flinched, arm over my face, split-second

wait for the crash and shards of glass. His nod
instead, satisfied he'd frightened me back down
into whatever place I'd slid from. Laughter

quaked the other men. At me, a she-dog, queer
enough to talk? At him, tricked by a stone-face
drag woman stealing his punch line, astonished

as if a rock'd come to life in his hand and slashed
him? He dropped his hand, smiled like he'd won.
Slammed into the car, I drove away, mad, ashamed.

All night I seethed, helpless, the scene replayed,
slow-motion film, until I heard my *Yes*, and the dream
violence cracked with laughter. I was shaken out

    on the street where my voice reared up her snout,
    unlikely as a blacksnake racing from a drain, fire-
    spitting, whistling like a siren, one word, *Yes*,

    and the men, balanced between terror and surprise,
    laugh as the voice rolls like a hoopsnake, tail
    in her mouth, obscure spinning blur, quiet howl,

    a mouth like a conjuring trick, a black hole
    that swallows their story and turns it inside out.

    For a split second we are all clenched, suspended:
    upraised fist, approving hoots, my inverted ending.

From "Crime Against Nature"

6

I could have been mentally ill or committed
adultery, yet not been judged unfit. Or criminal
but feminine: prostitution, passing bad checks.

Or criminally unnatural with women, and escaped,
but only if I'd repented and pretended
like Susan S., who became a convincing fiction:

Rented a two-bedroom, poolside apartment, nice,
on Country Club Road, sang in the choir at Trinity,
got the kids into Scouts, arranged her job to walk
them to school in the morning, meet them at 3:00 p.m.,
a respected, well-dressed, professional woman
with several advanced degrees and correct answers
for the psychiatrist who would declare her *normal,*
in the ordinary sense of the word. No boyfriend
for cover, but her impersonation tricked the court.
In six months she got the children back: *custody.*
It's a prison term, isn't it? Someone being guarded.

I did none of that. In the end my children visit me
as I am. But I didn't write this story until now when
they are too old for either law or father to seize
or prevent from hearing my words, or from watching
as I advance in the scandalous ancient way of women:

Our assault on enemies, walking forward, skirts lifted,
to show the silent mouth, the terrible power, our secret.

Walking Back Up Depot Street

In Hollywood, California (she'd been told) women travel
on roller skates, pull a string of children, grinning, gaudy-
eyed as merry-go-round horses, brass-wheeled
under a blue canopy of sky.

               Beatrice had never
lived in such a place. This morning, for instance, beside
Roxboro Road, she'd seen a woman with no feet wheel
her chair into fragile clumps of new grass. Her legs ended
at the ankle, old brown cypress knees. She furrowed herself
by hand through the ground. Cars passed. The sky stared down.
At the center of the world's blue eye, the woman stared back.

Years revolved, began to circle Beatrice like a ring of burning eyes.
They flared and smoked like the sawmill fires she walked past

    as a child, in the afternoon at 4 o'clock, she and a dark woman,
    past the cotton gin, onto the bridge above the railroad tracks.
    There they waited for wheels to rush like the wings of an iron angel,
    for the white man at the engine to blow the whistle. Beatrice had waited
    to stand in the tremble of power.

                          Thirty years later she saw
the scar, the woman who had walked beside her then, split,
but determined to live, raising mustard greens to get through
the winter. Whether she had, this spring, Beatrice did not know.
If she was sitting, knotted feet to the stove, if the coal had lasted,
if she cared for her company, pictures under table glass,
the eyes of children she had raised for others.

                        If Beatrice went back
to visit at her house, sat unsteady in a chair in the smoky room,
they'd be divided by past belief, the town's parallel tracks,
people never to meet even in distance. They would be joined
by the memory of walking back up Depot Street.

                              She could sit
and say: *I have changed, have tried to replace the iron heart*
with a heart of flesh.

            But the woman whose hands had washed her,
had pulled a brush through her hair, whose hands had brought her maypops,
the green fruit and purple flowers, fierce eyes of living creatures—
What had she given her, that woman, anything, all these years?

Words would not remake the past. She could not make it
vanish like an old photograph thrown onto live coals.

If she meant to live in the present, she would have to work, do
without, send money, call home long distance about the heat.

Chopping Peppers

The slice across the top, at right angles, and
I am inside. If I did this for a job, where would I be?
Sitting on a milk crate in a restaurant kitchen. Who
would I be? Someone chopping green peppers for
sweet-and-sour chicken. I hold the slippery bowl
and inside is the secret, an island of seeds, a palisade,
a reef, an outcropping of the future waiting for decay,
for the collapse of walls, for escape. Instead, I filigree
the flesh into odd bits of ribbon with the little paring knife,
the gesture effortless, no more than a minute, time to play
with these words, and my fingers and wrist don't feel a thing.

I was no metaphor when I fed a machine eight hours a day.
I was what came before words, my hands the spring,
setting metal jaws to shut, the same synapses to snap
together every second all day again and again
until what is being done can be named.

Paisley Rekdal is the author of a book of essays, *The Night My Mother Met Bruce Lee*, and three books of poetry, *A Crash of Rhinos*, *Six Girls Without Pants*, and *The Invention of the Kaleidoscope*. Her honors include a National Endowment for the Arts Fellowship, a Fulbright Fellowship, and several Pushcart Prize nominations.

A Pornography

There was a time when I watched it happen.
Strangers pressed to other strangers
in one bed, clothes on, air humid
with the cloying scent of fruit juice
and vodka; none of us
giving into another and yet unwilling to leave the scene
of that possibility,
pretending to sleep, actually sleeping.
Then waking again to slip a hand
over a shoulder, slide a finger
inside the waistband of a skirt; so young
(we are even now still
so young) in that hotel room
turning blue then lighter blue.
We wouldn't have tried for more:
the kiss, the button; firm, white shape
of an image slipped wholly into the mind,
acted upon, dreamed upon,
filling the thin vessels of the lungs.

Earlier, a film, its forced sounds
of lovemaking. The tension I felt winding
into the muscles of some of the others in the room.
I remember I left for awhile.
We all left for awhile;
even the music was frightening. How
to strip ourselves like that, point
at the places that were wanted, plucked
and peeled; speaking the words, hearing them form us,
the nature of what we were
and could do to each other?
The music, the rocking, the sobbing.
The man called the woman by parts of herself.
Some laughed at this. I remember
I must have been one of them.

In the morning, the hotel room was turning white.
After the long night, hands were slipping

and unslipping, moving over the flattened pillows
as if in hopes something small could still satisfy us.
Someone turned and looked at someone else;
we all heard it. Legs
shifted, sheets slid themselves down waists
or shoulders, tightened again at the necks
of those pretending to sleep as the unblinking sun
crawled in our window.
From another room, coughing.
We all heard it.
Someone looked at someone else.
The room turned white. The air began clearing.

Dear Lacuna, Dear Lard:

I'm here, one fat cherry
        blossom blooming like a clod,

one sad groat glazing, a needle puling thread,
        so what, so sue me. These days what else to do but leer

at any boy with just the right hairline. *Hey!* I say.
        That's one tasty piece of nature. Tart Darkling,

if I could I'd gin, I'd bargain, I'd take a little troll
        this moolit night, let you radish me awhile,

let you gag and confound me. How much I've struggled
        with despicing you, always; your false poppets, relentless

distances. Yet plea-bargaining and lack of conversation
        continue to make me

your faithful indefile. I'm lonely. I've turned
        all rage to rag, all pratfalls fast to fatfalls for you,

My Farmer in the Dwell. So struggle, strife,
        so strew me, to bell with these clucking mediocrities,

these anxieties over such beings thirty, still smitten
        with this heaven never meant for, never heard from.

You've said we're each pockmarked like a golf course
        with what can't be said of us, bred in us,

isn't our tasty piece of nature. But I tell you
        I've stars, I've true blue depths, have learned to use

the loo, the crew, the whole slough of pill-popping
        devices without you, your intelligent and pitiless graze.

Everyone knows *love* is just a euphemism
        for *you've failed me anyway.* So screw me.

Bartering Yam, regardless of want I'm nothing
        without scope, hope, nothing

without your possibility. So let's laugh
        like the thieves we are together, the sieves:

you, my janus gate, my Sigmund Fraud,
        my crawling, crack-crazed street sprawled out,

revisible, spell-bound.
        Hello, joy. I'm thirsty. I'm Pasty Rectum.

In your absence I've learned to fill myself
        with starts. Here's my paters. Here's my blue.

I just wanted to write again and say
        how much I've failed you.

Ode

And now the silver, ripping sound of white on white, the satin,
light snow torn
under wheels, car bang metallically grenading, and the wood poles,
whipping, loom—

•   •   •

I have always wanted to sing a song of praise

for the unscathed: myself
stepping from the fractured car whose black axle's one inch
from gone; slim pole slicing cable

up to sheet metal, seat foam, corduroy
(*like butter*, the mechanic will later
tell me, poking a stiff finger through the cloth),
to pierce the exact point

I was supposed to sit, stopping
because praise begins where pain
transfigures itself,
stoppered by a deeper kind of joy: so I
transfigure myself from driver

to survivor, the blessed Lazarine failure

bolting up and opening her eyes.
And here are the thousand wrecks
from a life configured in snow before me: myself,
at five, pulled from the burning car seat;
at twelve, bleeding from the scalp
after the car throws me from my bike; at fourteen,
tumbling over the slick hood rushing;

sockets of windows with glass
bashed out into a translucent, toothy ring; lights
and bumpers clipped clean off; tires burst; deer
gravitationally hurled through my windshield; brakes
given out and worse,

the icy loop de loops
on roads, the trucker's 18 fat wheels squealing—
All the ways technology should have killed me

and didn't.
Praise for my death-hungry luck!
And all the manner in which I've failed it—
marriage lost,

---

buried in the blanks of white space, my solitude
at the Greyhound station
knowing no one to retrieve me,
carless among the others pressed tight
to their own disaster or boredom—
unbearably young mothers,

drifters, boy soldiers
shoulder to shoulder with the insane, weaving
the same thread of conversation back and forth
between ourselves. How

could this happen to me
at this age, at this stage, how
did I not notice, and will you put this seat up?
and will you lend me this quarter? and will you
call me a cab when we get back home?

The young man in the seat before me, head
full of zigzagging tight braids says,
Sure you can dig up that ballot box in Florida
and while you're at it look up all the bones
buried in the Everglades, repeats it

for the amusement of the woman across from him,
who knows a presidential failure like she knows herself,
and when we pass my accident on the road points
and whistles, snickers: *Bet you no one walked away from that one.*

For this, and for all these things: praise

to the white plains of Wyoming, highway coiled
like a length of rime-colored rope; to snow
broiling in the sunlight so that the landscape
takes on a nuclear glow, so bright

we have to shield our eyes from it. Praise
for myself playing at morbidity
because I thought I had a right to it

as if flesh had to follow spirit
to such a pure depth the bones themselves
could not rest but must be broken, nerves
singed then ripped out, the heart clenched madly in its chest.

As if I had nothing except this white earth, this
smashed car to praise

what I knew before and know
even better now, the hills
cold as a hip bone and tufted with ice. Praise
to my youth and to my age, praise

to ambition and small-mindedness,
the kind I recognize and the kind
I am soon to recognize; praise

to self-hatred for it keeps me alive, and praise
for the splinters of delight that can pierce it.
Praise for wood pole, praise for glass.
Praise for muscle, praise for bone.

The sky is bright as a bowl on a nurse's table today.

And the sun gleams into it as our bus slides by,
the light of us a wash of gold illuminating
bodies lost, bodies regained; gleaming

like my heart here, on this earth,
bloody and still beating.

Richard Shelton is the author of ten books of poetry, including *The Last Person to Hear Your Voice, The Other Side of the Story, Hohokam,* and *Selected Poems, 1969–1981,* as well as the nonfiction books *A Poet Goes to Hell: Three Decades as a Volunteer in Prison* and *Going Back to Bisbee,* six chapbooks, and three documentary films. He received the International Poetry Forum's United States Award for *The Tattooed Desert,* and *The Bus to Veracruz* was nominated for the Pulitzer Prize and the National Book Award. In 1974 Shelton established, under the auspices of the Arizona Commission on the Arts, a Creative Writers' Workshop at the Arizona State Prison. Shelton is a Regents Professor in the English Department at the University of Arizona, where he was director of the creative writing program from 1979 to 1981. He has lived in southern Arizona since 1956.

The Creep

his compass has no needle
he is everywhere at once
arriving at the wrong moment
dragging an embarrassed shadow

if he does not come by he will call
if he does not call he will come by
if he comes by he will not leave
and if he leaves he will return
too soon it takes several weeks
to spend an hour with him

he is the one subject of all
his conversations but his life
is garbled like a bad translation
his mind is a series of interruptions
his voice an insult to silence

he is needy he wants
to tell you about himself
wants to hang himself on your wall
like a coat somebody forgot
just hanging there you can't
wear it can't throw it away
and each time he returns for it
he will forget it again

at parties he violates your space
when you step back he steps forward
when you look down you feel guilty
his shoes are ashamed of his feet

ambition's blue vein twitches
in his eyelid he wants
to be famous for something
for anything to sign autographs
to be recognized wherever he goes
and eventually he is

If I Were a Dog

I would trot down this road sniffing
on one side and then the other
peeing a little here and there
wherever I felt the urge
having a good time what the hell
saving some because it's a long road

but since I'm not a dog
I walk straight down the road
trying to get home before dark

if I were a dog and I had a master
who beat me I would run away
and go hungry and sniff around
until I found a master who loved me
I could tell by his smell and I
would lick his face so he knew

or maybe it would be a woman
I would protect her we could go
everywhere together even down this
dark road and I wouldn't run from side
to side sniffing I would always
be protecting her and I would stop
to pee only once in awhile

sometimes in the afternoon we could
go to the park and she would throw
a stick I would bring it back to her

each time I put the stick at her feet
I would say *this is my heart*
and she would say *I will make it fly*
but you must bring it back to me
I would always bring it back to her
and to no other if I were a dog

The Little Towns of West Texas

know all the roads go somewhere else
and never come back. They know
Heaven is directly above them
and from it comes great suffering.
In their fierce localities they suffer
without complaint. They believe
in their names and in the Holy Ghost
whose tongues of fire surround them.

They are covered with cotton silt,
insulated from the cold and the world
as if wearing a coat of frost all year.
They are mirages of mica shimmering
in the distance, moving always ahead
of the traveler. No stranger
can enter them, no native can leave.

Their seasons are summer and winter,
the hot wind and the cold. Spring
avoids them and goes a different way.
At night the wind spins them upward
into the darkness. At dawn it drops them
back to earth in no particular order.
If a house is found closer to the road
or at a different angle, nobody notices.
The horizon is always the same.
The wind flays everything equally.

Near the graveyards of the little towns
of West Texas beer cans are crucified
on fence posts and shot full of holes.
The wind plays them like flutes. Coyotes
answer with voices that could wake
the dead. But the dead sleep on,
having everything they ever wanted,
a cool, dark place to rest where the wind
cannot rattle the lids of their coffins
and the sun no longer torments them.

Their mouths are pale crescent moons
drawn down over teeth they paid for
and intend to keep. They await
no other transfiguration, having heard
a voice roaring out of the desert
and it was not a comfort to them.
Now they sleep without dreams,
rocked by the rhythm of the pump's
heartbeat and the faint susurrus of oil
sliding like silk from beneath them.

In Search of History

We go in search of history and find
a guillotine at a garage sale where the lady
of the house in curlers and stretch pants
sits in a lawn chair knitting, knitting.

The guillotine is ugly but has historic
value, we say, and take it home
to replace the wagon wheel in the yard,
but we can't get the damned thing to work.

Nobody told us the lubricant of history
is blood. We thought it was money.
Is Grandma's pickle crock historical?
How much is it worth? Could we convert

the rusted old tricycle into a fountain?
But history sings like a chainsaw
in the woods, a freight train
in the night. History is the grizzled

Vietnam veteran with his dog and sign,
begging at the intersection. History
is the yellow detritus of used condoms
at the edge of Lovers' Lane.

History is a lottery ticket, a truck full
of cocaine approaching the border crossing,
a drunk on the wrong side of the highway.
History is hallucination, fantasy, a mirage

in the desert, as blind as justice.
Historians suffer from the fever of time
but never know what time it is.
They are mad poets making up stories.

The history of war passes a hat and we
put our children in it. Then somebody
gives us stars to put in our windows,
one star for each child.

Politics Last Summer

The pederasts were pederasting,
the sycophants were sycophanting
and Washington was awash in the slime of politics

when suddenly the three wise monkeys
burst into the committee room
beating on drums and demanding

an end to the teaching of Darwinism or any
theory that related them, even distantly,
to such a debauched creature as man.

Meanwhile, the homeless were trying
to form a union so each of them
could have a pot and a window.
Can you imagine the gall? A pot and a window!

Miranda of the Sorrows

do you like my ponytail
I got it off a real pony who died
but I have always been a real literal
person things would be easier for me
if I didn't tell the truth so much
like my mother said a thousand times
Miranda don't tell the truth so much
it will only get you into trouble
but I always told her to screw it
what did she know about how precious
the truth is and she never knew
nothing about all the sorrows

just because I always tell the truth
don't mean I ain't understanding
see how I wear makeup on only one
side of my face that makes me able
to understand both sides of every issue
but we suffer Lord we all suffer
some more than others and I have been
chosen to understand the sufferings
and will probably live forever
which is why I always keep one eye
closed so my eyes will last and each one
works a four-hour shift it's only fair

sometimes children throw rocks at me
but they are mostly feral and sniff
paint from spray cans they steal
otherwise life on the streets ain't
too bad if you keep your wits about you
and don't have serious bowel problems
like I often do that's the worst
if you're willing to be honest and suffer
for others as I am we all suffer
Lord some more than others
but I was always strong in the legs

I dance sometimes to cheer everybody up
a kind of belly dance and I lift up
my shirt so they can see my belly dancing
but that's all I do because if you take off
your clothes they put you in the wagon
and take you to a place where everybody
is throwing up all over the floor
I pray for all of them but it smells bad
Lord sometimes it's hard to suffer

once when I was listening to the preacher
on the corner a man stopped and asked me
if I had a personal savior and I told
him there can't be no personal savior
because suffering ain't personal it's
general and I wanted to talk to him
for a long time but he was just passing
through the neighborhood the way
everybody does since the stores have all
gone out of business or to be literal
the business has all gone out of the stores
we suffer Lord some more than others
on the streets where we live nobody is home

Photo by Robert Giard

Reginald Shepherd is the editor of *The Iowa Anthology of New American Poetries*. He is the author of five volumes of poetry: *Fata Morgana; Otherhood*, a finalist for the 2004 Lenore Marshall Poetry Prize; *Wrong; Angel, Interrupted;* and *Some Are Drowning*, winner of the 1993 Associated Writing Programs Award in Poetry. His other honors include grants from the National Endowment for the Arts and the Illinois Arts Council. He lives, writes, and dodges hurricanes in Pensacola, Florida.

Maritime

—For Jocelyn Emerson

There's always been this dream that reason has, shearing off
from the conceivable like pollen or Sahara dust: a windy day
along Lake Michigan, cold water, cold war won. The ferroconcrete
lakefront where yuppies jog with dogs and clouds of midges
hover mating is a second nature, like the city it defines
by exclusion. People sun themselves on yellow
terry cloth across cement, water too clear
to be clean. The mind, unable to rest in such fragments
capital has shored up or left behind (man-made rock
fissured to exposed steel rods, absence filled in with lichen
and a sudden fear of heights: the undertow
of Lincoln Park a marsh, contradiction
buried in an unstable foundation), would be an inland gull or kite
convenient to the lowest clouds, flat roofs
of residential high rises across Lake Shore Drive
and lunchtime traffic: crippled by a rising wind,
untimely car: tethered or tangled there. Would be a sign, NO DIVING
SHALLOW WATER SUBMERGED ROCKS. Enlightenment
comes later, or not at all, lampposts flaring on in orderly rows
in summer, when days are long and promise
stalls like a gull against prevailing currents and falling
barometric pressures: every third bulb dead, burned
out. Would be anywhere, almost. Over there, the real
world of elevated trains and the Chicago school
of architecture rises into the sphere of possession,
claims the view south: the Carbide and Carbon Building
or U.S. Gypsum tower. Market fluctuations and assorted
human rights violations are duly noted in the ledger, cement
that holds society together, the concrete world
of what's smashed in order to make other things
whole. That's what this afternoon America tastes of, floating
tar particles and pulverized quartz on the tongue, wet sand
trucked in from building sites to make a beach, closer to mud
without the salt to desiccate and keep it fresh: glass silicates

and contained local conflicts, the debris disposed of
carelessly (a rusting corrugated breakwater, collapsed causeway
green-yellow algae plashes over, a drifting Fritos bag
or this old woman asking if anyone can spare some
coffee), also called the Third World here at home, but not in this
neighborhood. The wind employs each cardinal point
in turn, or pushes a low-pressure zone across the Great Divide:
of which I thought I caught a whisper, echo, or response,
anchor, answerer, or worse. Also, you figure.

A Plague for Kit Marlowe

—*In Memory of Derek Jarman:*
"I place a delphinium, Blue, upon your grave."

I

I don't trust beauty anymore, when will I stop
believing it, repeating wilted petals? He loves
me not. Delphinium, cornflower, lupine, flowers
I've never seen: forget-me-not, fringed gentian,
lobelia, love-in-a-mist, old names of a world
that never was mine, the last of England's green
and pleasant island, sheer blue above the whited
Dover cliffs. Blue fog spelled out across an August sky
the blinded retina keeps, blue frost of a February
dawn, blue hour where you're dead. Agapanthus, also
called lily-of-the-Nile, closer to my lost continent. Pressed
in this anthology of hours, the serifed letters keep
for years of pages, film on water. Scilla, flax, large periwinkle.
Nothing is wasted but regret. Bluebell, blue flag.

II

The gardens of Adonis wither like burnt pages. Beauty
is an infection, I see now, the paper-thin skin written on water
like hyacinth, lily and anemone floating to decay. The filmy blossoms
fall apart like my hands, like *shallow rivers to whose falls*
Melodious birds sing madrigals. Narcissus was pushed, drowned in

a flood of song; Leander's white shoulder is coral echoing
the Dardanelles. *For in his looks were all that men desire.*

I tramp through a closed garden of cures, Foscarnet, Retrovir,
Zovirax, gaudy bouquets which wilt expensively
before ever reaching you. Roferon, Sporonox,
Leukine and Cytovene: those plastic flowers lose color
in the windows of a funeral home, pink wax and wire
accumulating dust like any dead. *And I will make thee*
beds of roses And a thousand fragrant posies.

III

Saw ye him whom my soul loveth? Will culture cure me, keep me
from harm? It let him die. I wanted some white immortality,
but find *I from myself am banish'd* in these lines, ghost body
of the light I poured away. My hands are stained and helpless
here, black ink spilled uselessly as any blood. The heart
is attached to a branching tree of capillaries, veins and arteries,
oxygen flowering like amaryllis, rose of Sharon, vermilion trumpets
forced in January, Sebastian's month. *Why should you love him*
whom the world hates so? The heart wants to keep opening
for seven years of any kind of luck, for any body's blood. Small bells
of paperwhite narcissus fill someone's winter with an idea of scent,
released of color, shape, or sense of touch. Who wouldn't wish
to linger in the sensual world that won't spare me, or let me hold
a living hand to him, *the king in whose bosom let me die.*

IV

I wanted something musical for you, notes floating
on the margins of a stranger's days and works: a lark, an air
of spring somewhere, my voice not clouded under error
just this once. How fine the song I wanted then,
changing from major to minor and, strangely,
back again. The knowing gods must think so little
of my minor wishes, all the sentimental tunes
I've memorized off-key: repeating every error helplessly
to make a song's my one refrain. I suppose I die
a little every day, not noticing it yet. I'm gathering dust

from an occasional shaft of light, I'm dotting all the i's
whole notes repeat, like why or cry. There's no finer tune
than afternoons clouded with luck all spring, the margin of error
I'd call a song. This happens every time I try to say good-bye.

World

—For Lawrence White

The man in my dream said, *Let me live*, but that
was too much of a sacrifice, and I was never
just, like you; he was working for the infidel,
his domino mask said that, blue turban with one
black feather and a ruby set exactly
in the center: entitled to his own sedan chair
with four bearers. An unlikely forebear.
Venice perhaps, betraying anybody's lovers
to sell more of the sea, body of cold
salt water warming in the sun. An heirloom
brooch my mother never owned
is waiting for me when I wake up: *Honi soit*
qui mal y pense, it says in French that no one
speaks any more, medieval as the patience
it takes to go blind coaxing these raised letters
out of hammered gold and ivory filigree, a full year
of travel and expense: someone waited the entire
fourteenth century for this; he's dead
by now, still waiting for that final shipment
from Bukhara, Samarkand, or the Tarim
basin. Shame, indeed. I should think evil of the man
who could command such labor, but
my ancestors weren't involved, and it was
just a gift, passed down like a secret
or a kiss from mouth to mouth: by the time
it's come to me it's been forgotten what it
was, what that man's lips could possibly
have tasted of. Who knows who he stole it

from, who knows who he is now, or
where. This amulet, charm, or medallion
against shames never to be named never was
my mother's, never belonged to anyone
I could mistake for mine. My mother
had nothing she could hand down; I lost it
centuries ago. In my dream he kissed me (I forgot
to say), begged that I not think evil of him
for what he had to take. I won't forgive you, world
I won't survive.

Semantics at Four P.M.

He smiles, says *What's happening?*
and I say somewhere
someone's setting electrodes to someone's testicles
who's been immersed two hours in ice water

up to his shoulders, he can't remember
what day it used to be. Somewhere someone
is being disemboweled with a
serrated blade, fish-knife

to slit open two fresh trout
he had for dinner last
week, Wednesday celebration
sizzling in its battered aluminum pan

over an open campfire
in a clearing, gleaming
pan and fish and fire and the water
that put out the fire, and

he looks down at his intestines, small
and large uncoiling, spoiling
by the unpaved road, surprised
the slick should glisten so, even

at noon, this close
to the equator, is it still summer
there, I never can remember
seasons. Several things are

happening, someone is being kicked repeatedly
in the ribs by three cops (he's black, blue
by now too, purple boot
marks, bruise treads), someone else

keeps falling against the wet cement floor
of his holding cell, he can't stop
falling, somebody
stop him, then he does, stopped watch, old

-fashioned, with a broken
spring coil mechanism, and someone
could find it facedown on the sidewalk, hold it
up to the light, say *I can fix this,*

but doesn't. Somewhere four teenaged boys
are playing hackeysack by a stream bed
on the verge of story, one
has an erection he wants

to go down, and someone thinks about
dinner, someone says *Sure looks like rain.*

Photo by John Eddy

Cathy Song is the author of *Cloud Moving Hands; Picture Bride,* nominated
for a National Book Critics Circle Award; *Frameless Windows; Squares of
Light;* and *School Figures.* Her work has been widely anthologized and has
appeared on the buses of Atlanta, the subway cars of New York, and in *The
Best American Poetry 2000.* The recipient of numerous awards, including a
fellowship from the National Endowment for the Arts, and a Pushcart Prize,
Song lives in Honolulu with her husband and three children.

The Day Has Come When My Mother

The day has come when my mother
no longer knows me.
It comes on a day of dying
paperwhites, crumpled
like words torn from a typewriter.
Weightless, they scatter, generous
as sighs, across the table, the patio,
where the attendant wheels her,
leaning into the dead
weight of her,
through so many
blossoms it actually
looks like snow.

My Beautiful Daughter Calls to Tell Me It's Snowing

She knows, an ocean and a continent away,
I carry a picture of her,
a locket close to my heart
that revolves like a prism
hung in a window to catch the ever-changing light.

It's beautiful, she says, and a little sad.
Snow feathers her eyelashes,
dusts the collar of her coat
as I move with her, and through her, to a younger self,
hurrying as she must back to the dorm,
books slipping into satchel in the gathering dusk.
Along Severance Green the shepherd
lampposts light her way as they did mine.

She will never feel the sense of exile
I did, out of my league among young women
who had a clarity of purpose and strong
opinions that they voiced regularly.
I sought out others of my kind in the outer regions

of foreign exchange, transfer students, and financial aid,
the ones dressed matronly in Filene's Basement coats
and hand-knitted lavender sweaters
donated to the annual clothes cupboard sale.

I'm sorry you were so poor, my beautiful daughter has said
at tales of my arrival, standing like a refugee
beneath the ivy-encrusted archways, flanked
by two avocado-green suitcases,
care of my mother and Sears, Roebuck and Co.,
wondering where I would find the courage
to climb the stairs to my room
and introduce myself to the others.

Having never gone to college
or lived in a cold place,
my mother had sent me packing
with enough blankets to survive a Siberian winter.
Like making sure I had exact change for the bus,
it was the best she could do.
As we existed the best we could
somehow together,
the curve of her life having succeeded
in the trajectory of mine,
for the cultivation of an inner life
I have her to thank.

Letters sent home she bundled.
I found them stashed after her death
at the bottom drawer of her bureau
beside the last wallet she carried, holding still
a few coins and a plastic sleeve of snapshots,
photos of me at ages one, three, five, and nine,
ages when she could still mother me.

I will never know what she thought of my time
in college, in exile, a self-imposed solitary
confinement, an ocean and a continent away.
The best she could do was write in cheerful

schoolgirl cursive that she hoped
I was eating well, keeping warm.
She never replied to the pages scrawled
in late-night misery of loneliness and doubt,
the struggle over finals and papers long after
the others had gone to bed.

At some point the letters changed, a gradual
easing of mind, like soil turned over in a garden bed.
Rather than my usual complaints,
one letter in particular described opening
a book of paintings by Georgia O'Keeffe,
picked off the library shelf of new arrivals.
The presence of light suffusing each plate
rose out of the book itself,
like a formless intelligence,
gathering force over distance
to funnel into a single transmittal
words that sparked skin to metal.
Hours passed, or minutes—
when I looked up, outside the wall of glass,
it was snowing.

The Souls We Carry Hunger for Our Light

The souls we carry hunger for our light.
They who feel unfortunate, close in
on the fields, convene around happiness.
They hear the sound of it like laughter,
on roads, through rain-blurred trees,
the smell of it boiled through bones
and cartilage, the taste of earth
deep and darkly rooted.

Drawn to those sleeping skin to skin,
they shiver, wanting fur, wanting in,
the closeness of animals

sharing heat, sharing fire.
They want to be let back in.

The muscular ache of the man splitting wood,
the muscular ache of the woman
tidying the beds of messy children
bring desire for tenderness so intense
they would gladly return home
to houses that indifferently bred them.

The souls we carry hunger for our light,
the music of that open door calling them
as they thrash through realms of enslavement
thick as honey.
It's the first bite of sweetness they crave,
and the last.
Gathered around the kitchen table
they thrill to the clamoring.
They remember the woman sighing
opening her blouse and the man cutting into pieces
small mouthfuls of his own sweet cake.

I Hated the Hairy Ones

> …he was a very good hater.
> —SAMUEL JOHNSON

I hated the hairy ones
of the graceless shuffle,
arms stretched past knees,
knuckles grazing the ground.
They lurched as if on wobbly crutches,
limping, unseemly as the pelts
they sprouted, flagrant patches
I wanted to bleach and uproot.

I hated the fat ones
of the uninspired hunger,

dull teeth butchering
charred slabs of beast.
They hauled unwashed flesh
from unmade beds
to barbecues at sundown, hurling
bones and beer bottles like ineffectual spears.

I hated the pale ones
of the self-inflated arrogance,
pink as plucked chickens,
aggressively pecking the air.
They squabbled among themselves,
catapulting assertions
right through the roof of the henhouse.
They thought they were smarter than me.

I hated the leather-skinned ones
of the foreign tongue,
tribes of these garlic eaters and stone haulers
mowing across neighborhood lawns.
Turbans of rags, nomadic tents of loose-fitting
hand-me-downs kept them faceless from me,
faceless and poor,
nameless and dumb.

I hated the old ones
of the prying porches,
old biddies with nothing better to do
than to see what I was up to
with my boxes of razors, my jugs of bleach,
my potent teas, my nightly purges.
I never waved hello.
Old biddies with nothing better to do
than rock on front porches,
silently judging me.

Cloud Moving Hands

Cloud moving hands,
hand moving clouds—
in the water, boundaries shift,
the skin sheds its tight perspective,
stretched into a vast shimmering.
I enter the sea to the level
where my vision brims at the surface.
The position of swimmers and small
boats skim across the field,
supported by an imperceptible current.
On a platform a woman performs
a series of movements.
She seems to float yet remain
deeply grounded.
She appears to be walking on water.

With one kick
I bob between earth and sky,
suspended in a blue globe,
gently rocking.
Everything is as it should be.
To leave the body
when it is time
must be like this,
nothing more than giving one's self
over to what is always
holding us, the soft lapping.

My mother lies on her back,
compressed into a pocket of bones.
At the appointed hour,
nurses flip her to one side
and then the other, to release
the pressure such tiny bones
leave on the skin, sores
that leak like grapes.

When they roll her over, her eyelids
flash open like a doll's.

I drift, and in drifting, think of her.
I surround her with a circle of light.
Out of this intention,
the girl who has smiled at me
from the picture on my desk
emerges, vibrant and lithe, just shy
of sixteen, a year before she is to meet my father.
She slips out of bed, hair curled, already
dressed, as if she has been waiting
for the signal.

She sheds the old body
like a nightgown she is sick of wearing.
She walks out the door,
down the sunlit hall, like a teenager
tiptoeing past her parents' room.
Once safely by the nurses' station,
she begins to run.
I am afraid in her haste
she will not remember me,
but she does.
She does remember.
She turns and waves.
And then, into the skylight
she leaves in earnest,
she exits,
swimming toward the surface.

Clouds move hands,
hands move clouds—
gently lifted, gently supported.
Everything is as it should be.
I stroke through air,
I fly through water,
I send my mother home.

Photo by Jason Flom

Virgil Suárez was born in Havana, Cuba in 1962. Since 1972 he has lived in the United States as a naturalized citizen. Suárez is the author of four novels, two collections of stories, two memoirs, and eight collections of poetry, including most recently *90 Miles: Selected and New*. Currently he is working on a new novel about Elian Gonzalez. Suárez lives in and loves the city of Miami, Florida, where he shares a home with his wife and two daughters in Key Biscayne.

In the House of White Light

When my grandmother left the house
    to live with my aunts, my grandfather,

who spent so much time in the sugar-
    cane fields, returned daily to the emptiness

of the clapboard house he built
    with his own hands, and he sat in the dark

to eat beans he cooked right in the can.
    There in the half-light he thought of all he'd lost,

including family, country, land; sometimes
    he slept upright on that same chair,

only stirred awake by the restlessness
    of his horse. One night during a lightning

storm, my grandfather stripped naked
    and walked out into the fields around

the house saying *"que me parta un rayo,"*
    may lightning strike me, and he stood

with his arms out; the hard rain pelted
    his face, and then the bolts fell

about him, and he danced and cradled
    these filaments in his arms, but they

kept falling, these flashes of white light,
    and he ran back inside and brought out

an armful of large mason jars my grandmother
    used for pickling, and he filled them

with fractal light. Like babies, he carried
    the jars inside and set them all about the house,

and the house filled with the immense
      blinding light that swallowed everything,

including the memories of how each nail
      sunk into the wood, the water level rose

in the well, the loss of this country,
      the family who refused to accept him now,

that in this perpetual waking, the world
      belonged to those who believed in the power

of electricity, those moments zapped
      of anguish, isolation, this clean and pure

act of snatching lightning out of heavy air,
      plucking lightning like flowers from a hillside.

Recitative after Rembrandt's "The Anatomy Lesson of Dr. Nicolaes Tulp"

how the whiteness of flesh beckons the doctor's eyes averted
from the flash of muscle, tendon like pulleys, rubber
bands useless now in death, and in the brightest light,

the good doctor's hands shine, one holding a pair of tweezers,
the other in explanatory gesture as if to say look how the red
of exposed arteries, darkened in crimson light, contrasts

against corpse-pale, moments when corporeal secrets
still held the curiosity of those gathered to study how the body
works, functions, even in this futility of the laid-out, another

corpse donated by the city morgue, a drunkard, a wayward soul,
and I think of my own father, a hard-working man, dead
of complications in surgery, or rather, how a blood clot choked

his heart into submission, and his eyes closing to the world,
a fluorescence of white doves aflutter on the roof of a train
station, my father a young man of fifteen on the way to Havana

to seek his fortunes, and fifty years later, in another country,
in the bark of a foreign tongue, in the whirlwind of exile,
his ears surrender to the sound of a muted cry, his own,

and the hospital's ICU doctors and nurses flock to him, his heart
will not start up again, and they paddle it with electricity, paddle
again, but his heart knows its calling, a royal palm tree

calls it home, where the rivers teem with the silver of fish,
fiery beings under the water's mirror, and he wants to go home,
he yearns for this place of his youth, the doctors and nurses

stand dumbfounded because Dr. Tulp, despite a lifetime
of practice and a steady hand, is too late; science has failed him,
my father, as science fails us all.

Isla

In Los Angeles I grew up watching *The Three Stooges*,
The Little Rascals, Speed Racer, and the Godzilla movies,

those my mother called *"Los monstruos,"* and though I didn't
yet speak English, I understood why such a creature would,

upon being woken up from its centuries-long slumber, rise
and destroy Tokyo's buildings, cars, people—I understood

by the age of twelve what it meant to be unwanted, exiled,
how you move from one country to another where nobody

wants you, nobody knows you, and I sat in front of the TV,
transfixed by the snow-fizz on our old black and white,

and when Godzilla bellows his eardrum-crushing growl,
I screamed back, this victory-holler from one so rejected

and cursed to another. When the monster whipped its tail
and destroyed, I threw a pillow across my room; each time

my mother stormed into the room and asked me what,
what I thought I was doing throwing things at the walls.

"*¡Ese monstruo, esa isla!*" she'd say. That monster, that island,
and I knew she wasn't talking about the movie. She meant

her country, mine, that island in the Caribbean we left behind,
itself a reptile-looking mass on each map, on my globe,

a crocodile-like creature rising again, eating us so completely.

—for Jarret Keene

American Drag Rhapsody: J. Edgar Hoover in Havana

He always came to the Tropicana Night Club in Old Havana,
a touch of Yves St. Laurent perfume behind the ears; a contact
would meet him there and then take him to the underground

gay nightclubs, where the free-for-all made his head spin,
after the *mojitos,* and all the bump-and-grind action he'd go
home with the blond who caressed his face with smooth dove-

feather hands, tickled him on the soft backs of his knees, licked
him there where the sultry Cuban men liked to give *la espuela,*
a trick they learned from the French, that much he was sure

of—Ah, those nights in Havana, those young men who knew him
better than his own mother. Music pulsing behind stucco walls,
a light glinting off a chandelier … these nights of release

from daily tensions. The games he played. His favorite scene
of any movie was Ava Gardner's scene with the two dark
and handsome boys in *Night of the Iguana,* shot in Acapulco.

He liked this bite-squeeze of flesh, no doubt. One night
he painted his lips bright red, put on a flamenco dress, sunset
red, white polka dots the size of quarters on the ruffles, onyx shiny

pumps, and he danced in front of mirrors; some distant guitar
weep and clatter of castanets helped him keep the rhythm. Nobody
knew him at the Havana Hilton, not here, not there at the clubs.

He loved this anonymity, this disappearing act of vanishing
before mirrors. Silk scarves around his neck, cotton blouses
rubbing against his nipples. Oh those glorious Havana

mornings when he opened the windows to let some light sneak in:
people below on the move, the bakery boys coming in to work
the dough with their rough fingers, pigeons on the wires, a man

on a balcony with a cigarette in his mouth, smoke wisping
in the wind. Holy Evanescence. How many mornings like this
would he have left in the world? How many nights would he feel

this rapture of passion, unbridled, free? The young man behind
him embracing him to greet the day like lovers, the way men
have held each other into an eternity.

La Florida

Lugubrious days pass with the amplitude of manatees,
hibiscus unfold their smiling vortex to confused bees,

somewhere near Turkey Point a crocodile grows a foot
by the day, tourists mistake the big ones for logs,

anhingas play Jesus on the Spanish moss-riddled branches
of oaks and junipers, crucified in the sun. Feral Quaker

parrots build nests high up in the banyan trees. Orchids,
capuchin monkeys loosed from an animal distributor

warehouse, memories of the bearded lady and the lizard
man, retired now in Palatka, holding court in the shade

of a parasol by their trailer. Russian midgets, rockets
shot into the eye of the moon, this magic of fireflies

zapping their phosphorescence in the night air, jasmine,
gardenia—somewhere a man barbecues 4-inch-thick steaks

in a thing called the Green Egg. A firefighter, a player
of handball. When his son visits once a year from Vegas

he asks when will he return to Tampa, his home. Who isn't
lured by so much sun, heat? The permanence of weather—

or by the mystery of sun showers when the sky opens up
and pelts the earth with a momentary lapse of crying.

Right now, somewhere in the Everglades, a fish jumps
out of the water and into the mouth of an alligator.

Nobody's there to witness it, but it happens again and again.

Purple Finch

Los cien enamorados
duermen para siempre
bajo la tierra seca.
—FEDERICO GARCÍA LORCA
FROM "DE PROFUNDIS"

My student and I are sitting out on the deck of my house
        in Tallahassee, the machinery of spring in full
    stride, wisteria lavender choking the chain-link
        fence, azaleas crowning oak trees, when a bird

flies up onto the post office-shaped bird feeder,
        a red-throated sparrow, Laura informs me later,
    that isn't a sparrow at all but a purple finch. (She looks
        it up and sends me its description from the North

American Field Guide to Birds where it says
        it's an easy misnomer made by amateur birders.)
    One can tell because the purple finch looks "dipped
        in raspberry juice." The image stays with me days

after Laura sends me the E-mail. I look out beyond
        the deck at the feeders, searching for and yearning
    for that purple finch to reappear so that I can see
        the striations of purple wisped on its feathers....

I think of the man who took his son to the hillside
        whorehouse, how a rosewater-scented woman, skin
    whiter than moonglow, unhooked the boy's belt,
        lowered his pants, all along whispering some tune

in Spanish from long-ago days, a *bolero* about lost
        love, and she cuddles with the boy in bed, feeling
    the soft, warm skin of his belly and loins. The boy's
        nerves prevent him from speaking, but for some reason he feels

safe in her bosom, that place where he can see traces
        of talcum powder mixed in with glitter, tiny specks
    of it catching the light just so. Heaven's wink. In minutes
        he's dressed and out in the lobby, his father not

finished. The boy looks outside a window and there:
        a row of hummingbird feeders, the plastic red kind
    with yellow flowers to fool the birds into thinking
        of real flowers. But the empty feeders sway in a breeze.

The boy hears his father coming down the stairs.
        The boy thinks of the woman who held him, her face.
    The boy speaks the name of a red-throated sparrow
        better known as a purple finch, the kind that sings once

right before he dies, maybe, or the kind that flutters
        about before the last kiss, the last blink, the last breath.

                                            —*for Laura Newton*

The What of Rocks

Everywhere I travel I stop to pick up a rock,
a hard-kept promise to my mother who needs
the foundation of hard things in my life,
some certainty at my hand. So I walk, keep
my eye on the ground—a red-ticked pebble
here, an ochre-hued, polished stone there.
I gather them at night in darkness; only
then do they feel smooth enough to carry
back. They are the eyes of my father
in moonlight. I want to say rocks know
the truth about a wicked tongue. Some,
and I know this is far-fetched, blink
at me, wink as if in approval. "Pick me,"
says the one near the tree. "I weigh
nothing, for in me is the hollow air you
need." A rock held in the night does feel
as light as a dead father, a tongue gone dry,
a mouth so thirsty for words that when
you say "rock," something grounds you
to the spot, though it could simply be
the earth mistaking you for its own hunger.

Ronald Wallace is the author of many books of poetry and criticism, including *People and Dog in the Sun*, *The Makings of Happiness*, and *God Be with the Clown: Humor in American Poetry*, and the editor of *Vital Signs: Contemporary American Poetry from the University Presses*. Wallace directs the creative writing program at the University of Wisconsin, Madison. He is married and has two daughters and divides his time between Madison and his farm in Bear Valley, Wisconsin.

A Hot Property

I am not. I am
an also-ran,
a bridesmaid, a finalist,
a second-best bed. I am
the one they could just
as easily have given it to
but didn't.
I'm a near miss, a close second,
an understudy, a runner-up.
I'm the one who was just
edged, shaded, bested, nosed out.
I made the final cut,
the short list,
the long deliberation.
I'm good, very good,
but I'm not good enough.
I'm an alternate, a backup,
a very close decision,
a red ribbon, a handshake,
a glowing commendation.
You don't know me.
I've a dozen names,
all honorably mentioned.
I could be anybody.

Sestina for the House

October. They decide it is time to move.
The family has grown too large, the house
too small. The father smokes his pipe.
He says, I know that you all love
this house. He turns to his child
who is crying. She doesn't want to leave.

Outside in the large bight yard the leaves
are turning. They know it is time to move
down onto the ground where the child
will rake them together and make a house
for her dolls to play in. They love
the child. A small bird starts to pipe

his song to the leaves while the pipe
in the father's hand sputters. The father leaves
no doubt that he's made up his mind. He loves
his family; that's why they must move.
The child says, this is a wonderful house.
But nobody listens. She's only a child.

The father continues to talk. The child
cries, staring out at the Indian pipes
in her backyard, wondering if the birds of this house
will pack up their children, their nests, and leave
the old yard. Do birds ever move?
Do they know her sadness, her love?

Her father is smoking and talking of love.
Does he know what it's like being a child?
He knows she doesn't want to move.
She hates him sitting there smoking his pipe.
When has he ever been forced to leave
something he loved? He can't love this house.

The father sits by himself in the house
thinking how painful it is to love
a daughter, a house. He's watched her leave
saying she hates him. She's just a child
but it hurts nonetheless. Smoking his pipe
he wonders if he is wrong about the move.

Outside the bird pipes: Don't move. Don't move.
The bright leaves fall on the wonderful house.
And the child sits crying, learning about love.

Nightline: An Interview with the General

The retired general is talking about restraint,
how he could have blown them all to kingdom come.
Read between the lines: this man's a saint.

War is, after all, not for the faint-
hearted. It's more than glory, fife, and drum,
and tired generals talking of restraint.

Make no mistake. He's never been one to paint
a rosy picture, mince words, or play dumb.
Caught behind the lines no man's a saint.

But why should strong offensives ever taint
a country pressed by Leftist, Red, and Hun?
He's generally tired of talking about restraint,

tired of being muzzled by every constraint
put on him. He thinks the time has come
to draw the line between the devil and the saint,

to silence protest, demonstration, and complaint,
beneath a smooth, efficient, military hum.
The general's retired all talk of restraint.
He aligns himself with God. And God's no saint.

Fielding

I like to see him out in center field
fifty years ago, at twenty-two,
waiting for that towering fly ball—
August, Williamsburg, a lazy afternoon—
dreaming how he'd one day be a pro
and how he'd have a wide-eyed son to throw
a few fat pitches to. An easy catch.
He drifts back deeper into a small patch

of weeds at the fence and waits. In a second or two
the ball is going to stagger in the air,
the future take him to his knees: wheelchair,
MS, paralysis, grief. But for now
he's camped out under happiness. Life is good.
For at least one second more he owns the world.

The Friday Night Fights

Every Friday night we watched the fights.
Me, ten years old and stretched out on the couch;
my father, in his wheelchair, looking on
as Rocky Marciano, Sonny Liston, Floyd Patterson
fought and won the battles we could not.
Him, twenty-nine, and beat up with disease;
me, counting God among my enemies
for what he'd done to us. We never touched.

But in between the rounds we'd sing how we'd
Look sharp! Feel sharp! & Be sharp! with Gillette
and Howard Cosell, the Bela Lugosi of boxing.
Out in the kitchen, my mother never understood
our need for blood, how this was as close as we'd get
to love—bobbing and weaving, feinting and sparring.

Off the Record

In the attic I find the notes
he kept in college
over forty years ago: *Hooray
for Thanksgiving vacation!* he wrote
in the margin of Psych 102.
And for a moment I can see him there,

feel the exuberance surge through
that odd cell of his body
where I am still

a secret code uncompleted, a piece
of DNA, some ancient star-stuff.
And then I find a recording of me

from 1948, when he was twenty-two
and I was three, and I can see,
from my perch up on his shoulders,
him stopping at the gaudy arcade,
plugging his lucky quarter into
the future where we'd always be.

Maybe imagination is just
a form of memory after all, locked
deep in the double helix of eternity.
Or maybe the past is but one more
phantasmagoric invention we use
to fool ourselves into someone else's shoes.

It is not my voice I want to hear
on memory's fading page, on imagination's disk.
It is my father's in the background
prompting me, doing his best
to stay off the record, his hushed
instructions vanishing in static.

In the Amish Bakery

I don't know why what comes to mind
when I imagine my wife and daughters,
off on a separate vacation
in the family car,
crashing—no survivors—
in one of those godless snowstorms
of Northern Illinois,
is that Amish bakery
in Sauk County, Wisconsin, where,
on Saturday mornings in summer,
we used to go—

all powdered sugar and honey in
the glazed caramel air. And O
the browned loaves rising,
the donuts, buns, and pies, the ripe
strawberry stain of an oven burn
on the cheek of one of the wives.
And outside in the yard
that trampoline
where we'd imagine them—
the whole blessed family in
their black topcoats and frocks,
their severe hair and beards,
their foolish half-baked grins,
so much flour dust and leaven—
leaping all together on
their stiff sweet legs toward heaven.

Pantoum: The Sturdy of Worry

In the paper today I read [sic]
about "a sturdy of worry"
at the local psychiatric clinic.
They are prepared to pay money

to study the sturdy who worry
though there's nothing to worry about.
If they're prepared to pay money,
I'll sign up. I worry a lot.

Though there's nothing to worry about,
I'm continually sick to my stomach.
Signing up to worry—my lot
in life. No confidence. No pluck.

I'm continually sick to my stomach.
Meet anxiety, my oldest friend,
Mr. No Confidence, Mr. No Pluck.
But what if my anxiety ends?

If anxiety, my oldest friend,
at the local psychiatric clinic,
ends? *What if my anxiety ends?*
I read today's paper, worried sick.

Man Sleeping

He lay awake. He tossed and turned. He could
not get to sleep. The place eluded him
as if it were some far-off destination
he'd lost the map to. If the neighbor's lamp would
just go out, the errant leopard frog
stop his protestations, the garish nightjar
leave off celebrating whatever star
it was that burned its hole in sleep's thick bog.

Minutes passed. Hours. It could have been
years. His father gone. His mother. Even his
daughters passed through sleep. The lamp turned off,
the bird, the star, the bright amphibian.
And then they all were gone, these lights of his.
And he, at last, was left with dark enough.

Blessings

occur.
Some days I find myself
putting my foot in
the same stream twice;
leading a horse to water
and making him drink.
I have a clue.
I can see the forest
for the trees.

All around me people
are making silk purses

out of sows' ears,
getting blood from turnips,
building Rome in a day.
There's a business
like show business.
There's something new
under the sun.

Some days misery
no longer loves company;
it puts itself out of its.
There's rest for the weary.
There's turning back.
There are guarantees.
I can be serious.
I can mean that.
You can quite
put your finger on it.

Some days I know
I am long for this world.
I can go home again.
And when I go
I can
take it with me.

Photo by Karen A. Mauch Photography

Afaa Michael Weaver is the author of ten books of poetry, including *Plum Flower Dance, Multitudes, Sandy Point, The Ten Lights of God,* and *Water Song*. His full-length play *Rosa* was produced in 1993 at Venture Theater in Philadelphia, and his short fiction appears in Gloria Naylor's *Children of the Night* and in Maria Gillan's *Identity Lessons*. Weaver has been a Pew Fellow in poetry and has taught at National Taiwan University and Taipei National University of the Arts in Taiwan as a Fulbright Scholar. At Simmons College in Boston, Massachusetts, he is the Alumnae Professor of English and director of the Zora Neale Hurston Literary Center. In addition, he is chairman of the Simmons International Chinese Poetry Conference.

Ego

God's voice
is caught in
the crackling commotion
of thought,
like dried leaves—
breaking

Sidney Bechet

No one could ever *call* the way
Bechet did. He squeezed that soprano sax
so that a vision from our own lax
recollections poured forth in a display.

We all tried to call back then.
We summoned like *meisters* the private
moments curled up inside ultimate,
forgotten corners of us, tucked, hidden.

While Bubber Miley cut him,
Bechet would step backstage to drink.
He yelled out who he was gonna think
to call next, what soul, what whim.

The people sitting at their tables
didn't know that he was a conjurer.
He told tales by making murals stir
with messages that hung like a jazz fable.

We were in our own dimension,
as we made a deliberate suspension.

The Picnic, an Homage to Civil Rights

We spread torn quilts and blankets,
mashing the grass under us until it was hard,
piled the baskets of steamed crabs
by the trees in columns that hid the trunk,
put our coolers of soda pop
on the edges to mark the encampment,
like gypsies settling in for revelry
in a forest in Romania or pioneers
blazing through the land of the Sioux,
the Apache, and the Arapaho, looking guardedly
over our perimeters for poachers
or the curious noses of fat women
ambling past on the backs of their shoes.
The sun crashed through the trees,
tumbling down and splattering in shadows
on the baseball diamond like mashed bananas.
We hunted for wild animals in the clumps
of forests, fried hot dogs until the odor
turned solid in our nostrils like wood.
We were in the park.

One uncle talked incessantly, because he knew
the universe; another was the griot
who stomped his foot in syncopation
to call the details from the base of his mind;
another was a cynic who doubted everything,
toasting everyone around with gin.
The patriarchal council mumbled on,
while the women took the evening to tune
their hearts to the slow air and buzzing flies,
to hold their hands out so angels could stand
in their palms and give dispensation,
as we played a rough game of softball
in the diamond with borrowed gloves,
singing Chuck Berry and Chubby Checker,
diving in long lines into the public pool,
throwing empty peanut shells to the lion,

buying cotton candy in the aviary
of the old mansion, laughing at monkeys,
running open-mouthed and full in the heat
until our smell was pungent and natural,
while the sun made our fathers and uncles
fall down in naps on their wives' laps, and
we frolicked like wealthy children on an English estate,
as reluctant laws and bloodied heads
tacked God's theses on wooden doors,
guaranteed the canopy of the firmament above us.

The Shaw Brothers

—for the Drunken Boxing Masters

If we had the space in the backyard we could have built
a Shaolin temple of our own, or at least one of the chambers,
the sun sparkling off the edge of those shiny blades,
silk outfits popping with that invisible power, iron palms,
golden shirts, eagle claws, death touches, and most of all,
flying, we would be flying, higher than after two gallons
of battery acid cheap wine, or Sunday's holiest dance,
the earth trembling when our bodies shake to ancient wisdom
when Hong Kong came to Black America and saved us
from the lack of answers in the box of riddles life came to be,
we cheered, ate popcorn or the contraband chicken taken
from the kitchen keeping place, and all else that made
Saturday kungfu the first level in Paradise, never mind Dante,
never mind the way the world turned flat at the edge
of where we lived, with the drowning river between us
and what lay all around us in a world that was round
we had secrets slid to us from the old connections
because Egyptian mystics sent the secrets to India and China
then back to us as we watched quadruple somersaults
ending in spinning triple twirl back kicks, masters who
melt iron and stop waterfalls, snatch dead warriors back
from six feet under, stomp their feet and make an army rise up
just when somebody ate the Baby Ruth without sharing

and we started practicing in the movie house, reverse
punches and steel fingers, eyeball staring contests to see
who could make the building shake, throwing steel darts
we made at home out of aluminum foil that won't fly,
letting loose the secrets this time in a world of Kool Aid,
blessed by eyes peeled to stars, touching nirvana with fingers
weaving the tapestry of what holds us together, what makes life.

19 Pages with No Promotion

The day you realize Tony Soprano's mama
is not like your mama, that you don't live in Dunkin' Donuts,
that you hate northern New Jersey because it is
not Philadelphia or St. Louis or anyplace other
than the grist in the air turnpike world of a television
show, it's that day you wake up healed, freed up
from another fascination with America making itself over
on a cathode-ray tube, and Junior won't show up
at your door with some nearsighted hit man carrying
tweezers who forgot his eyeglasses but is intent
on putting the squeeze on you, and you consider
your Italian friends who have to live with this as you
think of the limitations, gangster footnoting
when the world is being carved and shaped
by genius, so it is, you are free and don't have to weep
for Christopher, who wants so much to make a movie
out of his life, and that is the wheel of this carnival,
one real life in the center while the rest of us spin
on its reflections on itself, each one further away
from the way a body feels when it is alive until one day
we are healed, one at a time, from the need to be alive
inside a mass of things we create in a web of circuits
and electrons and invisible forces flying from satellite
to satellite & when it makes you wanna jump up inside
yourself, oh … just do it so the world will not forget
you once had real skin and breath and farted in real
time with all else that makes us more than television.

Photo by Noelle Watson

David Wojahn is professor of English and director of creative writing at Virginia Commonwealth University. He is the author of *Interrogation Palace: New and Selected Poems 1982–2004, Spirit Cabinet, The Falling Hour, Late Empire, Mystery Train, Glassworks,* and *Icehouse Lights.* Wojahn is the recipient of three Pushcart Prizes and the William Carlos Williams Book Award, among others. He has received fellowships from the Guggenheim Foundation and the National Endowment for the Arts.

E-mail (from "Dithyramb and Lamentation")

Loosen this guy up. Make sure he has a bad night.
Take away the mattress, clothes & sheets.

He'll break down real fast.
Make sure he gets the special treatment.

Take a few snaps of him if you want.
But loosen him up. Make sure he has a bad night.

Then he'll give out some real intelligence.
Let him lie there in his own sorry shit—

He'll break down real fast.
Wrap him in the hood & wrap it tight.

He won't know where the next hit's
coming from. Make sure he has a bad night.

The brass from Langley are coming tonight
& soldier, these guys need results.

He'll break down real fast
when you tape electrodes to his dick—

Sending an e-mail *is what we're calling it—*
he'll loosen up. Make sure he has another bad night.

He'll break down real fast.

"Mystery Train": Janis Joplin Leaves
Port Arthur for Points West, 1964
(from "Mystery Train: A Sequence")

Train she rides is sixteen coaches long,
    The long dark train that takes the girl away.
The silver wheels
                    click and sing along

The panhandle, the half-assed cattle towns
All night until the misty break of day.
    Dark train,
            dark train, sixteen coaches long.

Girl's looked out her window all night long,
    Bad dreams:
           couldn't sleep her thoughts away.
The wheels click, mournful, dream along.

    Amarillo, Paradise,
          Albuquerque still a long

Night's ride. Scrub pine, cactus, fog all gray
    Around the dark train
           sixteen coaches long.

A cardboard suitcase and she's dressed all wrong.
    Got some cousin's address,
          no skills, no smarts, no money.
The wheels mock her as they click along.

A half-pint of Four Roses,
        then she hums a Woody song,
    "I Ain't Got No Home."
          The whistle brays.
The Mystery Train is sixteen coaches long.

    The whistle howls, the wheels click along.

"It's Only Rock and Roll but I Like It": The Fall of Saigon, 1975 (from "Mystery Train: A Sequence")

The guttural stammer of the chopper blades
Raising arabesques of dust, tearing leaves
From the orange trees lining the embassy compound:
One chopper left, and a CBS cameraman leans
From inside its door, exploiting the artful

Mayhem. Somewhere a radio blares the Stones,
"I like it, like it, yes indeed …" Carts full
Of files blaze in the yard. Flak-jacketed marines
Gunpoint the crowd away. The overloaded chopper strains
And blunders from the roof. An ice-cream suited
Saigonese drops his briefcase; both hands
Now cling to the airborne skis. The camera gets
It all: the marine leaning out the copter bay,
His fists beating time. Then the hands giving way.

The Assassination of John Lennon as Depicted by the Madame Tussaud Wax Museum, Niagara Falls, Ontario, 1987 (from "Mystery Train: A Sequence")

Smuggled human hair from Mexico
Falls radiant upon the waxy O

Of her scream. Shades on, leather coat and pants, Yoko
On her knees—like the famous Kent State photo

Where the girl can't shriek her boyfriend alive, her arms
Wind-milling Ohio sky.
                              A pump in John's chest heaves

To mimic death-throes. The blood is made of latex.
His glasses: broken on the plastic sidewalk.

A scowling David Chapman, his arms outstretched,
His pistol barrel spiraling fake smoke

In a siren's red wash, completes the composition,
And somewhere background music plays "Imagine"

Before the tableau darkens. We push a button
To renew the scream.
                              The chest starts up again.

Excavation Photo

After making love she'd found it, asking me to touch the place
    as well:
her left breast, I remember that precisely, & just below the nipple
    I can also still recall,

half-dollar sized, a dusky pink that grew erect so often in
    my mouth and hands.
But the year, the details of the room, all blown apart in memory,
    broken vessels, potsherds

gleaming in the excavation photo's sepia, sunlight & long shadows;
    & if only my hand remains,
circling, pushing, probing, *it's a lump I'm sure of it* & if
    I could tell you what would happen

next, which sound from her throat, which sound from mine, the days
    & weeks to follow
& the bitter eschatologies of touch, what profit would
    such knowledge give you?

Would you hear our bedside clock? Cars outside in the rain? —
    & where is she now? Could you tell me
that much? Sand & gravel sifted & the sought thing rises,
    stroked & circled with a tiny

horsehair brush. Bead, shard, incised bone, it does not flare
    in the toothless worker's
whorled palm; & my hand keeps moving even now, the fine
    transparent hairs

erect as they waken from gooseflesh-speckled aureole, my circles
    tight, concentric. *Do you*
feel it now? The push & probe & spiral & the sudden
    yes I can feel it too.

Stammer

One by one I lift them to the mouth, the tongue
entwining them,
                the five smooth pebbles.

Speak now, speak now, say again.

Let the tongue know its place. This will,
according to Herodotus,
                      effect the cure for stammer.

Tongue contra world. Argot and glottal.

And memory, embabeled memory, is here
as well.
           The speech correction teacher Mrs. N.

looming back to me this morning as my neighbor

in black spandex cranks her Motown
up to ten, sunshine on a cloudy

day, in her yard as she lifts her hi-tech bow, and then

the target
              bristling arrows. Memory
of the tongue depressor, then its burrow

toward the tonsils. AH AH AH E E E,

good David good David good. Stereo
even louder now,
                Tempts, Four Tops
and Miracles, Cloud Nine Standing in the Shadows

of Love. *Talk when I say you can talk.*
Barnyard David barnyard.
                    Bright grail

of *R. Ruth* rang *Randy rarely. Stop.*

Rarely Randy rang. Rarely. Rarely. The stalled

train of the tongue, steaming

engine. Engine on the railroad on the winter trestle

Stalled. But then the grind and hiss and whistling.
I am speaking now I have permission.

Heat Wave, bull's-eye all the arrows bristle,

and she nods to herself. The tongue
set free, the pebbles spit down.

Speak now speak now again again.

And the Unclean Spirits Went Out of the Man, and Entered into Swine

> —Mark 5:13

Terrible to dwell within the body of a man
who squats in his own shit among the tombs.
Terrible his raiment, hair matted wild. Terrible the man
who wails his sorrow, scuttling in the grime
& litter of necropolis bone. O better instead to scurry
on these cloven feet, our tusks ashimmer,
better even this trance, this slither toward the sea,
the cliff where we hurl ourselves upon the breakers,
For we had tired of the ways of men & sought again
the Temple of the Four-Legged Thing, nave of sow-teat,
altar of snout & tusk, sacrament of bristle-hair, of penis bone
& musk gland. Here was our repose. But this God we bargained with,
as gods will do, had tricked us all. & to the precipice we came.
We the exiled, We the betrayed. We whose name is Legion.

Homage to Blind Willie Johnson

Past Phobos & Demos, past Mars & its gorges of fossil water,
Past the wheeling numberless moons of Jupiter,
Past asteroid, crater & absolute zero, past red gas thunderclaps

More massive than a dozen earths, celestial
Himalayas of ice, the bright coronal Saturn rings,
Past Neptune, Triton & storm-wracked Uranus,

Past spirochete comet head & the bleak realm
Of fallen sky gods, past darkling Pluto
Where sunlight is distant as a schoolroom

In the Alzheimer-riven midbrain of my grandfather,
Past color & conception, past sound wave
& the lavish carpal symmetries of gravity,

Past the Great Influenza of 1918 & the turbid
Bayous of East Texas seething cottonmouths, past
A training for salvation courtesy a bottle of lye

Burned into his six-year-old eyes by his stepmother,
Raging at his Daddy's stray cat low down ways,
Past urinous shack & sharecropper cotton,

A cigar-box guitar, fashioned of catgut & willow wood,
Past Beaumont & flophouse & Blood of the Lamb,
Past Jim Crow & Pentecost & Nacogdoches, past the Full Gospel

Tabernacle African Reformed & street-corner preaching
On the matter of John the Revelator, beholding His Book
Of Seven Seals, & the bees making honey in the lion's head,

past cylinder disk & quarter note, past undulating neon
& a primitive mike in a Dallas hotel, 3 December 1927,
A back-up band of foot stomp & the engineer coughing,

Blind Willie Johnson is flying.
On the Voyager Spacecraft he is flying,
With a Brandenburg concerto & Olivier

Intoning Hamlet, with the symbol for pi
He is flying, message in a bleeping whirring bottle
Hurled skyward for the delectation

Of extraterrestrials ten thousand years hence.
He is flying made of nothing but the otherworldly wail,
Of "Dark was the Night, Cold was the Ground,"

Wherein a hymnbook cliché is transfigured
& the afterlife commences with glissando,
Bottleneck & string, then the fretwork slowing

As the prayer-wheel cry emerges. The lyrics,
Like this earthly body, shed, replaced by feral moan.
Ah well, aaahhhh well, ah well ah well aaahhh well

Ah Lord. Our sorrows survive us, transfigured also.
Our sorrows lead us to the Promised Land.
Ah well, aahhh well. Bardo, Pleroma, Pearly Gate

& Shangri-la. Our sorrows pulse their sacred
Glossolalia up & down the strings. Ah well, aah well
Ah Lord. Long fingered are our sorrows

& the afterlife three minutes eighteen seconds long,
& the afterlife is flying endlessly
& the distance & the blackness & the cold immense,

Ah well aahh well, ummm ummm.
Ah Lord Ah Lord Lord
Permit our afterlives to be so blessed.

Dean Young has published several books of poetry, including his 2005 collection, *Elegy on Toy Piano,* a finalist for the Pulitzer Prize in Poetry. His collection *Skid* was a finalist for the Lenore Marshall Prize. Young has received two National Endowment for the Arts fellowships as well as a Guggenheim Fellowship. He teaches at The Writers' Workshop at the University of Iowa and in the Warren Wilson Low Residency Program.

Chapped Lips

The problem with childhood
is it's wasted on children.
Look at them all strung together
not being run over by the bus.
They're not neatly scared enough.
Just look how they color,
they think they'll be Matisses forever.
They think you can just get up in the morning
and put on velvet shoes. And they're small,
if they were any smaller you could stick them
to the ceiling like flies but no,
they keep lofting back down
like defeated balloons
but what do they know of defeat?
What do they know of the broken bathysphere?
In their little mittens and hats,
truly they look absorbent,
but just try using one to wipe up a spill
and there are so many spills:
spills that make ducks sick,
spills that dissolve railroads,
spills we don't even know what they're doing
but they're sure doing it.
Try explaining that to a child
and all you get is la la la.
Try getting one to sit for an hour
with her face in her hands.
They have almost nothing to remember
so what they forgive could be forgiven
by anyone. They don't pay taxes.
They're completely devoid of pubic hair.

Dog Toy

Master, how can I make a million dollars?
Cherry blossoms shake in the rain.
Have you tried decorative switch covers?
Yes, but the process was too expensive
with much breakage. Moon-dabbed
bush clover. Have you tried a dog toy
made from two tennis balls united
by a short length of rappeling rope?
So the novice goes off and does this
very cheaply and sells 35,000 in a week
at 200% above cost then Purina Dog Chow
offers to buy him out for a mill.
But still, as evening collapses
upon the orangeade drinkers carousing
the boutiques, he puts his hand down
his throat to touch his own heart
and it stings. A million isn't
all that much. So he goes back up
to the hut on the mountain and asks,
Is it the lion in the cave or
the lion coming out, roaring?
Neither in nor out, what is that?
suggests the Master. But isn't there
something more, pleads the novice.
Have you tried love? taunts the Master.
So the novice goes back to Berkeley
and eats crab with an undergraduate
who makes him feel in danger but
also volcanic, the crab cracks like fire,
her breasts shine like the sea glimpsed
through a broken wall but he's afraid
she won't leave and at the same time
afraid she won't stay and she keeps saying
she wants to be an aromatherapist so
the novice decides he must quit this world
and give everything he owns to a group
protecting the coyote. There are two kinds

of people and the right ones think it's okay
if a coyote eats the occasional chihuahua.
So the novice returns and says I have done
everything you said. What things? explains
the Master. There is no doing, no not doing.
No two kind of people. There is only the fluid
that drips from the dragon's mouth.
But what about the effect of glucosamine
on synovial joints? People actually say
they feel better. What about Beethoven's
deafness, cunnilingus, what is the best way
to cook fish? Cover with wax paper and marinate
for two hours then saute rapidly in hot
olive oil. Do you have any spare change?
proposes the Master. But what about
walking in the rain and being miserable,
what about being happy with nothing,
how the clouds that are nothing completely
consume the mountain? And they go on like this
for years, learning nothing, sleeping late,
getting drunk until the Master dies
like snow melting from a fence. So
the novice writes a book called *Dog Toy*
that becomes a bestseller then he goes
on a talk show with someone who fell
from an airplane and survived and
someone else who had been struck
by lightning many times and survived
and a woman who had exhausted all
conventional treatment but when
all hope seemed gone,
she just started concentrating
and drinking a lot of water
until she was completely healed
and able to move paperclips without
even touching them. What are you
waiting for? You've already
been given your free gift.

Sources of the Delaware

I love you he said but saying it took twenty years
so it was like listening to mountains grow.
I love you she says fifty times into a balloon
then releases the balloon into a room
whose volume she calculated to fit
the breath it would take to read
the complete works of Charlotte Brontë aloud.
Someone else pours green dust into the entryway
and puts rice paper on the floor. The door
is painted black. On the clothesline
shirttails snap above the berserk daffodils.
Hoagland says you've got to plunge the sword
into the charging bull. You've got
to sew yourself into a suit of light.
For the vacuum tube, it's easy,
just heat the metal to incandescence
and all that dark energy becomes a radiance.
A kind of hatching, syntactic and lull of buzz.
No contraindications, no laws forbidding
buying gin on Sundays. No if you're pregnant,
if you're operating heavy machinery because
who isn't towing the scuttled tonnage
of some self? Sometimes just rubbing
her feet is enough. Just putting out
a new cake of soap. Sure, the contents
are under pressure and everyone knows
that last step was never intended to bear
any weight but isn't that why we're standing there?
Ripples in her hair, I love you she hollers
over the propellers. Yellow scarf in mist.
When I planted all those daffodils,
I didn't know I was planting them
in my own chest Play irretrievably
with the lid closed, Satie wrote on the score.
But Hoagland says he's sick of opening
the door each morning not on diamonds
but piles of coal, and he's sick of being

responsible for the eons of pressure needed
and the sea is sick of being responsible
for the rain, and the river is sick of the sea.
So the people who need the river
to float waste to New Jersey
throw in antidepressants. So the river
is still sick but nervous now too,
its legs keep thrashing out involuntarily,
flooding going concerns, keeping the president
awake. So the people throw in beta-blockers
to make it sleep which it does, sort of,
dreaming it's a snake again but this time
with fifty heads belching ammonia
which is nothing like the dreams it once had
of children splashing in the blue of its eyes.
So the president gets on the airways
with positive vectors and vows
to give every child a computer
but all this time, behind the podium,
his penis is shouting, Put me in, Coach,
I can be the river! So I love you say
the flashbulbs but then the captions
say something else. I love you says
the hammer to the nail. I love Tamescha
someone sprays across the For Sale sign.
So I tell Hoagland it's a fucked-up ruined
world in such palatial detail, he's stuck
for hours on the phone. Look at those crows,
they think they're in on the joke and
they don't love a thing. They think
they have to be that black to keep
all their radiance inside. I love you
the man says as his mother dies
so now nothing ties him to the earth,
not fistials of dirt, not the silly songs
he remembers singing as a child.
I love you I say meaning lend me twenty bucks.

Lives of the Olympians

Here come the gymnasts, berserk
wind-up toys only a pasha could afford,
their parents in the stands like ill-risen
bread and usually some connection to
a horrible disease. Help, I can't stop
shrinking, I can't breathe but 2 years later,
watch me back-flipping at high speed.
Surely the ancients intended them
to perform naked. Or better yet,
their leotards fly off as they catapult.
Yahee! Put me on the Olympic Committee!
Definitely they shouldn't be allowed in
until they reach the age of consent.
I mean all these tiny children shooting
all over the *##@&$%!! place—it's
a bit much and does the rest of life
have to be anticlimactic after 13?

Now here come the swimmers like engineered
livestock you wouldn't want to eat the eggs of.
Why isn't there an event where we see
who can swallow the most pool water?
What about putting things up your nose?
Just sitting in a chair? Isn't it obvious
how difficult that is, how lousy
most people are at it? I once knew
a guy who excelled at breaking stuff
against his head. No one gave him a medal.
He probably wouldn't have been such a drunk
loser if someone had. Poor, misshapen
bloke, he had absolutely zero point zero
chance of achieving his dream which was,
he thought he told no one,
to dance a creditable tango.

Lives of the Robots

Green fluid drools from my shoulder.
I can't carry the tray I'm supposed to
and you know what they do to broken
robots, don't you? They pop their heads.
They yank out their uranium and belts.
They donate parts to art schools so
bug-brained sculptors can spot-weld
awful stupid things left to rust
in the backyards of houses where only
art students have lived so long,
the houses have forgotten everything
but the drunk names nicked into
their hardwood. The stars over such houses
don't bother. A crow made of the husks
of crows, police cruisers' mechanical
fins flicking out of the dark. You sleep
on rubber sheets because big genitalia
keep coming to get you, grasshoppers
clinging to the screens like transmitters,
you can hear the owls lying to you,
the brake factory releasing green steam,
the beautiful rhetoric pouring from
the conquerors' porcelain mouths.
They lied to you about what they knew
and they lied to you about what they didn't.
They told you to put down your sword
and welcomed you into the city. They said
you'd get used to the subterranean din,
the chalky residue, suspicious meats,
suspicious glues. And when what they told you
you wanted you got and stopped wanting?
And what they told you you needed
you didn't want to need? Which
of the swallowed poisons do you try
to bring back up, which best left
to pass through? There's the truth-sounding

lie and the lie that makes no sound,
dropped to depths unilluminable.
My father lied to me about the reward.
My mother lied to me for my own good.
At least turn me over so I can see the sky.

FROM *THE COLLECTED POEMS OF*
MURIEL RUKEYSER

Muriel Rukeyser, who died in 1980, was a Guggenheim Fellow and a fellow of the American Council of Learned Societies, a member of the American Academy and Institute of Arts and Letters, a winner of the Yale Series of Younger Poets award, and president of PEN American Center, among many other honors. She also was one of the judges for the Pitt Poetry Series's first book contests. It isn't easy to make a short selection of her work since many of her best and most characteristic poems are quite long, but I thought it was important to include her voice in this anthology. She was enormously influential for many of the poets who came of age during the 1960s and 1970s—particularly those influenced by second-wave feminism—and those poets in their turn influenced a younger generation. Erica Jong called Rukeyser "the mother of us all."

More particularly, over the course of a long life in poetry, Rukeyser wrote powerful and groundbreaking examples of the "political" poem. Since the 1950s, when Senator Joe McCarthy conducted witch hunts against supposed communists in government, the universities, and the arts, through the present, when prominent members of a proudly right-wing regime suggest that protest against the use of torture and the doctrine of unprovoked war is somehow un-American, the political poem has been in critical eclipse. In the middle of the last century the most influential academic critics airily dismissed the possibilities of the political poem. Rene Wellek and Austin Warren wrote, "literature is no substitute for sociology or politics. It has its own justification and aim" (*Theory of Literature*). Cleanth Brooks wrote that if "truth" is what we expect from poetry, we could "argue with the Marxist critics of the thirties for a propaganda art" ("Keats's Sylvan Historian").

These "new critics" were concerned with investigating and describing the structural principles of literature, and their work in that area is still valuable. But their prejudice against "political" subjects seems illogical unless we view it as a reflection of the political reaction of their time. Why should an elegy for a young, middle-class girl (John Crowe Ransom's "Bells for John Whiteside's Daughter," a good poem widely admired by such critics) be a proper subject for a poem, but an elegy for the victims of the My Lai massacre not be? In any event, many of the major poets of the twentieth century—Pablo Neruda, Bertolt Brecht, and Adrienne Rich, for example—have written about political and social issues, as do many of the poets in this anthology and other contemporaries. The antipolitical bias of last century's academics is still strong among some conservative critics, but—increasingly—it seems almost quaint.

Rukeyser's reputation, however, suffered because of that bias. Her courage in the face of it is one reason the poet Stanley Kunitz called her one of the bulwarks of twentieth-century American poetry.

The poems in this section appear in *The Collected Poems of Muriel Rukeyser,* ed. Janet Kaufman and Anne Herzog with Jan Heller Levi (Pittsburgh: University of Pittsburgh Press, 2005).

Poem

I lived in the first century of world wars.
Most mornings I would be more or less insane,
The newspapers would arrive with their careless stories,
The news would pour out of various devices
Interrupted by attempts to sell products to the unseen.
I would call my friends on other devices;
They would be more or less mad for similar reasons.
Slowly I would get to pen and paper,
Make my poems for others unseen and unborn.
In the day I would be reminded of those men and women
Brave, setting up signals across vast distances,
Considering a nameless way of living, of almost unimagined values.
As the lights darkened, as the lights of night brightened,
We would try to imagine them, try to find each other.
To construct peace, to make love, to reconcile
Waking with sleeping, ourselves with each other,
Ourselves with ourselves. We would try by any means
To reach the limits of ourselves, to reach beyond ourselves,
To let go the means, to wake.

I lived in the first century of these wars.

The Bill (from "The Book of the Dead")

The subcommittee submits:
Your committee held hearings, heard many witnesses; finds:

THAT the Hawk's Nest tunnel was constructed
        Dennis and Rinehart, Charlottesville, Va., for
        New Kanawha Power Co., subsidiary of
        Union Carbide & Carbon Co.

THAT a tunnel was drilled
        app. dist. 3.75 mis.
        to divert water (from New River)
        to hydroelectric plant (Gauley Junction).

THAT in most of the tunnel, drilled rock contained
            90—even 99 percent pure silica.

This is a fact that was known.

THAT silica is dangerous to lungs of human beings.
            When submitted to contact. Silicosis.

THAT the effects are well known.
            Disease incurable.
            Physical incapacity, cases fatal.

THAT the Bureau of Mines has warned for twenty years.

THAT prevention is: wet drilling, ventilation,
                    respirators, vacuum drills.
            Disregard : utter. Dust : collected. Visibility : low.
            Workmen left work, white with dust.
            Air system : inadequate.
            It was quite cloudy in there.
            When the drills were going, in all the smoke and dust,
            it seemed like a gang of airplanes going through
                    that tunnel.
            Respirators, not furnished.
            I have seen men with masks, but simply on their breasts.
            I have seen two wear them.
            Drills : dry drilling, for speed, for saving.
            A fellow could drill three holes dry for one hole wet.
            They went so fast they didn't square at the top.
            Locomotives : gasoline. Suffering from monoxide gas.
            There have been men that fell in the tunnel. They had
                    to be carried out.

The driving of the tunnel.
            It was begun, continued, completed, with gravest disregard.
            And the employees? Their health, lives, future?
Results and infection.
            Many died. Many are not yet dead.
            Of negligence. Wilful or inexcusable.

Further findings:
>>Prevalence : many States, mine, tunnel operations.
>>A greatest menace.
We suggest hearings be read.
>>This is the dark. Lights strung up all the way.
>>Depression; and, driven deeper in,
>>by hunger, pistols, and despair,
>>they took the tunnel.
Of the contracting firm
>>P. H. Faulconer, Pres.
>>E. J. Perkins, Vice-Pres.
>>have declined to appear.
>>They have no knowledge of deaths from silicosis.
>>However, their firm paid claims.
>>I want to point out that under the statute $500 or
>>$1000, but no more, may be recovered.

We recommend.
>>Bring them. Their books and records.
>>Investigate. Require.
Can do no more.
>>These citizens from many States
>>paying the price for electric power,
>>To Be Vindicated.

"If by their suffering and death they will have made a future life safer for
work beneath the earth, if they will have been able to establish a new
and greater regard for human life in industry, their suffering may not
have been in vain."
>>Respectfully,
>>Glenn Griswold
>>Chairman, Subcommittee
>>Vito Marcantonio
>>W. P. Lambertson
>>Matthew A. Dunn

The subcommittee subcommits.

Words on a monument.
Capitoline thunder. It cannot be enough.

The origin of storms is not in clouds,
our lightning strikes when the earth rises,
spillways free authentic power:
dead John Brown's body walking from a tunnel
to break the armored and concluded mind.

Bubble of Air

The bubbles in the blood sprang free,
crying from roots, from Darwin's beard.
The angel of the century
stood on the night and would be heard;
turned to my dream of tears and sang:
Woman, American, and Jew,
three guardians watch over you,
three lions of heritage
resist the evil of your age:
life, freedom, and memory.
And all the dreams cried from the camps
and all the steel of torture rang.
The angel of the century
stood on the night and cried the great
notes Give Create and Fight—
while war
runs through your veins, while life
a bubble of air stands in your throat,
answer the silence of the weak:
Speak!

Children, the Sandbar, that Summer

Sunlight the tall women may never have seen.
Men, perhaps, going headfirst into the breakers,
But certainly the children at the sandbar.
Shallow glints in the wave suspended
We knew at the breaker line, running that shore
At low tide, when it was safe. The grasses whipped

And nothing was what they said: not safety, nor the sea.
And the sand was not what they said, but various,
Lion-grained, beard-grey. And blue. And green.
And each grain casting its shadow down before
Childhood in tide-pools where all things are food.
Behind us the shores emerged and fed on tide.
We fed on summer, the round flowers in our hands
From the snowball bush entered us, and prisoner wings,
And shells in spirals, all food.
                              All keys to unlock
Some world, glinting as strong as noon on the sandbar,
Where men and women give each other children.

The Conjugation of the Paramecium

This has nothing
to do with
propagating

The species
is continued
as so many are
(among the smaller creatures)
by fission

(and this species
is very small
next in order to
the amoeba, the beginning one)

The paramecium
achieves, then,
immortality
by dividing

But when
the paramecium
desires renewal
strength   another joy

this is what
the paramecium does:

The paramecium
lies down beside
another
paramecium

Slowly   inexplicably
the exchange
takes place
in which
some bits
of the nucleus of each
are exchanged

for some bits
of the nucleus
of the other

This is called
the conjugation of the paramecium.

In Our Time

In our period, they say there is free speech.
They say there is no penalty for poets,
There is no penalty for writing poems.
They say this.   This is the penalty.

Endless

Under the tall black sky you look out of your body
lit by a white flare of the time between us
your body with its touch its weight   smelling of new wood
as on the day the news of battle reached us
falls beside the endless river

---

flowing to the endless sea
whose waves come to this shore a world away.

Your body of new wood your eyes alive barkbrown of treetrunks
the leaves and flowers of trees   stars all caught in crowns of trees
your life gone down, broken into endless earth
no longer a world away but under my feet and everywhere
I look down at the one earth under me,
through to you and all the fallen
the broken and their children born and unborn
of the endless war.

What Do We See?

When they're decent about women, they're frightful about children,
When they're decent about children, they're rotten about artists,
When they're decent about artists, they're vicious about whores,
        What do we see?   What do we not see?

When they're kind to whores, they're death on communists,
When they respect communists, they're foul to bastards,
When they're human to bastards, they mock at hysterectomy—
        What do we see?   What do we not see?

When they're decent about surgery, they bomb the Vietnamese,
When they're decent to Vietnamese, they're frightful to police,
When they're human to police, they rough up lesbians,
        What do we see?   What do we not see?

When they're decent to old women, they kick homosexuals,
When they're good to homosexuals, they can't stand drug people,
When they're calm about drug people, they hate all Germans,
        What do we see?   What do we not see?

Cadenza for the reader

When they're decent to Jews, they dread the blacks,
When they know blacks, there's always something :   roaches
And the future and children and all potential.   Can't stand themselves
        Will we never see?   Will we ever know?

Myth

Long afterward,   Oedipus, old and blinded, walked the
roads.   He smelled a familiar smell.   It was
the Sphinx.   Oedipus said, "I want to ask one question.
Why didn't I recognize my mother?"   "You gave the
wrong answer," said the Sphinx.   "But that was what
made everything possible," said Oedipus.   "No," she said.
"When I asked, What walks on four legs in the morning,
two at noon, and three in the evening, you answered,
Man.   You didn't say anything about woman."
"When you say Man," said Oedipus, "you include women
too. Everyone knows that."   She said, "That's what
you think."

From "Breaking Open (Rational Man)"

The marker at Auschwitz
The scientists torturing male genitals
The learned scientists, they torture female genitals
The 3-year-old girl, what she did to her kitten
The collar made of leather for drowning a man in his chair
The scatter-bomb with the nails that drive into the brain
The thread through the young man's splendid penis
The babies in flames.   The thrust
Infected reptile dead in the live wombs of girls
We did not know we were insane.
We do not know we are insane.
We say to them : you are insane
Anything you can imagine
        on punishable drugs, or calm and young
        with a fever of 105, or on your knees,
        with the word of Hanoi bombed
        with the legless boy in Bach Mai
        with the sons of man torn by man
Rational man has done.

Mercy, Lord.   On every living life.

Looking at Each Other

Yes, we were looking at each other
Yes, we knew each other very well
Yes, we had made love with each other many times
Yes, we had heard music together
Yes, we had gone to the sea together
Yes, we had cooked and eaten together
Yes, we had laughed often day and night
Yes, we fought violence and knew violence
Yes, we hated the inner and outer oppression
Yes, that day we were looking at each other
Yes, we saw the sunlight pouring down
Yes, the corner of the table was between us
Yes, bread and flowers were on the table
Yes, our eyes saw each other's eyes
Yes, our mouths saw each other's mouth
Yes, our breasts saw each other's breasts
Yes, our bodies entire saw each other
Yes, it was beginning in each
Yes, it threw waves across our lives
Yes, the pulses were becoming very strong
Yes, the beating became very delicate
Yes, the calling   the arousal
Yes, the arriving   the coming
Yes, there it was for both entire
Yes, we were looking at each other

SUGGESTIONS FOR FURTHER READING

There are many excellent resources on contemporary American poetry. References include *The International Directory of Little Magazines & Small Presses* and the similar but less comprehensive *The Directory of Poetry Publishers*. The two best magazines that feature news about poetry and poets, interviews, general articles, criticism, etc. are the *Writer's Chronicle* and *Poets & Writers Magazine*. Web sites from The Academy of American Poets (www.poets.org), Poetry Daily (www.poems.com), and Verse Daily (www.versedaily.org) sample poems from current books and magazines and much more.

The first part of the following list includes poets and books—not all of them American—that have been most influential for contemporary American poetry. The list contains many of the best poets of the last hundred years, and everything on it is a "must read" for any poetry fan.

The second part is a fairly comprehensive but not exhaustive list—the first of its kind, so far as I know—of mainly contemporary American poets very much worth knowing. Titles published by University of Pittsburgh Press as part of a prize series are so designated. A full list of titles in these prize series is available at www.upress.pitt.edu. The books I have recommended here are the most recent or the best and most characteristic examples of the authors' work. My advice is to take this as a checklist and guide for browsing—"browsing" because most of us can't read everything, and because poetry is a notoriously subjective art for the reader.

Finally, I've included a few recommendations for readable and important critical works on poetry. These are just brief samplings, but serve as a beginning for those interested in finding out more.

No one can tell you what will do it for you, but if you look you'll find works in this list that will change your life.

Essential Books of Poetry

W. H. Auden—*Selected Poems*

Elizabeth Bishop—*Complete Poems*

Robert Bly—*The Fifties; The Sixties; Eating the Honey of Words: New and Selected Poems*

Gwendolyn Brooks—*The World of Gwendolyn Brooks; Blacks*

Constantine Cavafy—*C. P. Cavafy: Collected Poems*

e. e. cummings—*50 Poems; 100 Selected Poems by e. e. cummings*

Emily Dickinson—*The Complete Poems of Emily Dickinson*

T. S. Eliot—*T. S. Eliot: Selected Poems*

Robert Frost—*Robert Frost: Selected Poems*

Allen Ginsberg—*The Fall of America; Howl and Other Poems; Kaddish and Other Poems: 1958–1960*

Thomas Hardy—*The Selected Poems of Thomas Hardy*

Nazim Hikmet—*Poems of Nazim Hikmet*

A. E. Housman—*A Shropshire Lad*

Langston Hughes—*Selected Poems of Langston Hughes*

Etheridge Knight—*The Essential Etheridge Knight*

Philip Larkin—*High Windows; The Whitsun Weddings*

Philip Levine—*The Names of the Lost: Poems; What Work Is; The Simple Truth*

Robert Lowell—*Lord Weary's Castle* and *The Mills of the Kavanaughs*

Edna St. Vincent Millay—*Edna St. Vincent Millay: Selected Poems*

Marianne Moore—*Complete Poems*

Pablo Neruda—*Neruda and Vallejo: Selected Poems*

Frank O'Hara—*The Selected Poems of Frank O'Hara; Lunch Poems*

Kenneth Patchen—*Selected Poems*

Sylvia Plath—*Ariel, Poems by Sylvia Plath*

Ezra Pound—*Selected Poems of Ezra Pound; ABC of Reading*

Adrienne Rich—*The Fact of a Doorframe: Poems Selected and New 1950–1984*

Rainer Maria Rilke—*The Selected Poetry of Ranier Maria Rilke* (trans. Stephen Mitchell); *Letters to a Young Poet*

Gerald Stern—*Lucky Life; The Red Coal; This Time: New and Selected Poems*

Wallace Stevens—*Selected Poems*

Walt Whitman—*The Complete Poems*

Richard Wilbur—*New and Collected Poems*

William Carlos Williams—*Selected Poems*

James Wright—*Selected Poems* (ed. Robert Bly and Anne Wright)

William Butler Yeats—*Selected Poems of William Butler Yeats*

Recommended Books of Poetry

Kim Addonizio—*Tell Me; What Is This Thing Called Love: Poems*

Ai—*Cruelty/Killing Floor; Vice: New and Selected Poems; Dread: Poems*

Elizabeth Alexander—*The Venus Hottentot: Poems*

Sherman Alexie—*One Stick Song*

Agha Shahid Ali—*The Country Without a Post Office: Poems*

A. R. Ammons—*The Selected Poems; Garbage: a poem*

Maggie Anderson—*Windfall: New and Selected Poems*

Nin Andrews—*The Book of Orgasms*

Ralph Angel—*Exceptions and Melancholies: Poems 1986–2006*

Maya Angelou—*The Complete Collected Poems*

John Ashbery—*Self-Portrait in a Convex Mirror; Selected Poems*

Renée Ashley—*Salt*

Margaret Atwood—*Selected Poems*

Jimmy Santiago Baca—*Black Mesa Poems*

David Baker—*The Truth about Small Towns: Poems*

Angela Ball—*Night Clerk at the Hotel of Both Worlds,* Donald Hall Prize (AWP)

Coleman Barks—*Gourd Seed: Poems; The Essential Rumi* (trans.)

Dorothy Barresi—*The Post-Rapture Diner; Rouge Pulp*

Quan Barry—*Asylum,* Starrett Prize

Jan Beatty—*Mad River,* Starrett Prize; *Boneshaker*

Robin Becker—*The Horse Fair: Poems; Domain of Perfect Affection*

Marvin Bell—*Nightworks: Poems 1962–2002*

April Bernard—*Psalms; Swan Electric: Poems*

Charles Bernstein—*Girly Man*

Wendell Berry—*The Selected Poems of Wendell Berry*

John Berryman—*77 Dream Songs*

Frank Bidart—*In the Western Night: Collected Poems 1965–1990*

Linda Bierds—*First Hand*

Peter Blair—*The Divine Salt*

Richard Blanco—*City of a Hundred Fires*, Starrett Prize

Louise Bogan—*The Blue Estuaries: Poems 1923–1968*

Michelle Boisseau—*Trembling Air: Poems*

Eavan Boland—*The Lost Land*

Philip Booth—*Lifelines: Selected Poems 1950–1999*

Laure-Anne Bosselaar—*The Hour Between Dog and Wolf*

David Bottoms—*Waltzing through the Endtime*

Lucie Brock-Broido—*A Hunger; Trouble in Mind: Poems*

Joseph Brodsky—*Collected Poems in English*

Olga Broumas—*Rave: Poems 1975–1999*

Joel Brouwer—*Centuries*

Christopher Buckley—*Sky; And the Sea*

Charles Bukowski—*Burning in Water, Drowning in Flame*

Michael Burkard—*Ruby for Grief*

Christopher Bursk—*The Improbable Swervings of Atoms*, Donald Hall Prize (AWP)

Anthony Butts—*Male Hysteria*

Nick Carbó—*Secret Asian Man*

Hayden Carruth—*Brothers, I Loved You All: Poems 1969–1977; The Selected Poetry of Hayden Carruth*

Anne Carson—*Men in the Off Hours*

Raymond Carver—*A New Path to the Waterfall; All of Us: The Collected Poems*

Lorna Dee Cervantes—*Emplumada*

Sandra Cisneros—*Loose Woman*

Amy Clampitt—*The Kingfisher; Westward*

Killarney Clary—*By Common Salt; Potential Stranger*

David Clewell—*The Low End of Higher Things*

Lucille Clifton—*Blessing the Boats: New and Selected Poems 1988–2000*

Henri Cole—*The Visible Man: Poems; Middle Earth: Poems*

Wanda Coleman—*Ostinato Vamps: Poems*

Billy Collins—*The Art of Drowning; Picnic, Lightning*

Victor Contoski—*Homecoming*

Jane Cooper—*The Flashboat*

Alfred Corn—*Contradictions*

Gregory Corso—*The Happy Birthday of Death*

Mark Cox—*Thirty-Seven Years from the Stone; Natural Causes*

Hart Crane—*The Complete Poems of Hart Crane*

Robert Creeley—*Selected Poems*

Jim Daniels—*Places/Everyone; M-80*

Kate Daniels—*The White Wave*, Starrett Prize; *The Niobe Poems*

Chard deNiord—*Night Mowing*

Carl Dennis—*Practical Gods*

Toi Derricotte—*Captivity; Tender*

James Dickey—*The Whole Motion: Collected Poems 1945–1992*

Deborah Digges—*Trapeze*

Diane DiPrima—*Revolutionary Letters; Selected Poems, 1956–1976*

Patricia Dobler—*Collected Poems*

Stephen Dobyns—*Black Dog, Red Dog; The Porcupine's Kisses*

Edward Dorn—*Gunslinger*

Mark Doty—*My Alexandria; Atlantis; Source*

Sharon Doubiago—*South America Mi Hija*

Rita Dove—*Thomas and Beulah; Grace Notes; Selected Poems*

Norman Dubie—*Selected and New Poems; Radio Sky*

Alan Dugan—*Collected Poems*

Denise Duhamel—*The Star-Spangled Banner; Queen for a Day: Selected and New Poems;
    Two and Two*

Robert Duncan—*Roots and Branches*

Stephen Dunn—*A Circus of Needs; The Insistence of Beauty*

Cornelius Eady—*Brutal Imagination*

Russell Edson—*The Very Thing that Happens; The Tormented Mirror*

Lynn Emanuel—*The Dig; Then, Suddenly—*

Martin Espada—*Imagine the Angels of Bread*

Peter Everwine—*Collecting the Animals; From the Meadow*

B. H. Fairchild—*Early Occult Memory Systems of the Lower Midwest*

D. W. Fenza—*The Interlude: Fables of the Twice-Fallen Angels*

Lawrence Ferlinghetti—*A Coney Island of the Mind*

Edward Field—*Stand Up, Friend, With Me; Variety Photoplays; New and Selected Poems from the Book of My Life*

Carolyn Forché—*Gathering the Tribes; The Country Between Us*

Daisy Fried—*She Didn't Mean to Do It,* Starrett Prize; *My Brother Is Getting Arrested Again*

Carol Frost—*I Will Say Beauty*

Alice Fulton—*Dance Script with Electric Ballerina,* AWP Prize; *Cascade Experiment: Selected Poems*

Tess Gallagher—*Instructions to the Double; Willingly; Amplitude: New and Selected Poems*

Richard Garcia—*The Flying Garcias*

Suzanne Gardinier—*The New World,* AWP Prize

Amy Gerstler—*Medicine; Crown of Weeds; Ghost Girl*

Jack Gilbert—*Monolithos; Refusing Heaven*

Gary Gildner—*Blue Like the Heavens: New and Selected Poems*

Elton Glaser—*Color Photographs of the Ruins; Here and Hereafter*

Michele Glazer—*It Is Hard to Look at What We Came to Think We'd Come to See,* AWP Prize

Louise Glück—*The Wild Iris; Averno*

Albert Goldbarth—*Popular Culture; Combinations of the Universe*

Jorie Graham—*Erosion; The End of Beauty; The Dream of the Unified Field: Selected Poems, 1974–1994*

Judy Grahn—*The Work of a Common Woman: The Collected Poetry of Judy Grahn, 1964–1977*

Linda Gregg—*Too Bright to See; In the Middle Distance*

Eamon Grennan—*The Quick of It*

Gabriel Gudding—*A Defense of Poetry,* Starrett Prize

Barbara Guest—*Rocks on a Platter; Miniatures and Other Poems*

Thom Gunn—*Collected Poems*

Tami Haaland—*Breath in Every Room*

Marilyn Hacker—*Selected Poems 1965–1990; Desesperanto: Poems 1999–2002*

Kimiko Hahn—*Mosquito and Ant; The Artist's Daughter*

Donald Hall—*Kicking the Leaves; The Painted Bed; White Apples and the Taste of Stone: Selected Poems 1946–2006*

Mark Halliday—*Jab*

Barbara Hamby—*Babel*, Donald Hall Prize (AWP)

C. G. Hanzlicek—*The Cave: Selected and New Poems*

Joy Harjo—*She Had Some Horses; How We Became Human: New and Selected Poems 1975–2001*

Michael Harper—*Dear John, Dear Coltrane; Songlines in Michaeltree: New and Collected Poems*

Matthea Harvey—*Sad Little Breathing Machine*

Robert Hass—*Field Guide; Human Wishes; Sun Under Wood*

Terrance Hayes—*Muscular Music; Wind in a Box*

Samuel Hazo—*A Flight to Elsewhere*

Seamus Heaney—*Selected Poems*

Anthony Hecht—*The Darkness and the Light*

Lynn Hejinian—*The Cold of Poetry*

Bob Hicok—*Insomnia Diary; This Clumsy Living*

Rick Hilles—*Brother Salvage*, Starrett Prize

Brenda Hillman—*Loose Sugar; Cascadia*

Edward Hirsch—*Wild Gratitude; Lay Back the Darkness: Poems*

Jane Hirshfield—*Lives of the Heart; Given Sugar, Given Salt; After*

Tony Hoagland—*Donkey Gospel; What Narcissism Means to Me*

John Hodgen—*Grace*, Donald Hall Prize (AWP)

Daniel Hoffman—*Darkening Water*

Garrett Hongo—*The River of Heaven*

Richard Howard—*Untitled Subjects*

Marie Howe—*What the Living Do; The Good Thief*

David Huddle—*Paper Boy*

Andrew Hudgins—*The Never-Ending: New Poems; Babylon in a Jar: New Poems*

Richard Hugo—*Selected Poems*

H. R. Hummer—*Useless Virtues; The Infinity Sessions*

David Ignatow—*Poems: 1934–1969*

Major Jackson—*Leaving Saturn; Hoops*

Josephine Jacobsen—*The Sisters: New and Selected Poems*

Gray Jacobik—*Brave Disguises,* AWP Prize

Randall Jarrell—*The Woman at the Washington Zoo*

Honorée Fanonne Jeffers—*Outlandish Blues*

Denis Johnson—*The Incognito Lounge and Other Poems*

Peter Johnson—*Miracles and Mortifications*

Rodney Jones—*Kingdom of the Instant: Poems*

June Jordan—*Naming Our Destiny: New and Selected Poems*

Allison Joseph—*In Every Seam*

Lawrence Joseph—*Shouting at No One,* Starrett Prize

Mary Karr—*Viper Rum; Sinners Welcome: Poems*

Julia Kasdorf—*Sleeping Preacher,* Starrett Prize; *Eve's Striptease*

Laura Kasischke—*Gardening in the Dark*

Weldon Kees—*The Collected Poems of Weldon Kees*

George Keithley—*The Starry Messenger: Poems*

Brigit Pegeen Kelly—*Song; The Orchard*

X. J. Kennedy—*Dark Horses: New Poems; The Lords of Misrule: Poems 1992–2001*

Jane Kenyon—*Otherwise: New and Selected Poems; Collected Poems*

Jesse Lee Kercheval—*Dog Angel*

Galway Kinnell—*A New Selected Poems*

Susan Kinsolving—*Dailies and Rushes*

David Kirby—*The Ha-Ha: Poems*

Carolyn Kizer—*Yin: New Poems; Cool, Calm, and Collected: Poems 1960–2000*

Bill Knott—*Poems 1963–1988*

Kenneth Koch—*Thank You and Other Poems*

Ronald Koertge—*Making Love to Roget's Wife: Poems New and Selected; Geography of the Forehead*

Sandra Kohler—*The Ceremonies of Longing*, AWP Prize

Yusef Komunyakaa—*Dien Cai Dau; Magic City; Neon Vernacular: New and Selected Poems*

Ted Kooser—*Sure Signs: New and Selected Poems; Flying at Night: Poems 1965–1985; Delights and Shadows*

Nancy Krygowski—*Velocity*, Starrett Prize

Maxine Kumin—*Selected Poems 1960–1990; Jack and Other New Poems*

Stanley Kunitz—*The Wellfleet Whale and Companion Poems; Passing Through: The Later Poems New and Selected*

Dorianne Laux—*What We Carry; Smoke*

Li-Young Lee—*Rose; The City in Which I Love You*

David Lehman—*Valentine Place; The Daily Mirror; The Evening Sun: A Journal in Poetry*

Denise Levertov—*The Jacob's Ladder; Selected Poems*

Larry Levis—*Winter Stars; The Widening Spell of the Leaves; Elegy*

Timothy Liu—*Of Thee I Sing; For Dust Thou Art*

John Logan—*John Logan: The Collected Poems*

Audre Lorde—*The Collected Poems of Audre Lorde*

Thomas Lux—*New and Selected Poems*

Anne Marie Macari—*Ivory Cradle; Gloryland*

Joanie Mackowski—*The Zoo*, AWP Prize

Gary Margolis—*Fire in the Orchard*

William Matthews—*Rising and Falling; A Happy Childhood; After All: Last Poems*

Mekeel McBride—*The Deepest Part of the River; Dog Star Delicatessen: New and Selected Poems, 1976–2006*

Shara McCallum—*The Water Between Us*, Starrett Prize; *Song of Thieves*

Lee McCarthy—*Good Girl*

J. D. McClatchy—*Ten Commandments; Hazmat*

Jo McDougall—*Dirt; Satisfied with Havoc*

Robert McDowell—*On Foot, In Flames*

Campbell McGrath—*Capitalism; Pax Atomica: Poems*

Thomas McGrath—*Selected Poems, 1938–1988*

Medbh McGuckian—*Selected Poems, 1978–1994*

Heather McHugh—*Hinge and Sign: Poems, 1968–1993; Eye Shot*

Peter Meinke—*Liquid Paper; The Contracted World: New and More Selected Poems*

William Meredith—*Effort at Speech: New and Selected Poems*

James Merrill—*Divine Comedies; The Inner Room*

W. S. Merwin—*Migration*

Josephine Miles—*Collected Poems*

E. Ethelbert Miller—*First Light: New and Selected Poems; How We Sleep on the Nights We Don't Make Love*

Czeslaw Milosz—*Selected Poems: 1931–2004*

Susan Mitchell—*Rapture*

Malena Mörling—*Ocean Avenue; Astoria*

Thylias Moss—*Slave Moth: A Narrative in Verse*

Lisel Mueller—*The Private Life; Alive Together: New and Selected Poems*

Paul Muldoon—*Moy Sand and Gravel*

Harryette Mullen—*Sleeping with the Dictionary*

Carol Muske—*Applause; Wyndmere*

Howard Nemerov—*New and Selected Poems*

Rick Noguchi—*The Ocean Inside Kenji Takezo*, AWP Prize

Kathleen Norris—*Little Girls in Church; Journey: New and Selected Poems, 1969–1999*

Alice Notley—*Grave of Night: New and Selected Poems, 1970–2005*

Naomi Shihab Nye—*Yellow Glove; Red Suitcase; You and Yours*

Ed Ochester—*The Land of Cockaigne; Unreconstructed*

Sharon Olds—*Satan Says; The Gold Cell; Strike Sparks: Selected Poems, 1980–2002*

Mary Oliver—*American Primitive; Dream Work*

Charles Olson—*The Maximus Poems*

George Oppen—*Of Being Numerous*

Gregory Orr—*City of Salt*

Simon J. Ortiz—*Out There Somewhere*

Alicia Ostriker—*The Little Space: Poems Selected and New, 1968–1998; The Volcano Sequence; No Heaven*

Eric Pankey—*Reliquaries*

Greg Pape—*Storm Pattern*

Linda Pastan—*Aspects of Eve; Pm/Am: New and Selected Poems*

Molly Peacock—*Cornucopia: New and Selected Poems*

Carl Phillips—*Rock Harbor; The Rest of Love*

Robert Pinsky—*The Figured Wheel: New and Collected Poems 1966–1996; Jersey Rain*

Stanley Plumly—*Out-of-the-Body Travel; Now that My Father Lies Down Beside Me: New and Selected Poems, 1970–2000*

Marie Ponsot—*The Bird Catcher; Springing: New and Selected Poems*

Minnie Bruce Pratt—*Walking Back Up Depot Street; The Dirt She Ate: Selected and New Poems*

Claudia Rankine—*Don't Let Me Be Lonely: An American Lyric*

Liam Rector—*The Executive Director of the Fallen World*

Spencer Reece—*The Clerk's Tale*

Ishmael Reed—*New and Collected Poems*

Paisley Rekdal—*The Invention of the Kaleidoscope*

Donald Revell—*Pennyweight Windows: New and Selected Poems*

Kenneth Rexroth—*One Hundred Poems from the Japanese*

Alberto Rios—*Teodoro Luna's Two Kisses; The Theater of Night*

Theodore Roethke—*Selected Poems*

Pattiann Rogers—*Firekeeper: Selected Poems*

Liz Rosenberg—*Children of Paradise*

Muriel Rukeyser—*The Collected Poems of Muriel Rukeyser*

Kay Ryan—*Say Uncle*

Natasha Sajé—*Red Under the Skin,* Starrett Prize; *Bend*

Tomaž Šalamun—*The Book for My Brother*

Sonia Sanchez—*Homegirls and Handgrenades*

Sherod Santos—*The Southern Reaches; The Perishing*

Gjertrud Schnackenberg—*Portraits and Elegies*

James Schuyler—*Selected Poems*

Maureen Seaton—*Venus Examines Her Breast*

Tim Seibles—*Buffalo Head Solos*

Vijay Seshadri—*The Long Meadow*

Anne Sexton—*The Complete Poems*

Alan Shapiro—*Song and Dance*

Richard Shelton—*The Last Person to Hear Your Voice*

Reginald Shepherd—*Wrong; Otherhood; Fata Morgana*

Jason Shinder—*Every Room We Ever Slept In; Among Women*

Betsy Sholl—*The Red Line*, AWP Prize; *Late Psalm*

David Shumate—*High Water Mark: Prose Poems*, Starrett Prize

Charles Simic—*Dismantling the Silence; Selected Poems*

Jim Simmerman—*Moon Go Away, I Don't Love You No More; Kingdom Come*

Michael Simms—*The Happiness of Animals*

Louis Simpson—*A Dream of Governors; The Owner of the House: New and Collected Poems 1940–2001*

Tom Sleigh—*The Dreamhouse; Far Side of the Earth*

Aaron Smith—*Blue on Blue Ground*, Starrett Prize

Dave Smith—*Cumberland Station*

W. D. Snodgrass—*Heart's Needle*

Gary Snyder—*Earth House Hold; Myths and Texts*

Sandy Solomon—*Pears, Lake, Sun*, Starrett Prize

Cathy Song—*The Land of Bliss; Cloud Moving Hands*

Gary Soto—*The Elements of San Joaquin*

William Stafford—*The Way It Is: New and Selected Poems*

Susan Stewart—*Columbarium*

David St. John—*Study for the World's Body*

Ruth Stone—*Second-Hand Coat; Ordinary Words; In the Dark*

Mark Strand—*Selected Poems*

Virgil Suárez—*90 Miles: Selected and New Poems*

Larissa Szporluk—*The Wind, Master Cherry, The Wind*

Wislawa Szymborska—*Poems New and Collected*

James Tate—*The Oblivion Ha-Ha; Selected Poems*

Amber Flora Thomas—*Eye of Water*, Cave Canem Prize

Sue Ellen Thompson—*The Golden Hour; The Leaving: New and Selected Poems*

Jean Valentine—*Door in the Mountain: New and Collected Poems 1965–2003*

Lyrae Van Clief-Stefanon—*Black Swan*, Cave Canem Prize

Mona Van Duyn—*Near Changes*

Michael Van Walleghen—*Tall Birds Stalking*

Ellen Bryant Voigt—*The Lotus Flowers; Two Trees; Shadow of Heaven*

Connie Voisine—*Cathedral of the North*, AWP Prize

Karen Volkman—*Spar*

Judith Vollmer—*Level Green; The Door Open to the Fire; Reactor*

Alice Walker—*Revolutionary Petunias*

Ronald Wallace—*The Uses of Adversity; Long for This World: New and Selected Poems*

BJ Ward—*Gravedigger's Birthday*

Belle Waring—*Refuge*, AWP Prize

Rosanna Warren—*Departure*

Michael Waters—*Darling Vulgarity*

Afaa Michael Weaver—*Multitudes: Poems Selected and New*

Charles Harper Webb—*Liver; Hot Popsicles*

Shao Wei—*Pulling a Dragon's Teeth*, Starrett Prize

Bruce Weigl—*Song of Napalm; Archeology of the Circle: New and Selected Poems*

Dara Wier—*Blood, Hook, and Eye; Reverse Rapture*

C. K. Williams—*Selected Poems; Repair; The Singing*

Crystal Williams—*Lunatic*

David Wojahn—*Mystery Train; Interrogation Palace: New and Selected Poems 1982–2004*

Baron Wormser—*Subject Matter*

C. D. Wright—*Further Adventures with You; Steal Away: Selected and New Poems*

Charles Wright—*China Trace; Zone Journals; Negative Blue: Selected Later Poems*

Franz Wright—*The Beforelife; Walking to Martha's Vineyard*

Jay Wright—*Transfigurations: Collected Poems*

Robert Wrigley—*Reign of Snakes; Lives of the Animals*

Mark Wunderlich—*The Anchorage: Poems*

Michael Wurster—*The Snake Charmer's Daughter*

Al Young—*Heaven: Collected Poems 1956–1990*

Dean Young—*First Course in Turbulence; Elegy on Toy Piano*

Kevin Young—*Jelly Roll: A Blues*

Paul Zimmer—*Family Reunion: Selected and New Poems*

Books of Criticism on Poetry

Donald Allen—*The Poetics of the New American Poetry* (contains many of the classic statements about "organic poetry")

Robert Bly—*Leaping Poetry: An Idea with Poems and Translations*

John Ciardi—*How Does a Poem Mean* (an older, "classic" text)

Stephen Dobyns—*Best Words, Best Order: Essays on Poetry*

Donald Hall—*Claims for Poetry* (critical essays on poetry by poets)

Robert Hass—*Twentieth Century Pleasures: Prose on Poetry*

David Wojahn—*Strange Good Fortune: Essays on Contemporary Poetry*